ON and OFF the FLOOR

ON and OFF the FLOOR

Samuel Shaffer

Thirty Years as a Correspondent
on Capitol Hill

NEWSWEEK BOOKS, New York

I am grateful to Katie Louchheim and Mary Costello for their
sustained critical enthusiasm, and to Ben Bradlee, Executive
Editor of the *Washington Post*, and Mel Elfin, *Newsweek*'s
Washington Bureau Chief, for making their research facilities
so freely available to me.

———————————

Printed in the United States of America

Library of Congress Cataloging in Publication Data

Shaffer, Samuel.
On and off the floor.

1. Legislators—United States.   2. United
Sates. Congress.   3. United States—Politics
and government—1945–   I. Title.
JK1041.S52   328.73'07'3   79-3541
ISBN 0-88225-289-5

Book Design: Mary Ann Joulwan

CONTENTS

To The Memory Of Helen

My Beloved Wife

CHAPTER 1

"The Lecky Principle"
& Related Matters

———

Although the first person singular will appear with some frequency in this narrative, the book is neither an autobiography nor an *apologia pro vita sua*. Though it will abound with anecdotes, its purpose is far from a remembrance of things past.

I have been a journalist for forty years. My first story dealt with fitting cow udders with brassieres at the Beltsville, Maryland, research station of the U.S. Department of Agriculture. I no longer remember whether this singular experiment was devised to trap parasites or keep them out.

The last story of my career explored the behind-the-scenes drama in which the least objectionable running mate for President Gerald R. Ford was chosen over a generally undistinguished lot. I have concluded that humanity was better served by the Beltsville experience than by the Kansas City roulette.

For the last three decades, I was *Newsweek*'s chief congressional correspondent, with time out for an occasional White House stint, fourteen nominating conventions, and four presidential campaigns.

This book concerns itself with some of the historic episodes of the last thirty years, ranging from the rise and fall of one of America's most dangerous demagogues, Sen. Joseph R. McCarthy, to the abdication of the thirty-seventh president of the United States.

There will be stories of lesser moment, but seen in their proper context, they help illuminate the nature of Congress, a body unique among the parliaments of mankind because of its constitutional equality and coordinate status with the presidency and the Supreme Court. The constant shifting of the balance of power among these institutions produces tension and out of that tension, drama.

I witnessed these events at first hand. Those which took place behind closed doors I was able to report in detail because of cooperative participants who took notes surreptitiously for their own archives and passed on copies to me.

The purpose of this narrative is to show not just how things happened, but why. The role played by such diverse circumstances as sheer happenstance, accidental timing, and the interplay of personalities involved cannot be underestimated. But there is also a unifying dynamic: legislative efforts to change the direction of American society or to correct inequities and injustices cannot succeed unless the public is ready to accept them.

The role of chance, I found, makes a mockery of Karl Marx's invocation of the "inevitable" laws of history. Certainly there was nothing "inevitable" about an indiscreet, overheard conversation conducted in a public telephone booth by Earl Warren, the fourteenth chief justice of the United States, which initiated a chain of events resulting in the failure of Associate Justice Abe Fortas to become the fifteenth chief justice. There was nothing "inevitable" in the series of misjudgments and blunders by the opponents of Joe McCarthy and the abandonment of standards of integrity and decency by otherwise honorable men that enabled McCarthy to wreak such havoc.

Nor was there anything "inevitable" about a dying senator staying alive just long enough to permit an obscure colleague, Robert C. Byrd of West Virginia, to cast a proxy vote that toppled Teddy Kennedy from the second highest leadership post in the Senate. Thus Byrd, not Kennedy, eventually became the majority leader of the Senate, one of the most influential and powerful positions in the American polity. And there was nothing "inevitable" about young Teddy's mishap at Chappaquiddick that weakened his Senate status to the point where Byrd would have seriously considered challenging him. Continuing this line of conjecture, one could say that Teddy could have been elected president in 1972 or 1976. Had he been elected in 1972, there would have been no Watergate leading to a certain impeachment by the House and a trial in the Senate which Richard Nixon escaped only by resignation. Or had Teddy been elected president in 1976, the name of James Earl Carter, Jr., would be found by future historians only in a listing of Georgia's one-term governors.

But all is not ruled by chance—not by a long shot. Einstein was certain that "God does not play dice with the universe." The logic of significant events that I witnessed as a journalist also appears to rule out celestial or human dice-throwing.

There are constants, and the most important of these I think of as "the Lecky Principle" after W. E. H. Lecky, the brilliant twenty-seven-year-old Victorian historian who wrote *The History of the Rise and Influence of the Spirit of Rationalism in Europe*, in which this concept is set forth. Noting the decline toward the close of the eighteenth century of the fierce passions that accompanied and followed the Reformation, he wrote:

> It was observed that every great change of belief had been preceded by a great change in the intellectual condition of Europe; that *the success of any opinion depended much less upon the force of its arguments, or upon the ability of its advocates, than upon the predisposition of society to receive it*, and that that predisposition resulted from the intellectual type of the age. (Italics added.)

After fifteen hundred years, the world finally rejected the "crime" of witchcraft. Lecky's explanation:

> ... It is the result, not of any series of definite arguments, or of new discoveries, but of a gradual, insensible yet profound modification of the habits of thought prevailing in Europe.... If we ask what new arguments were discovered during the decadence of the belief, we must admit that they were quite inadequate to account for the change.

The Lecky Principle helps to explain the McCarthy phenomenon. Fortunately, events take place more rapidly in the age of instant communication and nearly universal literacy—and there's always television for the functional illiterates. The Mc-

Carthy era lasted only five years instead of centuries. The Lecky Principle makes sense of the circumstances that led, finally, to the enactment of the Voting Rights Act of 1965, thus averting a mounting racial struggle that could have undermined the stability of the Republic. It even makes sense of the curious failure of the Republicans to profit politically from the release of the Yalta Papers. They had forced the most massive, *official* leak of government documents in American history in the vain hope these would prove that Franklin D. Roosevelt bartered away the freedom of much of the free world.

In addition to the constants of chance, timing, and the Lecky Principle, there is the significant, sometimes overriding factor of personality and the interplay of personalities. In some ways, politicians are a breed apart and often larger than life.

To close this chapter, which is the stage setting for the recounting of the events that follow, some generalizations about politicians could be helpful—and almost unavoidable. It is easy to be cynical about politicians. Few temptations are more difficult for newsmen to resist in covering Washington than the resort to cynicism.

It's part of the national tradition to take easy shots at politicians. As men and women who have chosen public life, they cannot—they often dare not—stake a claim to the privacy the rest of us expect as an inalienable right. Also, the Supreme Court decision in *Sullivan* v. *The New York Times* makes it almost impossible to sue successfully for libel unless actual malice is established.

Of course, Congress has its share of poltroons, timeservers, unblemished hacks, and even felons. But these are a distinct minority. Some of the ablest men and women and some of the most brilliant minds in the nation are to be found in the Senate and the House.

This is a representative democracy, and the Congress represents a nearly perfect mirror of America. A significant reason is the factor of accountability by the members to the thousands, even millions, who voted them into office. Each member of the House must face his constituency every two years; each senator, every six years.

To condemn out of hand the 535 men and women chosen to represent us in Congress would be foolish, for they are no better and no worse than the rest of us. But, in a number of respects, they *are* different. They possess an extraordinary stamina, far out of proportion to that of the generality of Americans. I have watched septuagenarians orate in all-night Senate sessions while their aides, half or even a third their age, crumple with fatigue. It's the Darwinian law of natural selection at work. Without that stamina, they would never have made it to Washington.

Anyone who has ever traveled with a candidate for national office soon finds out the tremendous expenditure involved. He hustles for votes at county fairs and in shopping centers. He goes on to address a dinner group, is rushed out to a radio or TV studio for an interview, and then must be up and dressed before dawn to shake hands with the early shift at the factory gate. And this goes on day after day.

Once in office, he cannot coast. He must maintain constant touch with his constituency; like the giant Antaeus, he loses strength when he fails to keep constant touch with the earth. If he neglects the overriding necessity of staying close to "the folks back home," he will find himself out of office, out of power, and out of countenance. It has happened to men of such worldwide stature as the former Rhodes scholar, J. William Fulbright of Arkansas, and skilled political infighter Tom Connally of Texas—both men of formidable intelligence; skillful, caustic, and even ruthless in debate; and among the ablest and most influential men ever to chair the prestigious Senate Foreign Relations Committee.

Both finally made the same mistake: they thought the clout they exercised in foreign affairs would impress their constituents—who actually cared far more about such homely matters as beef prices, soy bean futures, and "pork barrel" projects designed to irrigate dry lands, make streams navigable, and prevent floods.

Hubert H. Humphrey was a good example of a senator who never lost touch with his constituency and was unbeatable in Minnesota. He just never stopped campaigning. I recall an interrupted interview with him just a few weeks after he had been reelected to a second term. A Senate page handed him a note stating a constituent was waiting to see him. Humphrey leaped to his feet and started to walk away.

"For heaven's sake, Hubert," I said impatiently, "I haven't finished. You can let your constituent wait. You're not up again for six years."

"I know that, Sam," he said, "and I'm off and running for the next term right now."

Unfortunately for the ever-ebullient and always underfinanced Humphrey, his reach for the presidency in 1968, 1972, and 1976 exceeded his grasp. His highest post was vice president of the United States under President Lyndon B. Johnson, 1965–69. He then returned to the Senate again. After a valiant struggle against cancer, Humphrey died in January 1977. In his eulogy, President Carter called him "the most beloved of all Americans." He was one of the most innovative and creative legislators in American history. Among his accomplishments of international consequence are the Peace Corps and the Food for Peace program. He was a leader in all the civil rights legislative battles.

The successful legislator has an almost instinctive "feel" for the collective mood and desires of his constituency—a built-in political radar system infinitely more sensitive than the rest of us possess. It is more than the sum of local news stories, a sampling of the mail, and an occasional poll. It's more subtle and mysterious. And if he loses that "feel," he loses his seat in the next election.

Legislators have very little time for reflection. There are demands upon their attention literally every minute of the day— and these demands would be made every minute of the night too if not for unlisted telephone numbers. They are utterly dependent upon typed cards which they receive from their secretaries the moment they arrive in the office. These cards, broken down almost minute by minute, list every engagement of the day and every committee and subcommittee meeting, with a brief addendum of the agenda.

They are dependent upon hasty briefings from aides who scurry alongside as they dash about the Capitol. Too often, their only time for studying a complex legislative problem is when they are driven to and from their offices by aides, wives, or chauffeurs.

With singular exceptions, they possess almost no aesthetic sense or appreciation; if they did once, it has atrophied under the pressure of politics. One exception was the late Democratic Sen. Paul Douglas of Illinois, the author of about two dozen books, the best known of which was *The Theory of Wages* published in 1934.

Only moments before he was to give his presidential address to the American Economic Association in Chicago in 1947, Douglas was informed by Chicago political boss Col. Jake Arvey that he had been selected as the Democratic nominee for the Senate. He turned to his wife, Emily, and quoted from *Othello:* "Oh, now forever/Farewell the tranquil mind."

Douglas was almost sui generis in the Senate. Tall, erect, white-haired, with an arm crippled in battle in the Pacific in World War II in which he served as an overage marine—an arm whose pain seldom let up—he was erudite and steeped in the classics. His ever-pertinent quotations stemmed from his reading and not from riffling through the index of *Bartlett's Familiar Quotations.* He was too idealistic to make a memorably effective legislator. His ideas were usually five years ahead of time and were eventually appropriated by more practical colleagues.

Literary references in congressional speeches are few, repetitive, and most often inaccurate. Official Senate reporters, armed with *Bartlett's* and half a dozen similar compendiums, clean up the quotes before the *Congressional Record* goes to press.

Quotations and clichés have their fashionable runs in Congress. In the last few years, the following have been uttered almost daily:

"As Santayana said, 'He who doesn't remember the past is condemned to repeat it.'"

"As Victor Hugo said, 'Greater than all the armies is the power of an idea whose time has come.'"

For years, the late Sen. Everett M. Dirksen of Illinois regularly introduced legislation to make the marigold the national floral emblem. "As I think of these golden marigolds," he would tell the Senate in that rich, oleaginous voice, "a couplet comes to mind:

'Ten thousand saw I at a glance
Tossing their heads in a sprightly dance.'"

One day, when he came off the floor after delivering his standard speech, I told him, "Ev, that's Wordsworth, and he was writing about daffodils." Totally unfazed, Dirksen replied with a typical Dirksenian non sequitur, "But the principle remains the same."

Above: Howard Baker risked his
Senate career in Panama Canal
fight. To his left is John Rhodes.

Left: Paul Douglas, an erudite man
in a Senate where cliches often serve
for erudition, with wife, Emily.

Below: Low-keyed Congressman
Gerald Ford with hand-waving
Sen. Everett McKinley Dirksen.

Below: Irrepressibly ebullient Hubert Horatio Humphrey never stopped campaigning. The day after election he would start running again.

Above: Though not a household name, Gaylord Nelson of Wisconsin, has proved to be one of the most courageous men ever elected to the U.S. Senate.

Right: By any yardstick, the toughest and bravest woman to serve in the Senate was Margaret Chase Smith of Maine, here with Abe Fortas, then Supreme Court Justice.

In a powerful, concluding speech on the Public Accommodations Bill, a civil rights measure enacted in 1964, Dirksen—who had had a few celebratory drinks beforehand with Sen. Barry Goldwater, who refused to give him his vote but whose vote was no longer needed for passage—said: "As Don Byrne said, 'No man is an island unto himself. . . .'" Syndicated columnist Mary McGrory buttonholed him and said, "For heaven's sake, Ev, John Donne said that, not Don Byrne." For once, Dirksen had no riposte other than, "Oh, my God." And he rushed off to correct the *Record* before it went to press.

Dirksen, with his shock of unruly, wavy hair and perhaps the most mellifluous voice of modern times, was one of the most colorful characters ever to grace the Senate. He had a razor-sharp mind and loved few things better than to match wits with as many as one hundred newsmen in weekly press conferences in the Senate Press Gallery where he would sit cross-legged on a table cleared of press releases, sip cold coffee by choice, and bum cigarettes because he was trying to give up smoking. He could never be stumped in these bearbaiting sessions and rarely lost his cool. It was difficult to determine what Dirksen believed in. He could make an eloquent speech on either side of an issue. This stood him in good stead because he could flip-flop on issues with the greatest of ease.

He possessed a sense of timing tantamount to genius, and when the national welfare was clearly at stake—such as the need to end a Southern filibuster to move civil rights legislation while the nation was wracked with civil disorder—Dirksen would provide the needed push at exactly the right moment, even if it involved a reversal of a previous position.

When it comes to classical music, most legislators appear to have a tin ear. In the Coolidge Auditorium of the Library of Congress where some of the greatest classical music in the Western world is to be heard just a block from the Capitol and to which they have free entrée, I have seen only two senators over the years. One was the late Theodore Francis Green of Rhode Island who slept through every note—a partial deafness helped. The other was George Aiken of Vermont who attended just once, for a memorial service, and asked after hearing a Beethoven quartet, "Is this what they mean by soul music?"

As for the visual arts, a typical response was that of Sen. Jacob K. Javits of New York. When a friend criticized a Jasper Johns painting of the American flag, Javits asked with a note of irritation, "Don't you realize that is worth $65,000?"

To be fair to Javits, it should be pointed out that he is regarded by his colleagues as possessing one of the finest legal minds and debating skills in Congress. Though in the minority as a nominal Republican, he has been an influential legislator. One of his greatest accomplishments came during the Nixon era when he authored and pushed through the War Powers Act limiting the warmaking potential of the presidency.

A politician is almost always on stage. After going through a campaign with her husband, John Warner, who won a Senate seat in 1978, movie actress Elizabeth Taylor commented that "actors and politicians are always on."

The private person is very seldom seen. Once, in traveling around Minnesota with Hubert Humphrey, I saw him drop the public persona briefly. "Sometimes I feel I should get out of politics altogether," he said after a grueling day of campaigning. "I've been a bad father. My children are growing up, and I don't see them often enough." Within moments the public persona was back on. Like the "Happy Hypocrite" in Max Beerbohm's story, the average politician finds that the public mask he has worn for years cannot be removed. It has become his face.

Lastly, there is this aspect of the politician which is troublesome to many who tend to view life in terms of moral absolutes: the matter of conviction.

It is difficult at times to resist the conclusion that the effectiveness of a politician varies in inverse proportion to his commitment to principle. Some of the most effective politicians I have known have been, to put it charitably, "elastic" on matters of principle. And those who were rigid were sadly ineffective.

There's a virtue to that elasticity. For example, when the Public Accommodations Bill was introduced—a measure barring discrimination in public accommodations on grounds of race, color, religion, or national origin—Dirksen announced his opposition. "The first thing I do when I buy a dictionary," he told a press conference, "is to take a scissors and cut out the word 'compulsion.'" But as racial disorders continued to mount, Dirksen provided the push that broke a Southern filibuster and helped pass the measure.

When Ted and Bob Kennedy were both serving in the Senate, they voted in opposite ways on legislation to force a health warning to be printed on cigarette packages and in cigarette ads. Ted voted for the bill "because it's the best we can get." Bob voted against it because his amendment, which would have barred cigarette advertising altogether, failed. If Bob's amendment had carried, the bill very probably would have failed on final passage and there would have been no Surgeon General's warning on cigarette packages and ads.

In short, Ted was and is a good legislator. Bob, like his brother Jack, was a poor one—Bob, because the very concept of compromise was alien to him, and Jack, because he viewed the Senate as a stepping-stone to the presidency. Until the murder of his brothers, Ted viewed the Senate as his ultimate political goal, and he set about being good at it by hiring one of the best staffs in Congress and by immersing himself in the minutiae of the legislative process. He believed without question that Bob would exercise what the historian Edward Gibbon called "the insolent prerogative of primogeniture" and seek the presidency after Jack's second term expired.

The legislative process is necessarily a difficult and often tortuous one. Laws passed in haste under the pressure of an emergency are too often faulty and counterproductive. The essence of lawmaking is compromise. And that's where elasticity, even on matters of principle, counts.

I cannot conclude this chapter without a tribute to those members, admittedly a small band, who have shown grace under pressure and risked their careers for what they viewed as the overriding national interest.

Though his mail was running nine to one against it, much of it written in language of unparalleled abuse, and though ad hoc committees all over Tennessee ran hostile ads in every newspaper in his state, Sen. Howard Baker, Jr., voted for the ratification of the Panama Canal Treaties. There was not a single vote to be gained, and he risked losing tens of thousands of votes by his action. For a man who faced a reelection campaign that year and whose presidential ambitions might counsel expediency, Baker's action was an eloquent expression of statesmanship.

When Howard Baker, a bantamweight among senators of far larger frame and physical stature (he's only five feet seven inches tall), came to the Senate in 1967, his colleagues viewed him suspiciously as a "junior-grade Everett Dirksen." It was a heavy handicap to overcome. Their suspicion was understandable. Baker's wife, Joy, was the only daughter of the Senate's Republican leader.

It didn't take long for Baker to show his independence. Barely six months after the Ninetieth Congress convened, the forty-three-year-old Tennessee Republican courteously informed his father-in-law that he would oppose him on his efforts to overturn the Supreme Court's landmark "one-man one-vote" reapportionment decision.

"Howard," intoned Dirksen after a long silence, "my only advice to you is that when you fight, you try to win." Heeding the advice, Baker not only persuaded all but eight Republicans to back him but went on to outmaneuver Dirksen in two other major confrontations of 1968: the passage of open-housing legislation, and the rejection of Abe Fortas for chief justice of the United States.

In the early days of the war in Vietnam, Democratic Sen. Gaylord Nelson of Wisconsin cast one of the three votes against funds to finance our military involvement, an act of singular courage in the prevailing hawkish mood of the Congress and the nation. President Lyndon B. Johnson had asked for a supplemental appropriation of $700 million, not because it was needed at that moment, but because a vote for it would be a vote in support of the war. And a vote against it could be interpreted as "letting our brave boys down."

Nelson stayed up all night writing and rewriting his speech. Bleary-eyed, he addressed the Senate: "I need my conscience more than the president needs my vote."

This was to be the first of many stands against the prevailing tide. Three times in 1968 Nelson was just one of three legislators to vote against funds for the war, and on two additional occasions, he stood alone against such funding. He was also the *only* member of Congress to condemn President Ford's decision to send troops and combat planes into action in May 1975, to rescue the freighter *Mayaguez* and its crew after their capture by Cambodians. There were more casualties among the rescuers than the rescued: fifteen servicemen killed, fifty wounded, and three missing and presumed dead. Nelson told the Senate:

> There is no doubt about the popularity of the president's decision to recapture the *Mayaguez* by force. Reaction around the Congress is near unanimous. I have no doubt the public response is the same.

Hardly even a muted voice of doubt has been raised. After all, our honor and dignity were at stake.

Nevertheless, the real question remains. Was our government's action the right one? Did it serve the best interest of the nation? I think not. . . .

The test of the strength and maturity of a superpower is better measured by its restraint in minor incidents such as this rather than a demonstration of the power the world already knows we have at our command.

Thus I dissent from the conventional wisdom that tells us we must prove our virility and maintain our credibility whenever we may be challenged, however minor the insult.

Yet Nelson has none of the attributes normally associated with the legislative loner: irritability, suspicion of the motives of opponents, and an inability to work well with others. A liberal, Nelson works with conservatives who trust him unreservedly. A handsome, balding man, Nelson is jocular and has a ready wit which he turns upon himself rather than others. A popularity poll conducted in 1979 by a Rutgers professor showed Nelson to be the best-liked senator among his colleagues. Because he is somewhat lazy, it has been said of him that of the three attributes that go into the making of a good senator—intelligence, compassion, and drive—he rates a perfect score on the first two and a mediocre one on the third.

A memorable example of courage was exhibited on the Senate floor on June 1, 1950, when its only woman member, Margaret Chase Smith of Maine, rose to deliver her "Declaration of Conscience." A handsome, gray-haired woman with a soft voice that disguised a will of steel, and an ever-present red rose pinned to her dress near her right shoulder, Mrs. Smith blasted McCarthyism while a white-faced Joe McCarthy sat still.

I speak as briefly as possible [said the Maine Republican] because too much harm has already been done with irresponsible words of bitterness and selfish political opportunism.

I think it is high time for the United States Senate and its members to do some soul-searching . . . on the manner in which we are using and abusing our individual powers and privileges . . . I think that it is high time that we remember that the Constitution, as amended, speaks not only of freedom of speech but also of trial by jury instead of trial by accusation. . . .

Those of us who shout the loudest about Americanism in making character assassinations are all too frequently those who, by their own words and acts, ignore some of the basic principles of Americanism. . . .

The American people are sick and tired of seeing innocent people smeared. . . . I don't want to see the Republican Party ride to political victory on the four horsemen of calumny—fear, ignorance, bigotry, and smear.

Most of her colleagues were too craven or too opportunistic to support her. Only six of her fellow Republicans signed her "Declaration of Conscience." In this case, virtue went well-rewarded. Four years later, Joe McCarthy fielded and financed a personable, dynamic young man, Robert L. Jones, to run against her in the Republican primary. She beat him by a better than five-to-one margin. Jones, whom McCarthy called "that Maine boy who is going places," carried only two small precincts. The legend of McCarthy's political invincibility was destroyed. Six months later, he was censured by his colleagues, and the curtain was dropped on the era of McCarthyism.

CHAPTER 2

"The Swinish Blight of Ignorance"

"We know of no spectacle so ridiculous as the British public in one of its periodical fits of morality."

Thus wrote Thomas Babington Macauley nearly a century and a half ago. If he were reflecting today upon the five-year period—from February 9, 1950, to December 2, 1954—in which the late Sen. Joseph R. McCarthy of Wisconsin bestrode the national scene and blemished the image of the United States all over the world, he might have written: "We know of no spectacle so frightening as the American public in one of its periodical fits of national hysteria."

Joe McCarthy was one of the most gifted demagogues in our history but, fortunately for us and unfortunately for him, he had a fatal flaw in his makeup. He didn't believe in his own crusade. He was a Lord of Misrule. He was a poltergeist made flesh.

He did not consciously or deliberately seek to lead a movement or reach for the presidency. Former Secretary of State Henry Kissinger, in a jocular moment, described power as "the ultimate aphrodisiac." Joe McCarthy loved power after he achieved it; but, as those who knew him most intimately—and I knew him very well myself—could testify, power for him was a by-product. He loved to make mischief; he gloried in capturing headlines. The most charitable, not wholly inaccurate, description of him from an intimate was that he was a man who never grew up.

A once-admiring but later disillusioned newsman, Willard Edwards, veteran Senate correspondent for the *Chicago Tribune,* who was very close to Joe McCarthy, said of him, "He had intense ambition and drive, yet never planned ahead. While he was accused of long-range plans to make himself a national leader, he never knew at 9 P.M. what he would be doing at 9 A.M. the next day."

He loved to indulge in horseplay and practical jokes at social gatherings. He enjoyed trapping victims into a game in which a marble was dropped from the forehead into a funnel tucked into the belt. At the appropriate moment, he'd pour water down the victim's funnel.

He dreaded being alone in the evenings. In his early days in Washington, he would call me at home at night. The dialogue would go something like this:

"Guess who?"

"Oh, come off it, Joe. What's on your mind?"

"Well, I'm lonely," he'd say. "If you and your wife aren't busy, I'd like to come over and watch some wrestling matches on your television set."

"Come over," I'd reply unenthusiastically. "You can watch wrestling in the den. I'll shut the door, if you don't mind."

I'd set him up with a few beers or scotches, and he did just what he said he wanted to do: watch those fixed wrestling matches which used to pollute the airwaves in the early days of television.

Richard Rovere of the *New Yorker* magazine, who followed Joe McCarthy's rampages with close scrutiny, found in him a disassociation of public and private roles which allowed McCarthy to distort, misrepresent, even lie, and yet through it all to retain his "essential innocence."

Even after Joe McCarthy "discovered" the "Communist menace," or, to put it more nearly accurately, after he discovered the way to dominate the headlines by exploiting the "menace" of Communist infiltration into government and the domestic scene, he was often as childish as he was reckless.

There was a ritual about interviewing Joe at his office. As soon as one sat down in the chair opposite his desk, he'd get up, walk to the nearby bathroom, turn on the faucets in the sink, and go back to his desk. The sound of flowing water, he said, would interfere with any bugging of his office. On my second visit, I beat him to the bathroom and turned on the faucets, saying, "It's my turn this time, Joe."

Another habit was his tapping the mouthpiece of his telephone with a pencil. This was supposed to frustrate any bugs planted in his phone. Knowing Joe McCarthy, I concluded this was not paranoia, but sheer childish delight in playing spy games.

One day, when I was interviewing him in his office while the open faucets ran as usual, he suddenly launched into a disquisition on Marxism and Leninism. It was embarrassingly naïve and ill-informed. He saw the quizzical and bored look on my face, grinned sheepishly, and said, dropping the subject, "Oh, you know more about it than I do."

Joe McCarthy didn't discover the Communist menace until after he had been in the Senate for three years and began to worry about reelection three years hence. To put it as charitably as possible, his Senate record at that point was undistinguished. He fought with such vigor against legislation extending sugar price controls that he was known as "the Pepsi-Cola Kid." (He had an unsecured loan of $20,000 from the Washington lobbyist for Pepsi-Cola.)

While a member of the Joint Committee on Housing, Joe accepted $10,000 from the Lustron Corporation for an article he wrote for a Lustron brochure. Lustron made prefabricated houses. McCarthy wrote parts of the Housing Act, one of the provisions of which gave the Reconstruction Finance Corporation additional funds and authority to make a loan of $7 million to Lustron.

What well may have been the actual genesis of McCarthyism took place in my presence around the first of February 1950. George Waters, McCarthy's press secretary and speechwriter, approached Willard Edwards's desk in a corner of the Senate Press Gallery while I was chatting with him.

"Bill," said Waters, "the boss has got to make one of those Lincoln Day speeches in Wheeling, West-by-God-Virginia, on February 9. He wants to talk about Communist subversion. Nobody's interested in public housing anymore. You did some articles on it for the *Trib.* You got anything in your files I can use?"

"Yes, as a matter of fact, I have," Edwards replied. "I just finished a six-part series. And it's libel-proof. I name fifty-seven people who've been in the government as Communist or pro-Communist and every one has been identified either in court or has taken the Fifth Amendment before a congressional committee."

George Waters's entry and departure from the stage of history is brief, for shortly after the Wheeling speech, he went on leave and never returned. In our youth both he and I worked on the now-defunct *Washington Herald,* first under Hearst and afterwards under Eleanor "Cissie" Patterson who bought the paper. George, an impish, curly-haired Irishman with poorly fitted dentures, was our police reporter. His principal assignment was springing our drunken managing editor from the local precinct lockup where he was thrown on numerous occasions on charges of disorderly conduct and resisting arrest.

George wrote the Wheeling speech from Edwards's files—or rather, he wrote it in disjunct sections, allowing McCarthy to bridge gaps with the usual Republican clichés that make these annual fund-raising dinners in Lincoln's name such dreary affairs.

Unfortunately, it may never be known *exactly* what McCarthy said in the Colonnade Room of the McClure Hotel, one of the leading hostelries of Wheeling, after the creamed-chicken-on-patty-shell had been cleared away. Some of the ineffable flavor remains, however, in samples from the undisputed text of the speech which was titled "The Cold War between the Christian Democratic World and the Communist Atheistic World."

Decrying Secretary of State Dean Acheson's statement that he would not "turn my back on Alger Hiss," McCarthy said:

> When this pompous diplomat in striped pants with a phony British accent proclaimed to the American people that Christ on the Mount endorsed communism, high treason, and betrayal of a sacred trust, the blasphemy was so great that it awakened the dormant indignation of the American people. He has lighted the spark which is resulting in a moral uprising and will end only when the whole sorry mess of twisted, warped thinkers are swept from the national scene so that we may have a new birth of national honesty and decency in government.

Then, holding aloft in his hand a sheaf of papers, he moved into history by saying:

> In my opinion, the State Department, which is one of the most important government departments, is thoroughly infested with Communists. I have in my hand 57 cases of individuals who would appear to be either card-carrying members or certainly loyal to the Communist party, but who nevertheless are still helping to shape our foreign policy.

But did he say "57" or did he say "205"? Some of those present thought he gave the latter figure in his rambling address. The tape of that speech was erased, either by accident or design, and we'll never know.

At any rate, when he made his second Lincoln Day speech in Salt Lake City, he used both figures. The first was a list of 205 "bad risks" still working in the State Department. In addition, there were 57 "card-carrying Communists" in the State Department. In Reno the next day, the number 205 had been scratched from the rough draft and 57 written in its place.

As best as can be determined, McCarthy had no list, either of 205 or 57 names, when he went on that round of speechmaking.

The speeches made no impression in Washington. The wire services sent only a brief story out of Wheeling. The late John Peurifoy, then the dapper deputy secretary of state for security, didn't even learn about the Wheeling speech until two days after it was delivered. He wired McCarthy that he knew of no Communists in the State Department and asked for information. McCarthy didn't answer the telegram.

Then came a first-class blunder on the part of Senate Majority Leader Scott Lucas of Illinois. On Saturday, February 18, he was in Chicago to receive an honorary degree of Doctor of Law from the John Marshall Law School. An AP reporter asked him for a comment on Acheson's defense of Alger Hiss. "I told President Truman," Lucas said, "I would not defend Acheson if the matter comes up on the Senate floor. Acheson got emotional, but I don't think it will become a campaign issue—not a big one, anyway."

Then the two got to chatting, and Lucas thought he was now speaking off the record. The talk veered to the McCarthy charges. Lucas called McCarthy "the greatest headline-hunter in the world," said he didn't have the facts to back up his charges, and doubted whether he would produce the names. "If I made a charge like that," Lucas added, "I would be ashamed of myself for the rest of my life."

Lucas told me shortly after those words appeared in print that he felt "a little sick at the stomach." A cautious man, Lucas would not have attacked a Senate colleague in this manner when speaking for quotation.

It was not surprising that Lucas, a slim, handsome senator of mediocre ability, whose record as the Senate Democratic leader was unmemorable, was to commit not just one but a series of blunders which propelled McCarthy into national, even international, prominence. (After his defeat by Dirksen, Lucas, like so many defeated legislators, stayed on in Washington, becoming a lawyer-lobbyist for the outdoor advertising interests who fought against the placing of restrictions on billboards that polluted the landscape along federal highways. He didn't do very well at this, either.)

Meanwhile, the AP called McCarthy and asked for comment. McCarthy announced that he would make a speech on the Senate floor "to present considerable detailed information" to support his charges. And so he moved into the national arena.

The wisest thing to have done, of course, would have been to ignore McCarthy's absurd and baseless Lincoln Day speeches. Instead, Lucas, pushed by the State Department, went in for overkill. And here they badly misjudged their man, for even if they could prove the inaccuracy or even downright mendacity of one set of McCarthy's allegations, he would pop up with some others.

To intimates, Peurifoy said, "I've got the son of a bitch, and I'm going to let him have it." He telephoned Lucas urging that McCarthy's charges be submitted to a congressional committee. "Let's have the charges investigated," he told Lucas and several other senators. "We can hang McCarthy with them."

McCarthy made his speech on the Senate floor. No one wanted to listen to the rambling melange of tissueless allegations. A quorum was finally obtained when Lucas moved that the Senate sergeant at arms be "compelled" to bring in absent members. His voice dripping with acid, Lucas replied to the speech:

> I guarantee that a committee will be formed at once and the Senator from Wisconsin will have an opportunity to come before the com-

mittee to tell who these persons are. Before the committee, he will not be able to hide behind numbers. . . . In view of what has been said on the floor of the Senate tonight, it becomes absolutely necessary to clear this matter up as soon as possible.

The Senate voted for the investigation, and a subcommittee of the Senate Foreign Relations Committee, chaired by Millard Tydings of Maryland, finally concluded that McCarthy had imposed "a fraud and a hoax" on the Senate. Even before he saw the report, McCarthy said it would be "a disgrace to the Senate"; after he saw it he called it "a green light for the Reds."

When McCarthy was asked to produce his evidence, he said it was in State Department files. After a monumental struggle between the Tydings Committee and President Truman, the files were made available to the committee members—who found nothing to substantiate Joe's charges. McCarthy said the files had been rifled. J. Edgar Hoover, the FBI chief, said the files had not been rifled. Then McCarthy went off in another direction. It was like trying to pin down a blob of mercury.

Peurifoy, Lucas, Tydings, in fact most of Congress, had not only underestimated Joe McCarthy but had failed to measure the temperature of the nation. The issue of Communists-in-government took hold in the country. It was not alone the kooks who saw conspiracies everywhere. Patriotic organizations were quickly caught up in the hysteria. Even major segments of the Catholic hierarchy—in particular, Francis Cardinal Spellman, the most influential Catholic prelate in the country—were embracing Joe McCarthy. (At McCarthy's marriage three years later in St. Matthew's Cathedral in Washington, to which President Eisenhower sent his top aide, Gov. Sherman Adams, as his representative, the officiating priest read a cable from the Vatican in which Pope Pius XII cordially imparted his "paternal apostolic blessing" to the couple.)

McCarthy seemed invincible and thus became a great asset to the Republicans. He campaigned against and helped defeat Tydings, using in the process a faked photograph in which Tydings was shown listening intently to Earl Browder, the head of the Communist party in this country. Another outspoken Senate critic, William Benton of Connecticut, was defeated. Scott Lucas and his second-in-command, Francis Myers of Pennsylvania, lost their seats.

The defeat of Millard Tydings was particularly shocking to the Democrats. Patrician in appearance and manner, the lean, long-jawed Tydings was at the time the most powerful and influential member of the Senate. He was chairman of the Armed Services Committee which oversees the Pentagon and the entire national security scene. He was a senior member of the Foreign Relations Committee and thus bowed and scraped to by the foreign policy establishment. And he was a member, too, of the increasingly influential Atomic Energy Committee. As a debater, he was skillful and acerbic.

With hindsight, we can see that Tydings and the other senators lost their seats for reasons other than McCarthy's activities. At the time, a number of shrewd political observers noted this, but they were not listened to. Tydings had been losing touch with his constituency for years. Delegations from his state would call upon him only to learn he was "too busy" to see them and they would leave in anger. William Benton was a weak candidate—appointed, never elected, to his seat—and not tuned in well with his state. The same was true of Francis Myers. Scott Lucas was defeated by Everett Dirksen because a corrupt Cook County sheriff, exposed by an investigating committee headed by Lucas's colleague Sen. Estes Kefauver of Tennessee, was on the same ticket with Lucas. The exposé came late in the campaign, too late for Lucas to repair the damage.

While McCarthy was taking credit for Lucas's defeat, Lucas himself said to me as he pointed to Kefauver in the corridor of the Capitol, "There goes the son of a bitch who beat me."

It wasn't until the triumph of Margaret Chase Smith that McCarthy's alleged clout at the polls was seen to be largely mythical. But until then and until the censure not long thereafter, one could wonder how such a reckless and feckless man achieved such power. By his conduct he not only caused severe damage to the State Department and other government agencies; he even succeeded in humiliating the U.S. Army throughout the world. How could such things happen in our country?

It was the Lecky Principle in operation: a predisposition in America to accept the utterly ridiculous notion of widespread Communist infiltration of the government. Even the fact that McCarthy's sensational charges were based on a two-year-old list of State Department "suspects" which had been discredited by four congressional committees made no difference.

McCarthyism is not just a mid-twentieth-century aberration. A popular distrust and even fear of radicalism is as old as the Republic and as American as apple pie. As Robert Griffith pointed out in *The Politics of Fear,* it is "a natural expression of America's political culture . . . grounded in a set of attitudes, assumptions, and judgments with deep roots in American history."

It started with the Alien and Sedition Acts of 1798 which would have virtually nullified the First Amendment protection of freedom of speech and the press. The notorious Palmer Raids after World War I, in which U.S. Att. Gen. Alexander M. Palmer ordered the roundup of three thousand allegedly subversive aliens—most were subsequently set free—was a classical study in national hysteria. Immigration restrictions, anti-syndicalist laws, and the Sacco and Vanzetti case were also manifestations of this endemic malaise. Ever since the Russian Revolution of 1917, communism has been viewed as a threat to America. We didn't accord diplomatic recognition to the Soviet Union for sixteen years and to the People's Republic of China for thirty.

We came out of World War II with a self-confidence not often manifested in the American experience. Europe was in ruins and we were prosperous. Henry Luce's publications began trumpeting "the American Century." Then an erosion in our mind-set began and with it the Communists-in-government issue started to gather momentum with the frustrations and anxiety of the cold war and the revelations of Soviet espionage in Canada, Great Britain, and this country.

Almost on the eve of Joe McCarthy's Wheeling speech, a number of events took place which engendered the perfect conditions for the endemic malaise to erupt into a virulent fever.

On January 31, 1950, President Truman shocked the Congress—which had not been consulted—the country, and the entire world by announcing he had ordered the Atomic Energy Commission to proceed in the research and development of the hydrogen bomb.

I was present in the Press Gallery when Congressman Chet Holifield of California told a stunned House of Representatives that day:

> It is a decision which is fraught with the most terrible portent for the human race. In my opinion, unless an equally challenging statement is made at this time to the people of the world to obtain interna-

tional control of this weapon, which is estimated to be from ten to one thousand times greater than the A-bomb in destructive capacity, then it will make little difference as to the cotton-acreage allotment that we are so concerned with today in this House.

A number of members of Congress that day felt that Truman had missed a great opportunity, perhaps the last chance left to mankind, to use the hydrogen bomb announcement as an effective weapon for enduring peace. They believed, as did the entire nation, that we were so far ahead of the Soviets in atomic research and capability that we could demand international control of such a terrible weapon before proceeding with its construction.

The futility of this hope became frighteningly apparent on February 3, 1950, with the announcement of the arrest of Klaus Fuchs for atomic espionage. One of England's foremost atomic scientists, the mild-mannered little man had participated on the highest levels in all the work of the Manhattan Project from 1943 to 1946. When he visited Oak Ridge, Tennessee, the following year, he was given access to many of the postwar atomic secrets. Truman had rushed to make his announcement when he was informed Scotland Yard was planning to arrest Fuchs. He feared that the Soviet Union had already started work on the H-bomb and that the U.S. could afford no delay in its own effort. It was the end of any hope for an avenue of peace through American atomic preeminence.

The act that shocked the nation more than any other, causing not just an erosion but a landslide in American self-confidence, was the conviction of Alger Hiss on January 21, 1950, on two counts of perjury stemming from espionage for the Russians. After seventeen months and seventeen days of national suspense, a jury answered the question: "Who was lying, Hiss or Whittaker Chambers?"

In his senior class at Johns Hopkins University, Hiss was voted the man who had done most for the school. He was graduated cum laude from Harvard Law School and stepped into one of the most coveted jobs open at the time: secretary to U.S. Supreme Court Justice Oliver Wendell Holmes. He had been recommended to Holmes by his teacher, Felix Frankfurter, who was later elevated to the high court.

After practicing law in prestigious firms in Boston and on Wall Street, Hiss came to Washington, serving in the Agriculture Adjustment Administration; as legal assistant in the Senate investigation of the munitions industry; and as an attorney in the Solicitor General's Office in the Department of Justice. Then he went to the State Department, rising rapidly to the directorship of the Office of Special Political Affairs. He accompanied President Roosevelt to the Yalta Conference with Joseph Stalin and Winston Churchill in 1945 and was the principal adviser the next year to the U.S. delegation to the U.N. General Assembly.

Alger Hiss was the recipient of what we think of as "the American way of life" in which native talent, not class or bloodline, is the ticket to success. To repudiate it by selling out the nation in which he had been able to achieve so much was unthinkable. To this day, there are a number of people who refuse to accept Hiss's guilt.

If such a man could be an espionage agent for the Russians, asked many Americans, who could be trusted? It became easy to doubt the loyalty of one's next-door neighbor. The nation was now afflicted with one of its periodic bouts of hysteria and witch-hunting.

Wheeling, West Virginia, with its dreadful consequences, came nineteen days after Hiss's conviction; nine days after Truman's H-bomb announcement which shocked us to learn what a dangerous world we live in; and just six days after the Klaus Fuchs's arrest. Joe McCarthy's constituency was ready to be awakened with a demagogue's kiss.

If I were to pick the moment of the apogee of McCarthy's sway, it would be 12:30 P.M., February 24, 1954. And though it wasn't apparent then, it was also the moment that marked the beginning of the end for him.

The place: Ev Dirksen's Capitol hideaway, Room P-54. This was the scene of the famous "fried chicken luncheon" at which Army Secretary Robert T. Stevens was persuaded against his better judgment to avoid a head-on collision between the Eisenhower administration and Joe McCarthy. Present were Dirksen, McCarthy, and Sen. Karl Mundt of South Dakota, a McCarthy supporter.

Just six days earlier, McCarthy had hauled Brig. Gen. Ralph W. Zwicker, a much-decorated war veteran, before his investi-

At the height of his power, Senator Joseph R. McCarthy of Wisconsin is about to open hearings on his investigation of alleged Communist infiltration of the U.S. Army. He didn't know it at the time, but in taking on the Army, McCarthy started an ineluctable chain of events that was to lead to his destruction. With him is his cheif counsel, Roy Cohn, whose antics with another committee aide, G. David Schine, in an investigative trip abroad, horrified and amused all of Europe.

Brig. Gen. Ralph Zwicker, above, was blasted by McCarthy as "not fit to wear that uniform and "lacking the brains of a five-year-old." He refused to respond to interrogation on advice of Army Secretary Stevens, below, here with Gen. Mark

HOME TO STADIUM   RED PROBE IN FEUD

*Perhaps no event did more to launch
the witch-hunting wave with which
McCarthy rode to power than the
allegation that the brilliant young
State Department official, Alger
Hiss, was a Communist spy. He
maintained his innocence so
persuasively, left, that newsmen and
legislators believed him. Above,
released from prison he has
continued to proclaim his innocence.*

Senate Leader Scott Lucas of Illinois, left, underestimated McCarthy and the temper of the times. His effort to thrust McCarthy into oblivion had the unforseen effect of projecting him into national prominence. Soon McCarthy cowed virtually the entire Senate. An honorable exception was J. William Fulbright of Arkansas, right, who was the only Senator to refuse to vote for money to finance McCarthy's witch-hunts.

An upright, humorless and pious
Mormon, Republican Arthur Watkins of
Utah, above, was the perfect choice of
Senate leaders to chair the special
committee deciding whether the Senate
should censure their turbulent colleague.
It is a painful task to judge a fellow
Senator, but Watkins brought it off.
McCarthy's destruction was at hand.

On the way to the Senate via the Capitol
subway, the gentlemanly, soft-spoken
Senator Ralph Flanders of Vermont,
hands McCarthy the text of a resolution
he will introduce demanding his censure.
Joe was not impressed: "I think they
should get a net and take him to a good,
quiet place." But it was the beginning of
the end for McCarthy.

After serving nine years and three months of a 14-year sentence for relaying British and American atomic secrets to the Soviet Union, Klaus Fuchs, 47, boards a Polish airlines plane at a London airport for a flight to East Berlin, presumably to live with his aged father in Leipzig, East Germany, where he was granted asylum. By providing free access to U.S. atomic plants when the Soviet Union had no H-bomb, Fuchs's treachery had incalculable consequences for the free world's atomic supremacy.

gating committee to demand the names of all the officers involved in the promotion and subsequent honorable discharge of Maj. Irving Peress, a New York dentist who once had taken the Fifth Amendment against self-incrimination when questioned about his politics. When Zwicker, on advice of the army counsel, refused, McCarthy berated him as "not fit to wear that uniform" and said he did not have "the brains of a five-year-old." Stevens denounced McCarthy's behavior as unwarranted and ordered Zwicker not to reappear before the committee.

Over the underdone chicken, the moon-faced, bespectacled Stevens was conned into signing a "memorandum of understanding" in which he gave in to virtually all of McCarthy's demands under the naïve impression that McCarthy had made some concessions too. As he left the room, McCarthy bragged to waiting newsmen, "Stevens could not have surrendered more abjectly if he had got down on his knees." The army's "surrender" was trumpeted around the globe. The *Times* of London stated: "Senator McCarthy achieved today what General Burgoyne and General Cornwallis never achieved—the surrender of the American army."

At nine that evening, I was in Joe McCarthy's Capitol Hill home, at his invitation, to get an "exclusive" fill-in. He was in high spirits and just a little drunk as he opened the door and asked me to come into his kitchen because he had some guests in the living room.* He opened the door of the refrigerator, took out a quarter-pound stick of butter, bit off half of it, and swallowed it as I nearly gagged at the sight.

"What the hell are you doing?" I asked.

"Oh, this helps me hold my liquor better," he replied with a broad grin.

At that moment, the kitchen phone rang. His chief committee counsel, Roy Cohn, was calling him from Chicago. McCarthy said, "Sam Shaffer's here. I'm going to let him listen in." Cohn, chortling, then proceeded to read the lead in the *Chicago Tribune* story: "The United States Army, which never surrendered

---

* The guests to whom the ebullient McCarthy introduced me on the way out were Bob Kennedy, then a counsel on McCarthy's investigating committee, and his wife, Ethel. I said "Hi," for I had met the two before. As I was leaving the room, Joe said, "Stick with me, Bob, and you'll go places." Two years after McCarthy's censure by the Senate, Bob Kennedy flew out to Appleton, Wisconsin, to attend Joe's funeral.

in time of war, today capitulated to Sen. Joseph R. McCarthy of Wisconsin."

It was a grotesque spectacle—a "super-patriot" beside himself with joy at humiliating his nation's army. The most dedicated Communist saboteur could not have hoped for a greater achievement.

There was a curious consistency here. Joe McCarthy probably would never have made it to the Senate without Communist help in Wisconsin. The man he toppled in the primary, the young Bob La Follette, Jr., was "prematurely anti-Communist." On the Senate floor, he had been the first to attack the rough-shod subjugation of Eastern Europe by our wartime ally, the Soviet Union. Stalinists had penetrated the highest echelons of some of Wisconsin's most powerful unions. They did nothing to save La Follette's seat. In fact, they worked against him. After La Follette's defeat, the *Daily Worker* boasted, "The people will not mourn La Follette."

When he was accused of having Communist support in that race, McCarthy replied: "Communists have the same right to vote as anyone else, don't they?" This is not to suggest that McCarthy was himself a Communist "mole," though there was some random speculation about this when he was riding high. Joe was totally without principle and dedicated to nothing more than making mischief and grabbing headlines. And when he gained power as a result, he reveled in it for its own sake.

Characteristically, McCarthy could not restrain his havoc-making even after the Republicans triumphed in the 1952 elections, winning the Congress and the presidency. Now his rampaging was damaging his own party. Instead of "twenty years of treason," he spoke of "twenty-one years of treason," thus embracing the first year of the Eisenhower administration.

The army, which he had humiliated in February, now struck back, accusing McCarthy of seeking preferential treatment for Roy Cohn's close friend and assistant, G. David Schine, who had been drafted. The Army-McCarthy hearings consumed 35 sessions and 187 hours of live television over a period of 57 days. An estimated eighty million Americans watched McCarthy in action and most were enlightened and revolted by what they saw and heard. Among them were an increasing number of Republican politicians and voters who began to worry about a backlash at the polls in November.

Congressman George H. Bender, the normally jovial, extroverted, roly-poly—and eventually unsuccessful—Republican candidate for the Senate in Ohio, complained, "There is a growing impatience with the star-chamber methods and the denial of those civil liberties which have distinguished our country in its historic growth."

One man who could stomach it no longer was Republican Sen. Ralph E. Flanders of Vermont, a courtly, seventy-four-old conservative, an engineer, inventor, and internationally minded businessman who was one of the founders of the Committee for Economic Development.

A man of gentle mien, the avuncular, mustachioed Vermonter would appear to be the last member of the Senate likely to seek the destruction of Joe McCarthy. In fact, after the McCarthy censure, Flanders expressed regret and apologized to the Senate for earlier remarks in which he hinted at possible homosexuality as an explanation for McCarthy's assault upon the army. (The allegation that the Wisconsin senator was a homosexual was often bruited about. One would have to give a Scotch verdict of not proven.) Flanders acted because he could no longer abide McCarthy's assaults upon the dignity of the Senate.

On June 11, 1954, Flanders walked into the crowded Senate Caucus Room where the Army-McCarthy hearings were under way and handed McCarthy a copy of a resolution he planned to introduce in the Senate that afternoon to strip McCarthy of his committee chairmanships. After reading the draft aloud, McCarthy sneered, "I think they should get a net and take him to a good, quiet place."

The Republican leadership sidetracked the resolution by referring it to a committee—and oblivion. So on July 20, Flanders introduced a "privileged" resolution which, under the rules, could not be sidetracked easily. Senate Resolution 301 read:

> Resolved, That the conduct of the Senator from Wisconsin, Mr. McCarthy, is unbecoming a Member of the United States Senate, is contrary to senatorial traditions, and tends to bring the Senate into disrepute, and such conduct is hereby condemned.

A stand-up-and-be-counted vote before the elections was the last thing the Republican leadership wanted, for it would reveal a deep party split on McCarthyism. On the third day of debate, August 2, Republican leader William Knowland offered a motion to refer the Flanders resolution to a select committee of three members from each party. As amended before final passage, the resolution directed the committee to report back to the Senate before the Eighty-third Congress adjourned.

A final reckoning with McCarthy could no longer be dodged. The composition of the committee was almost beyond criticism from either side of the controversy. It was chaired by a thin, ascetic Mormon from Utah, Arthur Watkins, and had such highly regarded conservatives as Democrats John Stennis of Mississippi and Sam Ervin, Jr., of North Carolina on it.

On September 27, the committee unanimously recommended censure on two counts—for contempt of the Senate because of his refusal to appear before the subcommittee on Privileges and Elections in 1952, and for his abuse of General Zwicker.

But these counts weren't the ones that the Senate resorted to when it voted its condemnation by sixty-seven to twenty-two on December 2, 1954. By denouncing the Watkins Committee as "the unwitting handmaiden of the Communist conspiracy," McCarthy hanged himself.

"Do we have the manhood in the Senate to stand up to a challenge of that kind?" Watkins angrily demanded. McCarthy's attorney, Edward Bennett Williams, clutched his head in his hands. He knew McCarthy was doomed by his own words.

Of course the November elections helped too. Almost all the liberal Democratic incumbents won reelection. In vain did some Republicans, including Vice President Richard Nixon, accuse the Democrats of "bending to the Red wind." The Democrats recaptured control of both houses, and several of McCarthy's most vociferous supporters were defeated.

On the morning of the day the Senate was to vote its condemnation of one of its members—the fourth time such action was taken in 163 years—I asked a McCarthy foe, Democratic Sen. Mike Monroney of Oklahoma, what difference censure would make. His reply: "It means the difference from now on between Joe's getting on page one and being lucky to find space among the truss ads on page thirty-six."

He was prophetic. What Joe McCarthy had to say after the censure was ignored by the press. It was pathetic to watch him prowling the corridors of the Capitol, buttonholing newsmen and offering them stories they refused to file. His speeches on the Senate floor went virtually unreported, and his colleagues either deserted the chamber or gathered in small groups at the rear to chat among themselves.

Like Edward Arlington Robinson's "Miniver Cheevy" who mourned the passing of the age of chivalry, Joe "kept on drinking." But it was the silence as well as the whiskey that killed him by May 2, 1957.

It was odd to recall that only ten months before the condemnation, only one man in the Senate, J. William Fulbright, had the courage to vote against funds for Joe's investigating committee. Afterwards, he told his wife, Betty, "I could not live with myself if I voted a cent to support the swinish blight of ignorance."

CHAPTER 3

"What's Good for General Motors...."

The Truman administration was far from unique in misreading the public temper early in the McCarthy era. On a more benign level, the nascent Eisenhower administration embraced another misconception: that big businessmen necessarily make better government managers than professional politicians and "bumbling bureaucrats." As a result, the Great Crusade limped into the lists with its entire Defense Department team on the sidelines for a fortnight after the inauguration.

The spectacle of the leaders of industry selected by Ike insisting that conflict-of-interest laws apply to others but not to themselves awoke the combative instincts of the legislators, who were usually inclined to be cooperative during the "honeymoon" period of a new administration. And it certainly did not encourage competent men and women from the business world to risk participation in government.

The problem was Title 18 of the U.S. Code, a compilation of all federal crimes and criminal procedures. At least sixteen sections are devoted to the proper conduct of congressmen and other government officials. Section 434, which has been on the books since 1870, concerns "interested persons acting as government agents." It reads:

> Whoever, being an officer, agent, or member of, or directly or indirectly interested in the pecuniary profits or contracts of any corporation, joint-stock company, or association, or of any firm or partnership, or other business entity, is employed or acts as an officer or agent of the United States for the transaction of business with such entity, shall be fined not more than $2,000 or imprisoned not more than two years, or both.

On the eve of his inauguration as the thirty-fourth president of the United States, Ike learned he was going to have to take office with a truncated cabinet, lacking a secretary of defense, a deputy secretary of defense, and the secretaries for the army, navy, and air force.

There should have been no mystery about Section 434. Because of it, such wealthy former secretaries of defense as James Forrestal and Robert Lovett divested themselves at heavy financial sacrifice of stockholdings in corporations doing business with the armed services.

When the president-designate announced his cabinet choices, senators in both parties simply took it for granted that the appointees would conform with the law. In addition, the Democrats, who had lost control of Congress and the presidency, had little desire or intention to disturb the smooth transition of power. But not only did Ike's Defense team know nothing about Section 434; neither did the man he had chosen as the first lawyer of the Republic, Att. Gen.-designate Herbert Brownell; nor did the White House legal counsel-designate, Thomas Stephens.

On January 6, as the members of the Senate paraded in a body to the House of Representatives to participate in the vestigial practice of opening and counting the electoral ballots from the states, Majority Leader Robert A. Taft told his Democratic opposite, Lyndon B. Johnson, "General Eisenhower telephoned me and told me he was anxious to get his official family confirmed on inauguration day. I told him I saw no reason why it couldn't be done by unanimous consent of the Senate on January 20."

Johnson replied, "Bob, the Democrats are just as anxious as you to speed those confirmations. But somebody might raise a question about some of them and thus delay action. Why not get the committees into informal sessions as soon as they're organized? The questions could be asked and informal approval voted before the inauguration. Then, when the names are formally submitted, the nominees can be confirmed right away."

Informal approval of a number of the cabinet nominees was a quick matter. After volunteering the fact that he had resigned from the three automobile agencies he owned in Michigan, Arthur Summerfield was quickly approved for postmaster general. John Foster Dulles was informally approved for secretary of state after he volunteered that he had long cut himself off from any possible revenue from his former law firm of Sullivan and Cromwell.

Everything was going according to plan until the Defense Department designees appeared before the Senate Armed Services Committee, which met in closed session because military secrets might come up.

Charles E. Wilson, president of the General Motors Corporation and Ike's choice for secretary of defense, was not only frank but even garrulous about his finances. He owned $2.5 million in GM stock. In addition, he expected to receive $625,000 and an additional 1,800 shares of stock over the next five years as a bonus if he did "nothing inimical" to GM's interests. "Nothing inimical," he explained, really meant that he would not go with any rival corporation. GM's board of directors, he added, had already ruled that government service did not come under that prohibition.

The senators couldn't believe what they had just heard. One of them asked Wilson whether he had given any thought to disposing of his GM stockholdings. Wilson shook his head and explained that he had once thought of selling six hundred shares and discovered that the taxes involved would make it an unprofitable venture.

Lyndon Johnson asked, "Do you think you could act as secretary of defense on any contract involving General Motors that came across your desk? Or would you simply refuse to handle it yourself?"

"Of course I would act on the contract," Wilson replied, waving his arms forcefully. "Anything that's good for General Motors would be good for America, and anything that's good for America would be good for General Motors."

After that extraordinary declaration, which was to pass into

political folklore—Lyndon Johnson made sure of that by leaking
the statement to this writer and to Philip Geyelin, then of the
Wall Street Journal—the senators decided not to press the matter of divestiture at this time. It seemed futile.

Ike's nominees for deputy defense secretary and two designated service secretaries also revealed extensive holdings in corporations receiving defense orders. Questioned separately while
the others waited in an anteroom, these nominees differed with
Wilson in only one detail: though they would hold onto their
stock, they would not act personally on contracts involving their
corporations.

Charles Wilson's actions in the confirmation struggle could, in
an ordinary individual, be attributed to dim-wittedness. But
Wilson was not an ordinary individual, and he was anything but
dim-witted. He was an able businessman, a first-rate engineer,
and a successful president of the largest corporation in America.

Only Ike's choice for secretary of the navy, Texas oilman Robert B. Anderson, had no shares in U.S. corporations. Democratic
Sen. Lester Hunt of Wyoming afterwards remarked to this writer, "Anderson is as clean as a hound's tooth," recalling the unfortunate expression used by Ike during the campaign when
questions were asked about the secret fund raised by his running mate, Richard Nixon. But Anderson's installation would
have to wait until all were approved.

When the nominees had left, Sen. Harry F. Byrd, Sr., of Virginia brought up Section 434 of Title 18. A conservative who left
no doubt by his golden silence during the campaign that he favored Eisenhower over Adlai Stevenson, the ever-polite and
gracious Senate veteran was to prove the nemesis for Charles
Wilson and his aides. So far as he was concerned, the law was the
law.

Lester Hunt then turned to the very proper New Englander,
Sen. Leverett Saltonstall of Massachusetts, and said, "Lev, don't
you think Herb Brownell [the designated attorney general] or
some of those high-priced corporation attorneys could have told
these fellows about the law?"

Saltonstall, an Eisenhower loyalist, was visibly uncomfortable.
"It looks," he said, "as though none of them thought about it."

Lev Saltonstall, who died in June 1979 at the age of eighty-six,
retired in 1967 after twenty-two years in the Senate. A reserved

and genteel patrician with a lantern jaw and Yankee face, he was ill at ease at any unpleasant task such as the one in this instance of serving as a buffer between his colleagues and "Engine Charlie" Wilson.

Saltonstall wanted to cap his career by being chosen as the Senate Republican leader. He never knew why he didn't make it until he learned that one of his colleagues had passed the word that "the trouble with Lev is that he is such a gentleman, he agrees with the last man who speaks to him."

The committee recessed until the next day after instructing the Senate Legislative Counsel's Office to prepare a memorandum on the various laws showing the intent of Congress in this regard. No less than sixteen pertinent statutes were dug up.

Meanwhile, several senators made a quick check on the defense orders currently held by the corporations in which the nominees held stock. GM was revealed as the major contractor, holding $2,372 million in contracts. Roger M. Kyes, the proposed deputy secretary of defense, also held GM stock. Stevens and Co., a textile company in which Robert T. Stevens, the army secretary-designate, held stock, had $154 million in defense contracts. Chrysler Corporation, in which the proposed air force secretary, Harold E. Talbott, held stock, had $415 million in defense orders. In addition, the Du Pont Corporation, in which Talbott was a stockholder, had $56 million in such orders.

The next day, after an all-day session, the committee postponed any action on the nominations indefinitely. Saltonstall was instructed to confer with Brownell on the problem. Meanwhile, Lyndon Johnson sought out Taft, who knew nothing about the pending crisis, and told him, "I'm not the one who's going to jail, nor am I trying to form a cabinet. You better look into the situation."

New hearings were scheduled to "clarify" the views of Wilson and the others on corporation stockholdings. Saltonstall and Taft had the unpleasant duty of informing the new president he would have to take office without his Defense team.

Every senator will admit that there are at least ninety-nine prima donnas in the Senate and, if pressed, will include himself and raise the number to one hundred. The situation was no different in 1953 when there were only ninety-six in the Senate. Thus, even those senators most sympathetic with the plight of

Right: Leverett Saltonstall (gesturing), harried go-between in the fight over Charles Wilson's confirmation, smiles wanly after it's over, with Senate colleague Karl E. Mundt, South Dakota Republican.

Below: Defense Secretary Wilson (with hat) tells newsmen he's in trouble with Congress again because of his candor and asks forbearance.

Below: Senator Harry F. Byrd, Sr., a Virginia aristocrat and a bred-in-the-bone conservative, surprised Wilson by leading the fight to force him to give up his General Motors stock. Byrd's cocker-spaniel was a constant companion.

Charles Wilson bristled whenever he addressed the fifteen members of the Armed Services Committee as "you men." In his six-and-a-half hours of testimony covering three separate appearances, he seldom used any other form of address.

Even the gentlemanly Richard Russell of Georgia was moved to say to his colleagues in the Senate cloakroom, "Who the hell does he think we are? His board of directors?"

In his initial appearance after the formal hearings began, Wilson told the committee, "I would like to tell you men there is a change in the country. The people are not afraid of businessmen like me right now."

Several senators nodded their heads in apparent agreement. They added silently (so they told me later) that the absence of fear extended to senators, too. A test of strength was about to take place with unconditional surrender of one side or the other as the only conclusion.

Long afterwards, when asked why he didn't address them as "Senator," Wilson replied, "My dad taught me that it isn't important what you call a man, but what he is."

The test was launched when Wilson was asked whether he had divested himself of his 39,470 shares of GM stock, valued at some $2.5 million. He replied, "If there was a nice clear way without too much penalty for me personally to sell everything I had and put it in government bonds, I would do it; but the penalty is too great and I don't know why you should ask me to do it."

Lester Hunt pointed out that it had always been done in the past. Wilson said, "Well, I do not know just why you men should do that. I do not know just what a man can do. I do not particularly want to go into the apple business, for instance."

Wilson was unaware that Harry Byrd was one of the biggest apple growers in the country. Byrd interrupted Wilson to remark, "I advise you not to." Byrd went on to say that he was pro-Eisenhower. He wanted the new administration to succeed. But the fact remained that the possession of stock by the secretary of defense in a corporation doing billions of dollars' worth of defense business was a direct violation of a criminal statute. Not only that, Byrd added, but Wilson was compounding the violation of the law by insisting that he would have no reluctance in passing on GM contracts as secretary of defense. When

Lyndon Johnson asked him whether he would disqualify himself, Wilson replied firmly, "No, I will not."

The initial reaction of the Republican leaders in the Senate was that the Wilson matter could be smoothed over if he would "qualify" his testimony in a subsequent hearing by stating he would not personally handle contracts involving companies in which he retained a financial interest. Wilson reluctantly indicated he would accept the compromise. In a long conversation with the president while the two were sitting in a box at the inaugural ball, Wilson asked Ike whether he could delegate the responsibility involving such contracts to the president. Ike said he could.

But neither of them reckoned with the persistence of Harry Byrd nor the mounting public interest in the matter. Mail poured into senatorial offices complaining about Wilson's continued possession of GM stock. Those senators who had thought there might be a loophole in the law now failed to see any. On the day following the inauguration, Byrd placed excerpts from the National Defense Act of 1947 into the *Congressional Record.* They showed clearly that the secretary of defense couldn't dodge responsibility for anything taking place within his department.

A few hours later, after the news stories about Byrd's action appeared, Wilson telephoned him and asked him to come to his apartment in the Wardman Park Hotel where they could talk without interruption or interference. Since Byrd lived just two blocks away, he agreed to go over while walking his cocker spaniel. Without a particle of success, Wilson tried to convince Byrd that he should be permitted to retain his GM stock. He told him about Ike's agreement to make the decisions covering GM defense contracts. Byrd shook his head and said Wilson couldn't pass the buck that way.

Then Wilson tried a second proposition: he would place his holdings in escrow, giving any of the profits earned to charity. Byrd said that was no solution; Wilson would still own the stock and thus be in violation of Section 434 of Title 18, which forbids any officer of the government from being "directly or indirectly interested in the pecuniary profits" of a corporation doing business with the government.

The meeting ended in an impasse. The next morning, January

22, Byrd, accompanied by Russell, went to Saltonstall's office. They put the proposition bluntly: "Divestment or defeat." If Wilson didn't dispose of the stock, he would not be confirmed. Saltonstall called in former Gen. Wilton B. Persons, the president's legislative liaison officer, and told him the news. Persons telephoned Wilson at the Wardman Park Hotel and then informed the president.

Wilson wrestled with the problem for at least three hours before telephoning the White House and asking for an appointment with Eisenhower. It was set for 3:30 P.M. At 7:21 P.M., White House Press Secretary James Hagerty issued the following announcement: "The president has sent to the Senate the nomination of Charles E. Wilson as secretary of defense. Mr. Wilson visited the president this evening and volunteered his intention to dispose of all his stock in General Motors."

But Wilson's trials were not over yet. The following morning he appeared before a hastily summoned meeting of the committee. Chain-smoking cigarettes, the ashes falling upon the vest of his dark blue suit, Wilson read a prepared statement which said, in part:

> In these days when the whole free world is faced with such serious problems, it is imperative that the Department of Defense have the united support of the people of our country. In order to achieve this objective, I have decided, after carefully considering the matter, to dispose of all of the General Motors stock which I now own.... Mr. Kyes has authorized me to tell you that he will do the same thing.

Russell asked Wilson about the 1,800 shares of GM stock he was to receive as a bonus over the next five years for his work in the past as GM president. This stock was in addition to a bonus payment of some $625,000. "I am very frankly concerned about that phase of it," Russell said, "because it would seem that the value of that stock two years hence would be very directly related to the contracts that would be let by the Department of Defense."

Almost in despair, Wilson replied, "And I don't know what to do about it."

"I hope you understand," Russell went on, "that in none of these questions we have asked you here is anything personal. We do not pass these laws for good men; but we have to apply them equally to all men of all kinds when they come before this committee. . . . You say you haven't disposed of that stock. Have you exhausted every effort to see whether you can dispose of it?"

Exasperated, Wilson replied, "I would like to tell you this: I will make one more effort to see what can be done about it. I know what you are talking about, but I really feel you are giving me quite a pushing around. If I had come here to cheat, by God, I wouldn't be here."

With studied calmness, Russell said, "I am sorry you feel that way, Mr. Wilson. I am not trying to push you around, but I have my responsibilities too."

Wilson replied, "I understand that. But I am just human and, my God, I am making a great sacrifice to come down here."

Wilson then said he would make a commitment to turn over to charity any increase in the value of the bonus stock over the present market value. He was excused and the senators went into a huddle. They weren't satisfied. They wanted a specific guarantee on disposing of the bonus stock.

Wearily, Saltonstall telephoned Wilson at his hotel. Wilson put a call through to the legal counsel of the bonus and salary committee of GM in New York City. The lawyer replied he would recommend that the committee pay Wilson cash at the present market value of the stock he would receive in the future.

The next morning, Wilson spelled out this latest proposal, and unanimous approval of the nomination followed.

As secretary of defense, Charles Wilson did a very creditable job of managing the Pentagon in the difficult time of wind-down after the Korean War. President Eisenhower wanted less reliance on military manpower and a shift in emphasis to air power and nuclear weapons. Wilson, who was to carry out that policy, had to stand up to Army Chief of Staff Maxwell Taylor, his successor, Gen. Matthew Ridgeway, and Air Force Chief of Staff Hoyt Vandenberg. The first two fought against a reduction in conventional forces, and the third, for more air power than Ike sought.

Wilson's main problem was his inability to shift from the business to the political world. In the latter, as mentioned earlier, he could not bring himself to call a senator "Senator"—which caused him no end of trouble in the confirmation proceedings—

nor could he hide his contempt for the wheeling and dealing on Capitol Hill—which caused him even more trouble after he was installed at the Pentagon.

On one occasion, when he went to the U.S. Marine Base at Quantico, Virginia, he was notified by aides that the House of Representatives had voted more defense money than requested by the administration. Wilson's on-the-record comment whipped up a storm on the Hill when he said, "That's a little bit phony. I didn't see anyone vote to put up taxes to pay for it." Instead of calming the ensuing storm by claiming he was misquoted or misunderstood, Wilson, who had an excellent sense of humor, called newsmen in and said, "Fellows, we have a little problem." He rode out this storm as he did so many others while in office.

At the end of the second week of his administration, the president had a secretary of defense and a deputy secretary, but he was still lacking the service secretaries. He had been convinced by his attorney general, the White House counsel, and Wilson himself that the service secretaries would not have to sell their stock so long as they disassociated themselves from dealing with any of the corporations in which they had holdings. This could be accomplished legally, Ike was told, by a Defense Department directive permitting Wilson to assume the responsibilities in every case of "conflict of interest."

For two hours Army Secretary-Designate Robert Stevens pleaded with the committee not to compel him to sell his stock. For two hours he dodged the question as to whether he would sell his stock if it stood in the way of his confirmation.

Sen. Margaret Chase Smith of Maine said to him in a soft, but firm voice, "I would like your answer 'yes' or 'no.'"

Stevens, squirming in his seat and flushing, replied, "May I think about that as the discussion goes along?"

Sen. W. Stuart Symington of Missouri asked quietly, "Would you care to comment as to when you plan to tell the committee whether or not you are going to sell your stock?"

Stevens finally capitulated. "I will leave it with the committee as to whether I dispose of my Stevens stock." Talbott, who only the night before had told newsmen he hadn't made up his mind what to do about his stock, caved in when he saw Stevens surrender. There was no stock problem so far as Anderson was concerned. The service secretaries finally won approval after their unconditional surrender.

The mystique, if ever there was one, that big businessmen knew how to run things better than politicians died almost aborning with the start of the Eisenhower administration.

Some months later, Lyndon Johnson, in a casual conversation with me, said, "I've often wondered whether Charlie Wilson would have had so much trouble if he hadn't kept calling us 'you men.'"

CHAPTER 4

The Fiasco of
the Yalta Papers

It should have been so easy for Republicans, so long out of power, to translate the dream into reality.

The dream: the repudiation of the "infamous" secret agreements by which millions were "abandoned to Communist enslavement" by a sick and failing Democratic president outwitted by his wartime ally, the Soviet tyrant, Joseph Stalin.

All that was needed to make the dream come true was a sweep in which a Republican Congress and a Republican president could join hands in repudiating the Yalta Agreements as soon as possible after taking the oath of office on inaugural day.

It is difficult to comprehend today how intensely the Republican politicians clung to this article of faith. Whether the American people ever shared this passion is doubtful. The Republican policymakers believed they did share it and saw in the realization of the dream the solution that eluded these leaders in their flirtation with McCarthyism: becoming the permanent majority party once again in America.

The predisposition of the American people, as it turned out, was to let the dead past bury its dead. This chapter deals with the farcical effort to realize an insubstantial dream.

The Yalta Conference, attended by Franklin D. Roosevelt, Winston Churchill, and Joseph Stalin, was held at Yalta in the

Crimea for a week in February 1945. The three leaders insisted
on Germany's unconditional surrender. Plans were laid for di-
viding Germany into four zones of occupation—American, British, French, and Russian.

They agreed to ask France and China to join them in sponsor-
ing the founding conference of the United Nations to be convened in April. And agreement was reached on reorganizing
the Polish Lublin government (supported by Stalin) "on a broader democratic basis" that would include members of Poland's
London government-in-exile. On his part Stalin agreed to enter
the war against Japan within three months after Nazi Germany's
surrender.

The subsequent outbreak of the cold war and Soviet successes
in Eastern Europe led to much criticism in the United States of
the Yalta Conference and of Roosevelt, who was accused by Republicans of having delivered Eastern Europe to Communist
domination. The platform adopted by the Republican party in
Chicago in the summer of 1952 pledged:

> The Government of the United States, under Republican leader-
> ship, will repudiate all commitments contained in secret understand-
> ings such as those of Yalta which aid Communist enslavements. It will
> be made clear, on the highest authority of the President and the Con-
> gress, that United States policy, as one of its peaceful purposes, looks
> happily forward to the genuine independence of these captive peo-
> ples.

During his campaign, General Eisenhower had plenty to say
about Yalta. In his Madison Square Garden speech on October
20, he said, "They [the American people] want a brand new administration in Washington. They want men and women who
are not prisoners of past mistakes; men and women who are free
to work for and seek a solid and honorable peace; free of the
crushing handicap of having to justify Yalta and Potsdam. . . ."

In November, Republicans captured the presidency and the
Congress. Repudiation of Yalta was now at hand. In his first formal message to Congress, the State of the Union address which he
delivered February 2, President Eisenhower called for nullifica-
tion of commitments and agreements "contained in secret understandings of the past with foreign governments which
permit . . . enslavement" for "fancied gains."

But what Ike asked for on February 20 was something different, and it took a little time to sink in with the Republicans, especially in the Senate. Ike asked Congress to join him in a clear expression to the world that this nation would not acquiesce in the Soviet Union's perversion of wartime agreements which led to the enslavement of free people.

Such a resolution, backed by the unanimous sentiment of Congress, could be used as ammunition in psychological warfare against "totalitarian imperialism," to use the president's expression. By reminding the subjugated people that America had not forgotten their plight, the resolution would keep alive their hopes of eventual deliverance. And the stirring of such hopes would make more difficult the Soviet absorption of the subjugated areas.

In other words, what Ike was asking Congress to do was to condemn not the *substance* of Yalta, but its *perversion* by the Russians. The villain was to be Joe Stalin, not FDR (or Harry S. Truman at Potsdam).

And, as Secretary of State John Foster Dulles was careful to point out to the legislators, such a resolution would have no psychological value unless it had the unanimous and wholehearted backing of the Congress. To pass it by a narrow vote after a heated partisan fight would be "worse than useless."

The Democrats were delighted by the new approach and announced they would happily join the president in his request. The Republicans on the House Foreign Affairs Committee, though apprehensive at first, voted unanimously along with the Democrats after Dulles assured them the resolution "validated nothing that was invalid." But the Senate Republicans balked. The resolution struck them as an affirmation of Yalta, and this was intolerable.

What had happened in the interval between Ike's State of the Union address on February 2 and February 20? The legal counselor of the Department of State, Herman Phleger, pointed out to Dulles (and Dulles pointed out to the president) that repudiation of the Yalta Agreements would totally undermine the legality they established of our position in Berlin, Vienna, and even Korea!

The Republican members of the Senate Foreign Relations Committee insisted upon a closed door conference with Dulles. Something, they told him, had to be added to show that the Republicans weren't voting to approve Yalta when they supported the resolution. Since Dulles had told the House Republicans that the resolution "validated nothing that was invalid," why shouldn't such assurance be embodied in the resolution itself? Dulles replied that he wasn't insisting on rubber-stamping the resolution, but he was afraid of any change which would prevent a virtually unanimous vote.

Senate Majority Leader Robert A. Taft, a member of the committee, mulled the problem over during the weekend and concluded that an amendment was imperative. There simply had to be an escape clause for those members of his party who would rather be caught in a felony than discovered embracing Yalta. If he used all his power and persuasion to get the resolution past his fellow-committee Republicans and onto the floor without amendment, there was still no way he could keep any Republican from offering an amendment. And it would probably be one that repudiated Yalta outright. If the amendment was adopted, we'd lose our legal position in Berlin, etc. If it was rejected, the Senate would find itself in the position of approving Yalta, etc.

Taft outlined the dilemma at the White House in a meeting of Republican congressional leaders with the president. He said he would offer an amendment to the resolution running somewhat as follows: "The adoption of this resolution does not constitute any approval or confirmation of the provisions of the said agreements or understandings."

Ike asked Dulles what he thought. Dulles, looking very unhappy, said he would prefer no amendment. He was afraid that any changes in the original resolution would stir up a partisan fight which would nullify the effectiveness of the resolution as a weapon in psychological warfare.

In typical Ike fashion, the president resolved the dilemma by making it worse and washing his hands of it. "I will leave the wording of the resolution to you gentlemen."

The next morning, the Senate Foreign Relations Committee met behind closed doors on the resolution. Taft offered the amendment—and the fight was on. "During the campaign," Taft said, "we promised we would repudiate these pacts. Perhaps we can't go that far now, but this resolution must have language in it that shows that we don't affirm those agreements."

Sen. Theodore F. Green, Democrat of Rhode Island, said in a soft voice, "But hasn't the secretary of state expressed the opinion that we need those agreements to maintain our position in

Vienna, Berlin, and Korea?" Taft replied testily, "There's a wide variety of opinion on that. We Republicans are not for these agreements. We believe Roosevelt and Truman exceeded their authority when they signed those agreements."

In the light of the clear and uncontradicted warning from a Republican secretary of state that repudiation of the Yalta Agreements would undermine the legality of our position in Berlin, one wonders how someone as prominent and respected in his own party as Robert A. Taft of Ohio could have been so purblind. In simple truth, the humorless man with the flat, almost grating Midwest voice, who was known as "Mr. Republican" for his leadership role in the party, had long been an isolationist and had never been fully converted to internationalism by the flow of events. This was in sharp contrast to the late Arthur Vandenberg of Michigan, a former isolationist who led the Republican party in the Senate into a new bipartisan foreign policy stance in 1947 and 1948, making possible the Greek-Turkish aid program and the Marshall Plan which helped Europe in its postwar recovery. Also, Taft was a bitter man toward the end. The presidential nomination, which he thought had been his by right because of his years of service to and leadership of the party, was wrested from him by Dwight Eisenhower.

Sen. Walter F. George of Georgia spoke up (and it was clear the Democrats were beginning to enjoy the discomfiture of their Republican colleagues). "I didn't ask for this resolution. A Republican president asked for it. I feel this committee has been doing too much resoluting anyway. But since the president has asked us to join him in the resolution, and since he is the dominant figure in the making of American foreign policy, I feel obligated to support him."

Republican Sen. Alexander Smith of New Jersey said he had talked with Dulles only the night before and received the impression that Dulles wanted no amendment. But in light of the present discussion, he had decided to offer an amendment which would soften the impact of the Taft amendment. It read: "The adoption of this resolution does not constitute any determination by Congress as to the validity or invalidity of any of the provisions of the said agreements or understandings."

The meeting was beginning to take on an Alice-in-Wonderland quality as the logic-chopping grew steadily weirder.

In an angry riposte, Sen. George, normally the calmest of

men, said, "This amendment negates the entire resolution. If the wartime agreements were valid, there is no reason for an amendment. If their validity is in doubt, how can we criticize the Russians for perverting them? But more important than these considerations is that any expression of doubt undermines our position in Berlin." In his five terms in the Senate, George, a canny politician, became one of the most influential members of that body, especially in the field of foreign policy, though his critics felt that his main strength was in protecting two great Georgia industries—Coca-Cola and the Georgia Light and Power Company. He could thunder with the best of them. Nevertheless, his word carried great weight in the Senate, especially as former chairman of the Senate Foreign Relations Committee.

By contrast, Alex Smith, a mild, timid-mannered internationalist, had little impact in that body. The Smith amendment was put to a vote, and it was adopted eight to six, with only Democrat Guy Gillette of Iowa voting with the Republicans. None of his colleagues knew why Gillette crossed over; several expressed the opinion that Gillette didn't know himself. Gillette's greatest virtue was that with his handsome face and shock of white hair he looked like the quintessential senator. He was far from the brightest, however.

Next came the vote on the resolution as amended, and the vote was the same. Gone irrevocably was the unanimity sought by Ike and Dulles as the necessary psychological-war weapon. California Sen. William F. Knowland only worsened the situation by persuading the Senate Republican Policy Committee, which he chaired, to support the resolution as amended.

The Democratic leadership moved into action. Sam Rayburn, the House minority leader now that the Republicans were in control of Congress, telephoned the State Department to express his displeasure. Getting Undersecretary Walter B. Smith on the phone, Rayburn asked him rhetorically, "If you can't get cooperation from your own party in Congress on a simple resolution, what's going to happen when a major foreign policy issue is presented?"

At the same time, Senate Minority Leader Lyndon B. Johnson was telling Dulles on the phone that the amendment was unacceptable to the Democrats who had originally lost no time stating their willingness to join the president in the resolution he

Churchill, Roosevelt, and Stalin at Yalta on the eve of Russia's entry into the war against Japan. Later, as an article of political faith, Republicans accused F.D.R. of selling out Eastern Europe to the Communists and demanded the Yalta Papers to document their case. When they were finally "leaked" they proved to be politically worthless.

One of the principal actors in the fiasco of the Yalta Papers was Senator Styles Bridges, New Hampshire, holding umbrella over wife, Dolores, was chairman of the Senate Republican Policy Committee, the darling of the China Lobby, a champion of Chiang Kai-shek, an amiable man and a formidable party strategist and power.

"Mr. Republican", Robert A. Taft, above left, uncharacteristically smiling, found compromise on Yalta unacceptable. So did William F. Knowland, above right, who succeeded Taft as Senate leader. He was anything but brilliant. Both Secretary of State John Foster Dulles, below right, with Henry Cabot Lodge, were trapped by implacable, contending forces.

had requested from Congress. Johnson summoned his Democratic Policy Committee into session. It resolved unanimously to urge the proponents of the amendment to reconsider their position "so that the Congress can join the president in this, his first request in their field of foreign policy."

Thus, by 1 P.M., Wednesday, the position was a clear stalemate. Ike's first weapon in the psychological war with the Soviets was threatened with a premature explosion before it left the ground because of petty political tampering by his own party in Congress. The problem was solved by none other than Joe Stalin himself. He died. Republican leaders in both houses suddenly saw the wisdom of pigeonholing the resolution. A blast at the Soviet regime at this time could be used by the new rulers to consolidate their power. It might be used by the Soviet satellites for a premature attempt at revolt.

But the Yalta story didn't end there.

If the Republicans couldn't fulfill their campaign promise to repudiate the Yalta Agreements, the least they could accomplish while they controlled the White House and the State Department was to get the latter to release the Yalta Papers—the official papers and the working documents of the fateful conference. And they wanted them released before the 1954 congressional elections. They argued that since there was documentary evidence that Roosevelt had bartered away the freedom of millions of people when a man in better physical condition (and therefore more prudent) would have known Stalin would enter the war against Japan anyway, the American electorate would give the Republicans another lease of control of Congress.

Also, the Republicans had been tipped off that the Yalta Papers contained an anti-Semitic remark by FDR. In the margin of one galley proof, Walter Smith, then a general assigned to the European theater of operations at SHAEF (Supreme Headquarters, American Expeditionary Force) and afterwards undersecretary of state, had written, "Delete this. It is not pertinent history." Smith's reference was to a remark made by Roosevelt during the plenary meeting of February 10. It was a presumably jocular reply to a question by Stalin as to whether the president intended to make any concessions to King Ibn Saud of Saudi Arabia. According to the stenographic account, "The president replied that there was only one concession he thought he might offer, and that was to give him the six million Jews in the United States." The Republicans pressing for release of the Yalta Papers had visions of picking up the Jewish vote in the forthcoming elections as a result of this revelation.

The 1954 elections came and went. The Jewish vote didn't shift. The Democrats recaptured Congress. The Yalta Papers remained unreleased—because Sir Winston Churchill wanted them to remain secret. As a participant in the historic meeting, he had the absolute right of publication veto.

Another election was coming up in 1956. There was no certainty that Ike would run, and the Republicans were still harping on the need to release the Yalta Papers. The two most powerful members of the Republican party in Congress—Knowland, now the Senate Republican leader, and Styles Bridges of New Hampshire, the chairman of the Republican Policy Committee—started putting renewed pressure on Dulles with the convening of the Congress. By early March the heat on Dulles was intense.

William Knowland, who succeeded Taft as Senate Republican leader in 1953 after Taft died of cancer, was a stubborn man with cropped hair and a tendency toward beefiness. He was more of a headache than a help to President Eisenhower, insisting that his role was more properly that of the Senate's ambassador to the White House than the president's leader in the Senate. For genuine cooperation, especially on foreign policy matters, Ike had to lean more on the Democratic leadership in the Senate. A measure of Knowland's judgment—or rather, the lack of it—was demonstrated in 1958 when he retired from a "safe" Senate seat to run for the governorship of California, which he viewed as a certain springboard for the presidential nomination in 1960. He was defeated in the gubernatorial race, and his presidential ambitions sank without trace. Several years later he committed suicide; no one knows why.

Styles Bridges of New Hampshire was an entirely different breed of politician. Where Knowland was stubborn and abrasive, Bridges was as smooth as silk. He was without question one of the most astute politicians in recent Senate history. Seldom active on the floor or in committee, he preferred to operate behind the scenes, especially when it came to shaping a compromise or cutting a deal. A skillful operator, he admired this ability in his opponents. Once, outmaneuvered on the Senate floor by Lyndon Johnson, Bridges was asked by this writer whether he was angered by what Johnson did to him. "On the contrary," he replied. "I admire the way Lyndon operates." Like Knowland, Bridges was an arch conservative. He was perhaps the most effective instrument of the China Lobby that defended the government of Chiang Kai-shek and effectively delayed for years a rapprochement with the government of mainland China.

In the United Kingdom, Her Majesty's government remained adamant: the secret Yalta Papers were to remain just that, secret. After all, only ten years and thirty-three days had passed since the close of the Yalta Conference. So Dulles made a pathetic attempt at a Machiavellian tactic: he would "leak" the papers. It was unquestionably the most massive, *official* leak in U.S. history: more than 400 thousand carefully edited words of correspondence, notes, summaries, and stenographic reports. Packed into 834 pages were top-secret letters which passed among Churchill, Stalin, and Roosevelt; the classified messages of ambassadors and generals; the give and take of the conference table—a revealing picture of high diplomacy as it was practiced in the dramatic years of Allied "unity."

Dulles, a tall, slim, and slightly stooped man with some resemblance to the poet T. S. Eliot, was a successful Wall Street lawyer and a member of the so-called foreign policy establishment. More recent secretaries of state, such as Henry Kissinger and Cyrus Vance, have come from the same breeding ground. He was shrewd—some would say downright tricky—and brilliant. He could easily fend off and outwit an entire panel of hostile senators when testifying before their committees. An example: He was baited on one occasion by Hubert Humphrey because the U.S. government did not send Jewish members of the armed services to duty at the Dhahran Air Base in Saudi Arabia because of the official anti-Jewish policy of that country. After listening patiently while Humphrey denounced the policy of the Eisenhower administration in catering to Saudi Arabian prejudice, Dulles said quietly, "I believe that policy was instituted by President Franklin D. Roosevelt." Humphrey quickly changed the subject.

In defense of Dulles, it should be noted that he had to get along with powerful members of the Republican party in Congress who were isolationists or crypto-isolationists. In addition, McCarthyism was at its high tide. Nevertheless, one could sympathize with Senator Fulbright who, frustrated on one occasion by Dulles's deviousness in testimony, told this writer, "The truth is not in that man."

What happened after Dulles decided on the leak was farcical. On Wednesday morning, March 16, 1955, Dulles held a routine State Department press conference. At the close, his press officer, Carl McCardle, assistant secretary of state for public affairs, motioned with his finger to *New York Times* correspondent James "Scotty" Reston, to see him after the conference. Scotty stayed behind. McCardle handed him two bulky softbound volumes with the secrecy label crossed out, and asked him whether he would like to have the Yalta Papers.

This is an illustration of how most of the classic press scoops are obtained in Washington. For a variety of reasons they are given by government officials to newsmen, often to their vast surprise. Scotty did not expect such good fortune. The Washington bureau put on extra telegraphic help, but since the material was too voluminous to be handled entirely in this way, a courier was sent to New York by plane with a good portion of the text.

Meanwhile, Scotty was being scooped himself and by none other than his brother-in-law, William Fulton, a *Chicago Tribune* reporter assigned to New York City. His desk was on the third floor of the *New York Times* Annex close to the city room. He noticed the unusual activity and quickly discovered the cause: the *Times* was going to scoop the world on the Yalta Papers. This was staggering news to the *Chicago Tribune* which had always looked upon the Yalta story as its own. With the monomaniacal persistence of Cato demanding the destruction of Carthage, the *Trib* for years had been running editorials denouncing "America's diplomatic Waterloo" and demanding the release of the papers.

Fulton called his managing editor in Chicago, Don Maxwell, who called his *Times* opposite, Turner Catledge, suggesting that the two publications share the Yalta Papers and the cost of the special printing job so that both publications could appear simultaneously that night. Catledge, who had sole possession of the documents, turned him down.

Maxwell then alerted the Washington bureau of the *Trib,* instructing the staff to put maximum pressure upon senators Bridges, Knowland, Dirksen, and John Bricker of Ohio as well as congressmen Les Arends of Illinois, a member of the House Republican hierarchy, and Robert Chiperfield, the ranking Republican on the Foreign Affairs Committee, to demand White House release at once of the Yalta Papers.

Willard Edwards, the Senate correspondent for the *Trib*, told Bridges that his job depended on getting the papers. Bridges telephoned President Eisenhower, using the argument advanced by Maxwell: taxpayers' money was used to print the Yalta Papers and therefore it was against public policy to give them to only one newspaper.

By coincidence, Dulles was scheduled to have a private lunch in the Senate wing of the Capitol with Bridges and Knowland at noon; the meeting had been set up several days earlier on other matters. Before Dulles had finished chewing the first piece of cold roast beef (salad, ice cream, and coffee were also on the menu), the senators began berating him.

They knew, they said, that the Yalta Papers were being released to the *New York Times*. "If you have to leak," said Bridges, "why leak to a Democratic paper? Why not to a Republican paper like the *Chicago Tribune*?" Dulles lied, maintaining he knew nothing about the leak. He promised to look into the matter as soon as he returned to the State Department and report back. Dulles left most of his lunch on his plate. His appetite had deserted him.

Meanwhile, the *Trib*'s White House correspondent had gone to Ike's press secretary, James Hagerty. It was 2 P.M. "My office wants those papers," Laurence Burd told Hagerty, who said he would look into the situation. An hour later Burd told Hagerty, "If you don't give me the papers, I'll ask about the leak to the *Times* at the four-thirty briefing." Hagerty, shaken by now, said, "No, Larry, that's not the way to handle it. Trust in me."

In the meanwhile, the Washington bureau of the *Trib* made a reservation for Burd on every flight out of Washington for Chicago. At 4:30 P.M. Hagerty informed the White House press corps that the Yalta Papers were now generally available. Released at such a late hour, there was little that the wire services and the press generally could do with the story.

Exactly what happened in the interval between Dulles's return from his uneaten Senate lunch and Hagerty's release may never be known. Bridges informed me that Dulles telephoned Sir Winston Churchill and told him that "circumstances beyond my control" were forcing the release of the Yalta Papers. Churchill's response was said to be anything but tepid.

Burd caught the 5:30 plane. At Midway Airport, fifteen miles from the *Trib* building, he was met by a *Trib* part-time correspondent who was also a deputy sheriff for Lake County. His car had an official twirling red light. He made it in sixteen minutes, ignoring all traffic signals and Burd's plaintive pleas for a measure of caution.

Using a photoengraving technique first developed during a lengthy printers' strike, the *Trib* put out a thirty-two-page supplement within ten hours after Burd left the White House. Appearing almost simultaneously with the *New York Times,* the *Trib* had the satisfaction of not being scooped. A subscriber to the *Times* news service, the *Trib* had the further satisfaction of running the *Times*'s interpretative "sidebar" stories which the *Trib* hadn't had time to prepare itself. But it did have the time to run a blistering editorial which read, in part:

> The transcript ... was obtained through *Tribune* enterprise after this newspaper discovered the intention of the White House and the State Department to bootleg the suppressed record to favored Eastern newspapers. We were not disposed to permit this injustice to be consummated. Accordingly, we acted to obtain the record, in the belief that Administration transmission belts should not be privileged to enjoy a monopoly in matters of major public interest.

Carl McCardle paid the penalty for giving a *Trib* story to the *Times;* a reflex action, no doubt, for in Washington the first thought of a government official who wants to leak a story is to give it to the *Times.* Within a fortnight, the State Department press official announced he was returning to his paper, the *Philadelphia Bulletin. Newsweek* stated flatly he was "fired." Its story was never challenged.

After all the uproar that climaxed years of effort by Republicans to unveil the secrets of Yalta, the result was a yawning indifference by the American electorate. The Lecky Principle had been ignored. The American people were not predisposed to be excited about events a decade old.

When FDR and Churchill made their deals with Stalin, America did not have the atomic bomb. The price paid to get the Soviet Union into the war against Japan did not seem too high. Also, the foundations were laid for the creation of the United Nations.

The apathetic public response led a number of influential Republicans to regret that they had forced the disclosure. Bridges told me the Republicans would have been better off if the papers had remained secret through the 1956 campaign. The Republicans could have continued to hint that the contents were "too hot" to be published. The late Republican Sen. George W. Malone of Nevada, who had dwelt upon the iniquities of Yalta in his two Senate races, told me, "History is history. It's the future we're interested in. Why don't they dig up the Civil War?"

When newsmen asked an aide of Senate Democratic leader Lyndon B. Johnson for a comment, he replied, "I think it will be quote 'so what' end quote."

CHAPTER 5

Caliban & Tartuffe

———

Oscar Wilde once remarked that England was Caliban nine months of the year and Tartuffe the other three.

On occasion, Congress finds it possible—in fact, quite easy—to play both roles simultaneously: to be both the monster of Shakespeare's creation and Molière's engaging hypocrite. Seldom has it shown this versatility to greater advantage than in the rejection of Associate Justice Abe Fortas of the U.S. Supreme Court, nominated by his close friend and confidant President Lyndon B. Johnson in June 1968 to be the nation's fifteenth chief justice.

Political novels have seldom succeeded in America because the art of fiction can rarely compete with the reality of Washington. Allen Drury's *Advise and Consent* caught on because it was a roman à clef in which the actual personages and events could be traced with ease. Momentous constitutional struggles were reduced to malicious backbiting and the machinations of petty human beings. And what could be more titillating?

Fiction falters when it relies too much on sheer happenstance. Yet in politics, the accidental, the unplanned, or the unforeseen can be a deciding factor in fatal decisions. This is what happened in the Abe Fortas case. The Fortas nomination failed because of an improbable juxtaposition of (1) an injudicious telephone conversation from a public phone booth by the four-

teenth chief justice and (2) a reporter who happened to over-
hear it, struggled briefly with her conscience over the ethics of
eavesdropping, and decided that the "public interest" was
overriding.

As a result, the worst Republican suspicions about the surprise
resignation of Chief Justice Earl Warren were confirmed. He
was resigning not just because of age or health, but because he
was determined to keep his implacable enemy, former Vice
President Richard M. Nixon, from naming his successor should
Nixon, by now the likely Republican nominee, become the thirty-seventh president of the United States.

Even before they were known, Warren's motives came into
question among some Senate Republicans as soon as they became aware of the unconfirmed story of his resignation. This story began moving on the UPI ticker at 4:20 A.M., Friday, June 21.
But they didn't act on their suspicions, for they had nothing to
go on. When they raised their voices in opposition to any replacement of the chief justice by a "lame duck" president, they
did so, they said, as a matter of principle.

The first dissent was voiced by Republican Sen. Robert Griffin
of Michigan, who told the Senate that day:

> An unconfirmed report has been circulating this morning that
> Chief Justice Earl Warren has submitted his resignation.... While
> the report is still only a rumor which has not been confirmed or de-
> nied—and before we know what the next development, if any, may
> be—I want to indicate emphatically, as one U.S. senator, that I shall
> not vote to confirm an appointment of the next chief justice by a
> "lame duck" president....
>
> If a "lame duck" president should seek at this stage to appoint the
> leadership of the Supreme Court for many years in the future, I be-
> lieve he would be breaking faith with our system and that such a
> move would be an affront to the American people.

The flaw in Griffin's argument was that no fewer than five lame
duck presidents in American history have nominated men to
the Supreme Court and in each instance they were confirmed
by the Senate. The presidents were John Adams, Andrew Jackson, John Tyler, Rutherford Hayes, and Benjamin Harrison.
With a precedent so well established, it is difficult to argue con-
vincingly or logically that such nominations constitute "breaking faith with our system."

This was a prime example of Tartuffery. The blunt fact was that the Republicans expected to win the presidency in November and did not want to give up the greatest of all political plums. As events showed, Griffin was not to be underestimated. A short man with thinning black hair and the deceptive appearance of a mild-mannered schoolteacher or country parson, Griffin was one of the shrewdest political strategists in Congress. It was he who had organized the palace revolt, when he was a House member, that unseated Republican leader Charles Halleck, replacing him with Gerald R. Ford who later became the thirty-eighth president of the United States.

While there was widespread suspicion that Warren's timing was political and motivated by his well-known dislike of Nixon, the proof was lacking, and Griffin could rally few to his banner until the proof came, twenty-four hours later.

Warren was able to duck newsmen successfully when the story broke before dawn Friday morning. The next day he followed his usual practice, going to the University Club on 16th Street, four blocks north of the White House, for a rubdown and swim in the gymnasium. That same day, Malvina Stephenson, a Washington correspondent for the Swanco Broadcasting Company, with radio stations in Oklahoma, Kansas, Texas, and New Mexico, went to the University Club to attend a wedding of a friend, Beverly Updike, of Sapulpa, Oklahoma. While waiting for the ceremony to begin, she went over to the phone booth in the lobby to make a personal telephone call. The booth was occupied. While waiting for it to be free, she chatted with a friend, retired Army Col. John Orr, from Tulsa.

Faintly heard through the walls of the phone booth, the voice seemed familiar to Malvina. The words became distinct when the occupant opened the door from time to time to get some fresh air. What Malvina heard made her decide to forget about attending the wedding reception. Let me tell it in her own words, excerpted from the broadcast which she made shortly thereafter.

> I started out Saturday at a wedding of Beverly Updike from Sapulpa, but before it was over, I had the biggest story in Washington straight from Chief Justice Warren. In the lobby of the University Club, I was talking to retired Col. John Orr from Tulsa when I began to overhear a conversation of none other than the man most sought by reporters today, Chief Justice Warren.

It is true he did not see me. I had no bugging device, only my own ears. Col. Orr, a former intelligence officer and a lawyer, assured me I was within my constitutional rights as an individual reporter. So I believe this is the first direct, unrestricted report straight from the chief justice. He definitely—no doubt about that—and from all his chuckling—he is very relieved to get out.

The problem is, from what I HEARD [the word is capitalized in her copy, so I assume she stressed it in her soft, Southern drawl] is to get a suitable successor, that is, a liberal, not in the image of a Republican choice that might be dictated by a President Nixon and a Senate Republican leader Dirksen. . . .

I have just learned that Chief Justice Warren is rushing his retirement not only because he doesn't like Dick Nixon, but mainly because he doesn't want Republican Sen. Everett Dirksen to control the new Court appointments if Nixon gets elected president. . . .

Warren confided to a friend that if Nixon is elected president, Dirksen would be given the appointment and, said Warren, "Dirksen has already tried to ruin the Court."

The next day, Sunday, June 23, Malvina was interviewed by UPI reporter Jim Russell, who asked her whether she thought it was "entirely ethical to eavesdrop on a conversation by the chief justice." Her reply: "Would you have run from that kind of big news?" Relating the interview in her next broadcast, she said, "He laughed and said 'no.' I didn't run, I got the inside dope, from inside Warren. This is Malvina Stephenson, KRMG News, Washington, D.C."

Warren misjudged the situation slightly. Though Nixon, if and when elected, would certainly name a successor who would try to change the direction of the Warren Court, the role to be played by Dirksen was totally different from Warren's prediction. Dirksen was about to be cast in the role of the man who would be asked by President Johnson to help carry out Warren's scheme, not wreck it.

On Monday, the president asked Dirksen to come to the White House that evening for a secret talk. When Dirksen arrived, the president asked for his help. Johnson had learned about Malvina's scoop. He also knew that Dirksen's Republican colleagues were insisting that the matter of a Supreme Court appointment by a lame-duck president would be discussed at 12:30 P.M. the next day at the regular weekly meeting of the Senate Republican Policy Committee, a meeting always open to the entire Republican membership.

The president confided to Dirksen news that would not be made public for another forty-eight hours: Associate Justice Abe Fortas would be elevated to chief justice and another old friend of the president's, Texas Judge Homer Thornberry—with whom Dirksen served in the House—would be named to the vacancy created by Fortas's shift.

Johnson's strategy seemed foolproof. There was ample precedent, he told Dirksen, for a president to nominate a Supreme Court justice in the last year of his term. Stressing his high regard for Fortas, his intimate friend and adviser before and after he became president, Johnson said he didn't think the Fortas appointment would be contested after senators realized Fortas would be the first Jew to be appointed chief justice. It was an election year, Johnson went on, and even Republicans would see the folly of antagonizing Jewish voters—and fund raisers—by opposing Fortas. The Thornberry nomination, he added, would help dampen the opposition, if any, against Fortas. Members of Congress seldom oppose the judicial nomination of a colleague they had served with. Besides, since Thornberry had twice been approved for judicial posts by the Senate, it could hardly say now that he wasn't qualified to wear a justice's robes.

What the president wanted from Dirksen was to have the Senate Republican leader quell any revolt in his ranks before it could be organized. The president, as shrewd and slick a politician as Dirksen, also knew that logic alone would not do the trick. There had to be a payoff.

The payoff became clear soon enough. Dirksen feared only one possible opponent that fall—Adlai Stevenson III. Johnson asked Chicago's politically potent mayor, Richard Daley, to persuade Stevenson to wait. Since Ev's opponent turned out to be one of the weakest nominees who could be fielded against him, he had no difficulty winning another term. Two years later, when Dirksen died, Stevenson ran for the unexpired term and won handily.

Ev's first intimation that his task would be more difficult than he thought came during a dinner that same evening at the home of his son-in-law, Tennessee Sen. Howard Baker, Jr. Dirksen told him about his agreement to help the president and asked Baker to keep the names confidential until they were made public. Baker agreed to the request but balked at supporting the nominees. "Mr. D.," he said, using the form of address

he always employed with his father-in-law, "I can't go along
with you. I'll fight confirmation until we convene a new Congress and install a new administration."

At the Republican Policy Committee luncheon, Dirksen
stalled any discussion of Warren's reported resignation by discussing other matters until time nearly ran out. Then, briefly, he
left no doubt about where he stood. "There's nothing about
lame ducks in the Constitution."

As the Republicans hurried to the Senate floor in response to
bells announcing a vote, California's George Murphy, a former
Hollywood and Broadway song-and-dance man, turned to Griffin and said, "To hell with waiting a week for the next Policy
luncheon to decide on a position. Let's get up a statement declaring our opposition and get some of our colleagues to sign it."
Murphy's career as a one-term senator was distinguished by its
total lack of distinction, adding luster neither to his former occupation in show business nor his brief transit across the stage of
politics. He was elected to the Senate in 1964 because of a split
in the Democratic party in California. He was defeated for a second term after it was disclosed that he was on a $20,000 annual
retainer fee from the Technicolor Corporation and used its
credit card to pay for his numerous flights around the country.
His entry in *Who's Who* gives less than half a line to the fact that
he was a U.S. senator and an entire paragraph dealing principally with a listing of his films and Broadway shows.

That evening, in Griffin's office, Murphy and Griffin drew up
their statement:

> The undersigned Republican senators wish to indicate their strong
> view that the next Chief Justice of the Supreme Court should be des-
> ignated by the next President of the United States; and that if such an
> appointment should be made in the waning months of this Adminis-
> tration while the people are in the process of choosing a new govern-
> ment, we would not vote to confirm it.

Eight signatures were quickly obtained. Before more could be
sought, the president announced his nominations. There were
quick huddles in the Republican cloakroom. When someone remarked to Baker that the president had "pulled a fast one," Baker said, "By God, he did it in spades. But I'm going to oppose

confirmation. It's not personal; it's a matter of principle. I have nothing against Fortas, and I have nothing against Thornberry."

For a few moments there were qualms. Even though Thornberry was, as one senator put it, "an amiable mediocrity," could one oppose a former colleague, especially one deemed judicially qualified twice by the Senate? As for Fortas, the Senate had already deemed him qualified for a seat on the high court. Even before he went on the Court, Fortas had a reputation for possessing one of the finest legal minds in the nation. He had made his way up from immigrant's son to New Deal whiz kid to insider's insider around Washington, and had become a well-heeled, well-wired corporation lawyer with such clients as Pan Am, Philip Morris, and Coca-Cola. Lyndon Johnson met him in the 1930s when they were both new to Washington, and their intimate relationship continued after LBJ went to the White House.

That evening in Griffin's office, a new statement was drafted:

> It is the strongly held view of the undersigned Republican Senators that the next Chief Justice of the United States should be selected by the newly elected President of the United States after the people have expressed themselves in the November elections. We will, because of the above principle and absolutely with no reflection on any individuals involved, vote against confirming any Supreme Court nominees by the incumbent President.

This emphasis upon "principle" when the objective was to save the richest of all political plums for an anticipated Republican administration was also Tartuffery at its best. The petition quickly gathered eighteen signatures.

Thus, within less than seventy-two hours after the president had asked Dirksen for help, within twenty-four hours after Dirksen's appearance before the Senate GOP Policy Committee, and within minutes after the president submitted the names of his two nominees, Ev Dirksen had been deserted by half his troops in the Senate—including his own son-in-law.

Insiders knew that this bloc of eighteen senators was aiming at a filibuster. This would be easy to accomplish since Congress had a lot of "must" legislation to enact before its hoped-for adjournment in advance of the August 5 Republican Convention in Miami Beach, Florida. All they had to do was delay action in committee and on the floor for a mere three weeks and two

Abe Fortas, former Supreme Court Justice

Supreme Court Justice Abe Fortas in a happier time before Reporter Malvina Stephenson accidentally overheard a phone call by Earl Warren which started a chain of events that led to the first rejection in history of a nominated Chief Justice. Fortas was picked to be Warren's successor. By common consent, Fortas was believed to possess one of the keenest legal minds of the day. But he was nominated by a lame-duck President and thus became especially vulnerable in an election year. Nevertheless, if Malvina had been elsewhere that day, Fortas could well have made it and recent Supreme Court history would certainly have been vastly different.

Jack Miller, Iowa Republican Senator, made the high court's ambivalent attitude on pornography an issue in the confirmation battle.

Robert Griffin, Michigan Republican Senator, a shrewd political strategist, organized the fight against Fortas when it looked hopeless.

Earl Warren, Chief Justice, didn't want Richard Nixon, who was expected to become the next President, to name his successor.

days. The press of other legislation would compel the Senate leadership to lay the nominations aside. Of course, Johnson could make recess appointments after Congress adjourned, but he would do so in the face of a resolution adopted by the Senate on August 29, 1960, stating that "recess appointments to the Supreme Court of the United States should not be made except under unusual circumstances." Among those who had voted for this resolution was a senator from Texas named Lyndon B. Johnson.

On July 18, at a breakfast meeting with his congressional leaders, a grim president, whose anger was not very far below the surface, said, "I want Abe Fortas confirmed even if I have to keep Congress in session until Christmas." Adjournment plans had to be scrapped. The filibuster would continue after the two conventions were out of the way. What the president didn't know was that a telephone call made two weeks earlier had already doomed the Fortas nomination.

Bob Griffin was driving home to Traverse City, Michigan, for the July 4 recess. En route, he stopped off at the home of his mother near Pontiac. She told him he had had a telephone call from Winder, Georgia. There was only one citizen of prominence who lived in Winder—Richard Russell, the leader of the Southern bloc in the Senate.

"Bob," Russell said when Griffin returned his call, "how many votes have you got against cloture?" Cloture, always difficult to obtain, required a two-thirds vote to shut off debate.

"Well, Dick, I think I now have twenty to twenty-two votes on my side of the aisle. And I guess I can always count on some Western votes because those fellows just don't believe in cloture."

"Are you serious about this thing?" Russell asked. "Are you going to stick with it?"

"Yes, Dick, I'm dead serious about it."

"I'll be with you," Russell said.

That proved the turning point in Fortas's fortunes. Russell would deliver the Southern votes. Opposition to Fortas was no longer a partisan Republican issue. Griffin now figured he had thirty-eight votes, and only thirty-four were needed, under the existing rules, to prevent cloture. It didn't matter whether there was a majority in the Senate for Fortas; the majority wouldn't have the chance to cast their votes on confirmation.

LBJ had failed to touch base with Russell, a serious mistake in strategy. He didn't know that the Southerners were beginning to turn against Fortas because they, too, wanted a change in the permissive direction of the Warren Court. The president then began stepping up pressure on the senators. The methods used were classical examples of how arms are twisted in great political struggles.

At the behest of the White House, a Washington lobbyist for Coca-Cola telephoned Senator Russell Long of Louisiana, then the assistant Senate Democratic Leader, and asked him to vote for Fortas.

Long exploded. "Why, I just told the president of the Yew-nit-ed States that I was *not* going to vote to confirm Abe Fortas. How the hell do you expect me to tell the president of Coca-Cola that I *will* vote to confirm?"

Edgar Kaiser, the head of Kaiser Industries, a complex of steel, aluminum, and cement companies centered in Hawaii, telephoned GOP Senator Hiram Fong of that state so many times on behalf of the Fortas nomination that Fong hesitated to pick up the receiver.

One major industrialist visited GOP Senator John Williams of Delaware in his office to urge him to vote for Fortas.

"Why are you asking me to do this?" Williams asked.

After a pause, the industrialist replied, "Senator, I don't want to have any trouble with the Antitrust Division or any other branch of government. Besides, my corporation may have some cases before the Supreme Court."

"Be frank with me," Williams said. "What would you do if you were in the Senate?"

Another pause, then came the answer. "I'd vote against confirmation."

The president, it developed, was not only personally telephoning leaders of industry to enlist their lobbying support for Fortas, he was also on the phone with Jewish leaders asking them to phone their senators. The Republicans were concerned that they would be tagged with anti-Semitism, but Sen. Jacob K. Javits of New York told his colleagues he would personally get in touch with every Jewish leader who called them on Fortas's behalf to assert that the issue was *not* anti-Semitism. As the most prominent Jew in Congress, his pledge carried much weight and assurance.

One Southern senator, Ernest "Fritz" Hollings of South Carolina, told me he had received a phone call from "one of the most prominent Jewish leaders in Washington" urging him to vote for Fortas. When Hollings told him he couldn't because it would mean a continuation of the Warren Court, the caller said, "All right, Senator. The hell with Fortas. He hasn't been a religious Jew anyway, and he even married outside the faith. But I would appreciate it if you would do what you could to see that Israel gets those fifty F-4 Phantom jets."

When Fortas finally appeared before the Senate Judiciary Committee late in July, his position deteriorated sharply when he admitted that he had continued to advise the president on controversial issues. Even the newspapers most vocal in his behalf were critical: The *New York Times* said that Fortas "was injudicious in continuing to advise the President on controversial public issues"; the *Washington Post* editorialized, "The job of a member of the Supreme Court is to decide cases and expound the law, not to advise Presidents on matters of foreign and domestic policy, even if the President happens to be an old and dear friend."

Then the Senate began changing its role from Tartuffe to Caliban. Fortas came under attack for his permissive stand on a whole series of pornography cases. Under the prompting of GOP Sen. Strom Thurmond of South Carolina, a witness representing a group styled Citizens for Decent Literature, Inc., was brought before the committee to accuse Fortas of having provided the key vote the previous year in the five to four ruling that had decided that a particular peephole striptease film was not obscene. (The witness, Los Angeles attorney James J. Clancey, also accused Fortas of conflict of interest for having joined a six to three majority exonerating a book published by a man who, according to Clancey, had been represented by attorney Fortas in an obscenity case ten years earlier.)

The vote on the Fortas nomination in the committee was delayed for a week to give all the members who had not seen the film a chance to do so. The film was screened in the committee room behind locked doors. Thurmond, who was a few minutes late to his own showing, had to bang on the door to gain admittance. As a guest of Sen. Thurmond, I saw the film and wrote the following tongue-in-cheek critique for my editors—who never ran it:

The 14-minute film, while satisfying the Aristotelian precepts of unity of time, place, and action, and inducing the Coleridgean "willing suspension of disbelief," was singularly lacking in plot line, poorly directed, shabbily lighted, and excessively concentrated on closeup shots of the pubic region. It was certainly bereft of any redeeming social value. It was just plain, downright obscene, even by the standards of the artists who painted the frescoes in the brothels of Pompeii.

On July 26, GOP Sen. Jack Miller of Iowa carried the pornography issue to the Senate floor. He denounced Fortas's role in May and June 1967 in the reversal of twenty-three of twenty-six state and federal convictions for violating obscenity laws, upsetting the community standards of thirteen states. He said there were twenty-six more reversals in obscenity cases during the Court term that ended a month earlier. Miller said:

> Justice Fortas voted with the five to four majority in all of these cases. All but three were decided without opinion, and in the three with an opinion, there was only a brief majority opinion not written by Justice Fortas. In other words, we do not have his judicial philosophy on this subject; but we do have his judgment in the reversals of these cases, and the judgment is abhorrent to the maintenance of moral standards by our communities. It is a judgment which encourages the permissiveness and criminal activity which are plaguing our society.

The shoddiness of Miller's attack was shown by his admission that "we do not have his [Fortas's] judicial philosophy on this subject." Nearly all the reversals of the pornography convictions were made in unwritten opinions that overturn lower court findings.

Miller's flawed legal reasoning, however, was no barrier to his own service on the bench. Defeated in the 1972 elections after two terms in the Senate, he was rewarded by President Nixon with appointment to a cushy, lifetime job on the bench of the U.S. Court of Customs and Patent Appeals. A hard and diligent worker, he had a tendency to drive his colleagues to distraction by his earnest dullness and insistence on numerous and insignificant amendments to pending bills.

To discover the actual reasons for the Court's reversals, one would have to examine earlier opinions by the justices who constituted the majority. William O. Douglas and Hugo Black always argued that the First Amendment forbade any regulation of ideas, even those dealing with explicit sex. Potter Stewart confessed a total inability to define obscenity, saying in a memorable line, "I can't explain it, but I know it when I see it." William J. Brennan, Jr., believed obscenity could be regulated only when children were in the audience. Abe Fortas, whose judgment was condemned by Miller as "abhorrent to the maintenance of moral standards by our communities," had never even articulated his reasons for joining Douglas, Black, Stewart, and Brennan.

If there was any validity to Miller's attack, the stuffy Iowan owed it to his country to ask the House of Representatives to initiate impeachment proceedings against all five of the justices. Of course, he did nothing of the kind. Instead Miller went on to mention the film I have reviewed above and said he had seen it along with several members of the committee. "If this isn't hard-core pornography, we didn't know what it was. Now that these facts have been brought to public attention, I would hope that the president would withdraw the nomination."

More films were brought to Washington for the delectation of the senators. One was *Flaming Creatures,* which was seized by police on January 18, 1967, when it was shown on the University of Michigan campus. The Ann Arbor police flew it to Washington where it was screened behind the closed doors of the Judiciary Committee for the six senators who bothered to show up. It dealt unblushingly with transvestism and portrayed inter- and intra-sexual acts of sodomy. The case was moot by the time it reached the high court. Fortas merely noted that he would have voted to reverse the conviction. "That film," one of the viewing senators told me, "was so sick, I couldn't even get aroused."

By this time, the Fortas position was hopeless. The pornography issue had LBJ more worried than any other aspect of the nomination battle. Democratic Sen. Phil Hart of Michigan, an ardent Fortas defender, told me: "This is dynamite. As a lawyer, I could defend the Court's decisions on constitutional grounds, stating that state obscenity convictions ran counter to the First Amendment guarantees of free speech. But that's pretty hard to do when the material involved, by any common-sense standard, is hard-core pornography."

On October 1, 1968, the Senate voted forty-five to forty-three for cloture. The number of votes required that day to shut off the filibuster was fifty-nine. Three days later, the president withdrew the nomination. But Fortas's troubles weren't over yet. Seven and a half months later, he wrote a chapter in American history that had no precedent. He became the first member of the high court to resign in disgrace. And if he hadn't, his impeachment by the House and a trial and possible conviction by the Senate were inescapable.

Life magazine broke the story stating that in January 1966, three months after becoming an associate justice, Fortas had accepted a $20,000 fee from a foundation controlled by the family of industrialist Louis E. Wolfson. In September, Wolfson was indicted for selling unregistered securities. In December, Fortas returned the $20,000. Wolfson was convicted and sent to prison.

A tide of indignation and revulsion swept over Capitol Hill. It was intensified by Fortas's brief, written reply to the article in *Life*, a reply which struck the legislators as arrogant and disingenuous. Those who were angriest were those who had fought hardest for Fortas, such as Democratic Sen. Joseph Tydings of Maryland, who told the Senate, "The confidence of our citizenry in the federal judiciary must be preserved. Mr. Justice Fortas must resign. He must resign immediately." In the Senate dining room, Democratic Sen. William Proxmire of Wisconsin, who had also supported Fortas for chief justice, threw his arms up in the air and said, "I can't understand it. I just can't. What does he need that $20,000 for? He's a wealthy man. His wife has a lucrative law practice. They have no children to educate, to send through college. Why did he do it?"

Fortas resigned May 14. In a letter to Chief Justice Warren, Fortas said he had received no other compensation from Wolfson, his family, or his associates either "directly or indirectly." He added,

> Since I became a member of the Court, Mr. Wolfson on occasion would send me material relating to his problems, just as I think he did many other people, and on several occasions he mentioned them to me, but I have not interceded or taken part in any legal, administrative, or judicial matter affecting Mr. Wolfson or anyone associated with him.
>
> There has been no wrongdoing on my part. There has been no default in the performance of my judicial duties. . . .

History may well be kinder to Fortas than his contemporaries were. What he did, however unwise at the time, may eventually be judged as basically venial. The Court lost not only one of the most brilliant legal minds of the day; it lost a judge dedicated to the protection of First Amendment rights which today are under such a frightening siege.

Warren's indiscreet, overheard telephone conversation had tragic consequences indeed.

CHAPTER 6

"Troopers, Forward!"

―――――

"At times history and fate meet at a single time in a single place to shape a turning point in man's unending search for freedom. So it was at Lexington and Concord. So it was a century ago at Appomattox. So it was last week in Selma, Alabama."

These words were spoken at 9:04 P.M., Monday, March 15, 1965, by the first Southern president in a century, Lyndon B. Johnson, moments after he had begun a historic speech before a joint session of Congress. Millions of angry Americans were watching him in their homes on preempted prime television time.

Hanging on every word in the silent and jam-packed House chamber were the members of Congress, the president's cabinet, the members of the Supreme Court in their robes, and the entire diplomatic corps. In the President's Gallery to the left of the rostrum sat Lady Bird and members of the president's family, a number of the nation's religious leaders who had become involved in the current racial struggles, and even FBI Chief J. Edgar Hoover. Despite his implacable hatred of Martin Luther King, Jr., who had led the historic and bloody march in Selma, Hoover's agents at that very moment were gathering the evidence of the police brutality in Alabama which had led to the historic session.

Everyone present had the sense of participating in an extraordinary occasion, one which would mark a turning point in American history and lead to the ineluctable enfranchisement of the blacks.

As he told his listeners, the president had not come this night, as one of his predecessors had done, to veto a veterans' bonus bill, or as another had, to urge the passage of legislation to break a railroad strike that threatened to paralyze a nation. He had come to ask Congress to end a century of racial injustice by which the ballot had been denied the black citizens of America—and to propose a legislative remedy which even its advocates admitted privately stretched the outmost bounds of constitutionality.

What had only a short time ago seemed impossible was suddenly rendered possible when, on the soon-to-be blood-spattered streets of Selma, an Alabama state trooper, Major John Cloud, uttered two words: "Troopers, forward!"

Until then, the sole constitutional right of the states to set the qualifications for voters seemed to many in Congress and in the executive branch, too, to be an insuperable barrier to effective electoral reform.

The 1957 act, the first civil rights bill enacted since post-Reconstruction days, prohibited action to prevent persons from voting in federal elections and authorized the attorney general to bring suit when a person was deprived of his voting rights. The 1960 act strengthened provisions of the earlier measure for court enforcement of voting rights; Southern law enforcement officials had had no problem finding loopholes in the earlier law. The 1964 act effectively prohibited discrimination in public accommodations, but tougher voting rights provisions, aimed at plugging up even more newly discovered loopholes, were defeated by filibuster.

What was needed had been known for years, but the time had not been considered "ripe." Five years earlier, Sen. Paul Douglas had introduced legislation embodying the remedies finally adopted after Selma. Among those helping to sink the Douglas proposals was then-Sen. Lyndon B. Johnson.

The remedies finally written into law in 1965 provided for:

1. Federal "examiners" to supplant local registrars who abused their powers. (The term "registrars" had had a pejorative connotation in the South since Reconstruction days.)
2. The elimination of literacy tests which were used to disqualify black Ph.D.'s while granting the ballot to barely literate rednecks.
3. The defusing of poll taxes as a vote-denying device.
4. An automatic triggering device by which federal examiners would be dispatched to those areas where less than 50 percent of eligible voters were registered.

To blame small bands of "willful men," entrenched Southern legislative barons, or refractory congressional rules for the nation's failure to redress grave injustices prior to 1965 is to miss a vital aspect of lawmaking in a democracy. Without broad acceptance of major and basic change, a law to effect it will be ignored or flouted. This was the fate of Prohibition.

The same thing happens even in Vatican politics, as witness the failure of Pope Paul VI's encyclical, *Humanae Vitae,* prohibiting artificial means of birth control. Or the final collapse of the church's condemnation of lending money at interest, without which commercial civilization could never advance.

Until Selma, it seemed impossible to bypass Article One, Section Two of the federal Constitution without endangering the very fabric of American political life. The states were there given the *exclusive* right to set the qualifications of the voters. However, the swinging clubs and the tear-gas canisters of Selma caused a sudden change in the mental and moral climate in America, and therefore in Washington. Suddenly, lawmakers realized that Article One, Section Two had been modified—nay superseded—in 1870 with the adoption of the Fifteenth Amendment, which reads:

> 1. The rights of citizens of the United States to vote shall not be denied or abridged by the United States or by any state on account of race, color, or previous condition of servitude.
> 2. The Congress shall have power to enforce this article by appropriate legislation.

It was a perfect illustration of the Lecky Principle. At long last, the American people were predisposed to accept the dras-

tic change needed in the law to contain and alleviate social up-
heaval.

Veteran observers of Congress had never witnessed such anger since the Japanese bombed Pearl Harbor. The terrible
events of Selma triggered a wave of indignation greater than
any episode in the long civil rights struggle. There was a grim
determination in both parties to do the one thing they had
failed to do adequately in the three earlier civil rights bills: guarantee the right to vote. Impatience with judicial processes as the
guarantor of that right had grown to the point of legislative re-
bellion. Normal court delays were now viewed as intolerable.
Southern judges were now seen as men who had not doffed
their prejudices when they donned their legal robes. They had
to be circumvented.

Birmingham, Alabama's, former police commissioner, Eugene
"Bull" Conner, had paved the way for the 1964 Civil Rights Bill
by his brutal treatment of demonstrators. But the accomplishment of the storm troopers unleashed by Governor George Wallace far outdistanced Bull Conner's.

The wave of anger in Congress was a tribute to the impact of
visual journalism. The pictures of the troopers swinging their
clubs against prostrate blacks and marching like gas-masked au-
tomata through clouds of tear gas had a galvanizing impact
upon the legislators.

It is improper in congressional debate to cast unfavorable re-
flections upon any state of the Union. Senate Rule XIX, paragraph 4, states, "No Senator in debate shall refer offensively to
any State of the Union." In the House, there are a series of precedents forbidding invidious remarks about a state. No one invoked those rules and precedents after Selma. The columns of
the *Congressional Record* were studded with such subheads as
"Alabama's Shame" and "Shame at Alabama." Democratic Congressman Wayne Hays of Ohio, who had never commented on
civil rights on the floor of the House in his sixteen years in Congress, said: "We ought to cut the number of the Alabama delegation in half, and I am ready and willing to vote to do exactly
that." Several House members demanded that the federal government shut down all its military installations in the state. As
Democratic Congressman Charles Vanik of Ohio put it:

> If the state of Alabama chooses to declare war on the U.S. Constitu-
> tion and the rights which it confers on all of its citizens, our federal

government can take immediate steps ... to shut down and move military installations, and critical space and defense work, to areas of greater constitutional security. ... The shame of Selma is the shame of America.

Democratic Congresswoman Edith Green of Oregon said,

Was it to preserve the public safety to gas American citizens kneeling in prayer? Was it preserving the public safety to club and whip stumbling and panicked men and women fleeing for the safety of their homes?.... Everyone knows that it was in fact an exercise in oppression. Everyone knows, and yet the Justice Department announced it will investigate—investigate, if you will, whether unnecessary force was used by law officers and others.

Is this the U.S. government which dares the armed might of dangerous and powerful enemies abroad, but surrenders to storm troopers armed with tear gas and billy clubs? To say so is an offense against all sense and reason.

Even one Southerner, Democratic Sen. Ralph Yarborough of Texas, was moved to say on the Senate floor,

Shame on you, George Wallace, for the wet ropes that bruised the muscles, for the bullwhips which cut the flesh, for the clubs that broke the bones, for the tear gas that blinded, burned, and choked into insensibility.

The time was ripe for Johnson's historic speech. Eight days had passed since the column of 525 men and women filed across Edmund Pettis Bridge on the southern edge of Selma on its march to the seat of government in Montgomery to petition for a right that in the U.S. was supposed to be beyond debate—the right to vote. Eight days had passed since the troopers, acting under Governor Wallace's orders, used tear gas, nightsticks, and whips to halt the column, injuring forty marchers.

Wearing a dark blue suit and a light blue shirt (for the TV cameras), the president walked down the aisle to the rostrum in a withdrawn, somber manner. On the rostrum, he opened a black looseleaf notebook (in which key phrases were heavily underlined) and began to speak in a slow, subdued, even manner.

He had to read his speech from his notebook for the first fourteen minutes because the teleprompter didn't start functioning until 9:18. The text of the speech, written and rewritten almost up to the time of delivery, was so late in being prepared that the teleprompter rolls couldn't be readied in time. White House aide Jack Valenti told the teleprompter operator when he handed him the text, "I almost died a thousand deaths getting it here in time."

The speech was interrupted thirty-nine times by applause, and twice by standing ovations. Even one would have been unprecedented.

By the close of the speech, Johnson had sounded the anthem of the black revolt and turned it into a moral imperative for the nation: "Their cause must be our cause, too. Because it is not just Negroes but really it is all of us who must overcome the crippling legacy of bigotry and injustice." Then, raising his voice, he concluded with the words that sent a gasp of awe, surprise, and admiration through the chamber: "And we shall overcome."

As the president walked up the center aisle on the way out of the chamber, he spotted Democratic Congressman Emanuel Celler of New York, the chairman of the House Judiciary Committee which would handle the civil rights bill.

"Manny," the president said, "I want you to start hearings tonight."

Celler gulped, then said, "Mr. President, I can't push that committee or it might get out of hand. I'm scheduling hearings for three days next week, beginning Tuesday."

"Start them this week, Manny," the president said. "And hold night sessions, too."

Manny Celler, a civil rights advocate before Lyndon Johnson was born, served nearly half a century in Congress before he was finally defeated in 1972, at the age of eighty-four by a young woman, Elizabeth Holtzman. The voters in his New York City district decided he had been around long enough. At this time, he was seventy-seven and had already served in the House for forty-three years.

Two days later, without consulting Celler, Johnson told newsmen at the White House that Celler's committee would begin hearings the next morning with Attorney General Nicholas Katzenbach as the first witness. It was the first Celler had heard about it. So, two hours later, he rushed out a press release stating, in part, "In the light of the continuing shameful and tragic events in Alabama, the need for speedy action on the President's voting rights bill is essential. I have, therefore, scheduled hearings on the Administration Bill for Thursday, March 18. The restless mood of the country brooks no delay."

When Johnson asked the Congress Monday night to pass the bill without delay, there was no bill. It hadn't been written. In fact, until Selma, the president had had no intention of asking Congress to pass another civil rights bill. He had been elected three months earlier in a landslide and intended to capitalize upon that victory over Barry Goldwater with the enactment of a legislative program exceeding Franklin D. Roosevelt's One Hundred Days. (And he did.) A civil rights struggle, he feared, would slow down the rest of the program.

A bill was written on Capitol Hill in the office of Senate Republican leader Everett M. Dirksen of Illinois, just a few yards from the Senate chamber. The authors included Dirksen, Senate Democratic leader Mike Mansfield, and a bipartisan group of senators who had been pushing for a meaningful voting rights bill for months, despite White House resistance.

Room S-230, where the bill was drafted, is about fifty feet long and twenty feet wide. It has an arched ceiling supported by Romanesque arches nearly two stories high. It looks out upon a superb view of the city of Washington, taking in the entire sweep of the Mall, the Washington Monument, and the Lincoln Memorial on the banks of the Potomac. Hanging in the center of the room is a huge crystal chandelier that Thomas Jefferson had shipped over from Paris. Air from a nearby register blows upon the chandelier, and its pendants clink melodiously all day long. Just beneath the chandelier is an oblong mahogany table that normally seats ten—four on each side and one at each end. The table has extension leaves, and during the post-Selma deliberations, as many as sixteen senators, senatorial aides, and Justice Department officials (including Katzenbach and his deputy, Ramsey Clark) sat around it. Dirksen always sat at the head of the table with Katzenbach on his right.

Every day, new language was written or stricken. The president was constantly in touch either by telephone or through Dirksen's frequent trips to the White House. The bill was still several days short of completion when, on Sunday afternoon, March 14, a week after Selma, the Democratic congressional leaders met with the president. He told them he intended to send a civil rights message to Congress the next day and a draft bill as soon thereafter as possible. It was then that Speaker John McCormack and Mike Mansfield invited him to address a joint session Monday instead of sending a message.

At 11:45 A.M., Wednesday, the doors of Room S-230 were opened and newsmen poured in. "We have resolved our labors and put the finishing touches on the bill," Dirksen announced. "This is a bill that was written in Congress and not downtown [as government agencies are frequently described]. It was written by members from both sides of the political aisle with the consultative help of the Justice Department."

As he spoke, Katzenbach—who, until Selma was arguing that a constitutional amendment would be necessary to end literacy tests and provide federal registrars—was hurrying out of the room clutching a mimeographed copy of the bill which was marked up heavily with interlinear notations. He was driven by his departmental chauffeur to the White House, where he showed the draft to the president. The bill was copied in clean form by White House stenographers and then rushed back to Capitol Hill with accompanying letters to McCormack and Vice President Hubert H. Humphrey. Celler put the bill into the hopper (a small wooden box on the Speaker's rostrum) and he began the hearings the next morning, as announced by the president earlier.

The bill, the most comprehensive voting rights legislation to gain congressional approval in ninety-five years, was signed into law on August 6, signaling the end of the chain of events set into motion March 7, when Major John Cloud gave his order, "Troopers, forward!" But it was by no means the end of the civil rights struggle on the streets and in the halls of Congress. And, as we shall see in the next chapter, the Voting Rights Act came within a hairsbreadth of being scuttled by the Nixon administration five years later in the abortive effort to build a "Southern strategy" as a means of making the GOP once again the majority party of America.

CHAPTER 7

Civil Disorder: Challenge & Response

The Voting Rights Act of 1965 enfranchised the blacks; it did nothing to alleviate their economic condition. In the next three years, rioting, burning, and looting broke out in predominantly black sections of more than one hundred American cities.

Five days after President Johnson signed the bill, one of the worst racial disorders in the nation's history broke out in the Watts district of Los Angeles. The riot was touched off when a white California highway patrolman stopped a weaving car and gave its black driver a sobriety test. Six days of terrorism left 34 dead, 856 injured, and damage approaching $200 million. More than 3,100 people were arrested. A combined force of 15,000 National Guardsmen and 1,000 police was needed to restore order.

The same day saw the worst racial rioting in thirteen years in Chicago after a runaway fire engine killed a black woman bystander in a predominantly black west side neighborhood. In a two-day battle between police and blacks, 80 persons were injured and 123 arrested. More than 2,000 National Guardsmen were alerted to prevent a recurrence.

In the summer of 1966, rioting occurred in black sections of Chicago, Cleveland, Jacksonville, New York City, and South

103

Bend. A year later, there were riots and violent demonstrations in sixty-seven cities, the worst occurring in Newark and Detroit. In Newark, 25 were killed, an estimated 725 injured, 1,462 arrested, and property damage of $15 million was reported. The National Guard had to be called in to subdue the rioters. The Detroit riots followed within a week. From July 23 to July 28, more than 4,000 fires were set, extensive sniping occurred, 43 people died, and 657 were injured. The president had to send in federal troops because police and National Guardsmen were unable to control the situation.

And then, on April 4, 1968, the thirty-nine-year-old apostle of nonviolence, Martin Luther King, Jr., was slain in Memphis. President Johnson went on television to ask "every citizen to reject the blind violence that has struck Dr. King, who lived by nonviolence." More than 350,000 National Guardsmen and federal troops were activated; more than 60,000 were deployed as scores of cities, including the nation's capital—which still bears the scars more than a decade later—were put to the torch.

Only a month earlier, the president's National Advisory Commission on Civil Disorders cited "white racism" which has "long permeated much of American life" as the deep, underlying cause of urban riots. "This is our basic conclusion," reported the Kerner Commission (named for its chairman, Judge Otto Kerner). "Our nation is moving toward two societies, one black, one white—separate and unequal."

The congressional response was the enactment on April 10, 1968, of the first open housing law of the twentieth century. Signed the following day by the president, the law prohibited discrimination in the sale or rental of housing and was expected to cover eighty percent of all housing by 1970, when fully in effect.

Despite the background of a nation torn by civil disorder, the enactment of the open housing law had proved to be far more difficult than expected. The riots alerted many Americans to the underlying malaise of our society, but they also disaffected many who were determined not to reward those who resorted to violence. This dichotomy was reflected in the congressional debate; the bill came perilously close to defeat in both houses of Congress.

There wasn't a single vote to spare when the Senate voted, on

Monday, March 4, for the fourth and final time, to impose cloture to end the filibuster. The bill had been the only legislative business before the Senate since the second session of the Ninetieth Congress convened on January 15. Already thirty-one days—136 hours and 46 minutes—had been consumed by debate. "This is the moment of truth," Majority Leader Mike Mansfield told a colleague while the bells rang through the Senate wing of the Capitol for the climactic vote. "I feel like a cat on a hot tin roof." It was to be now or never, for Mansfield was going to shelve the bill if the fourth attempt since February 20 failed.

The story of how crucial votes were won and lost in the days, hours, and even last moments before the tally is worth relating and preserving for posterity—assuming there is a posterity in an unsettled world where we have 9,200 nuclear warheads, the Soviets 4,500, and more nations continue to enter the formerly exclusive nuclear club.*

The effort to line up sufficient votes began the previous Friday in the first of a series of conferences that continued almost around the clock that weekend in the office of Michigan Sen. Phil Hart, the gentle, soft-spoken floor manager of the bill. Among those present in the bipartisan group were Democratic Sen. (later Vice President) Walter Mondale of Minnesota; Republican senators Ed Brooke of Massachusetts, Jacob K. Javits of New York, and Charles Percy of Illinois; Attorney General Ramsey Clark and his deputy, Warren G. Christopher; and a slew of White House and congressional aides.

Absentees had to be corralled, if they were sure cloture votes, and persuaded to stay away if they opposed cloture. In addition, there were senators who had to be converted from a negative to a positive posture. In another office, Senate Republican leader Everett Dirksen was having little success in wooing votes from fellow Republicans who were offended by his sudden shift from opposition to support of cloture.

Dirksen was able to deliver only two votes: those of his son-in-law, Howard Baker, Jr., and Len Jordan of Idaho. Jordan, a

* This was the estimate advanced in congressional testimony by Defense Secretary Harold Brown in January 1979. The figures are certainly greater now, though the ratios may not have been appreciably altered.

rangy man who was very popular not only among fellow Republican conservatives but among members of both parties and of all shades of political opinion, was widely respected for his independence of mind. He deserves a footnote in history because of his self-enunciated "Jordan Rule." This came about one day shortly after the first Nixon administration came into office. Jordan disliked Nixon's Vice President, Spiro Agnew—not in itself a difficult or memorable attribute. A calm man under most circumstances, Jordan lost his temper when Agnew, ignorant of senatorial niceties, approached him on the Senate floor and asked him to vote a certain way because that represented the Nixon position. Jordan voted the opposite way and announced that hereafter he would follow the "Jordan Rule": to vote contrary to any Agnew request. He was never approached again by Agnew, on or off the floor.

One visitor in Dirksen's office heard Dirksen plead over the phone with Sen. George Murphy of California, "George, I want your vote. I need your vote. . . . All right, you pray over it, and I'll pray over you." He didn't get Murphy's vote. Salvation for the bill, then, depended upon the men gathered in Hart's office.

Phil Hart called AFL-CIO leaders in Washington and asked them to telephone the labor leaders in Missouri who, in turn, called Democratic Sen. Ed Long of that state and told him to cancel his official trip to Rio de Janeiro as the Senate Banking Committee's representative to the Sixth Inter-American Savings and Loan Conference. (Long, ample of jowl, stomach, and backside, had chaired a senatorial investigation into governmental invasions of privacy. As a result, the U.S. Post Office Department was compelled to stop snooping upon postal employees while they were in the toilet. Surveillance had been instituted by the postal service because of widespread thefts. After the practice was halted, the rate of thefts increased.)

The next two efforts failed. Organized labor got in touch with Roy Elson, the chief aide to Arizona's nonagenarian Sen. Carl Hayden to urge him to keep Hayden *off* the floor since Hayden always voted against cloture. Elson was reminded, not at all subtly, that if he was going to run as Hayden's successor, he would need labor's support and funds. Elson tried, but failed. At the age of ninety-one, the frail and totally bald Hayden, who bore an uncanny resemblance in his old age to a turtle tentatively poking its head out of its shell, retired from office. A former frontier sheriff, he had been a member of Congress—first the House and then the Senate—since Arizona became a state in 1912. From the eminence of his years of service, he was president pro tempore of the Senate—and hence third in line to the presidency—and chairman of the powerful Senate Appropriations Committee which, together with its House counterpart, controls the purse strings of the federal establishment. More often than not, he nodded off to sleep during committee and Senate sessions. He lived on another four years.

A call was put through to Vice Adm. George Buckley, the White House physician who was treating Democratic Sen. John Pastore of Rhode Island, who had had a heart attack earlier in the year. Could Pastore be allowed to make just one appearance Monday to cast his vote, a certain pro-cloture vote? Absolutely not, Buckley replied. He would not take the responsibility of risking the senator's life.

Ramsey Clark had better luck. Democratic Sen. Albert Gore had flown back to Tennessee in a huff after voting against cloture, to everyone's surprise. Gore was jealous of all the publicity his junior colleague, Baker, was getting because of Baker's support of open housing. Clark soothed Gore and persuaded him to fly back Monday to vote for cloture.

Then came two setbacks in a row. Percy telephoned Richard Nixon and asked him to put pressure upon Sen. Karl E. Mundt, a Nixon-for-President man and chairman of the South Dakota delegation to the Republican convention. Nixon couldn't budge Mundt. Percy also called George Romney and asked the Michigan governor to telephone his fellow Mormon, Sen. Wallace Bennett of Utah. Romney pleaded and argued, but Bennett stood firm in his opposition.

As the weekend proceeded, it became clear that it was necessary for the Hart group to zero in on Democratic senators George Smathers of Florida, Howard W. Cannon of Nevada, and Bob Bartlett of Alaska, and Republican senators Frank Carlson of Kansas and Jack Miller of Iowa. Each one was a most unlikely prospect.

Smathers, who was a sure anti-cloture vote, had to be persuaded to stay away, and the rest had to be "converted." Hart telephoned Hubert Humphrey at the vice president's favorite

hotel, the Seaview, in Miami Beach, where he was sunning himself, and asked him to telephone his good friend Smathers, who
was vacationing in Rio de Janeiro, and ask him to stay there until
after the crucial vote. Smathers didn't answer the phone, nor
did he respond to the urgent messages left by Humphrey. What
Humphrey didn't know was that Smathers's Florida colleague,
Spessard Holland, and Mississippi's John Stennis had reached
him earlier and obtained a commitment from him to return in
time to vote against cloture.

George Smathers is worth a footnote in history. Tall, slender,
debonair, and very handsome, his hair-dye job was one of the
most skillful in Congress. Only the sideburns gave a touch of
gray while the rest remained firmly black. A shrewd wheeler
and dealer, he became a power on the tax-writing Senate Finance Committee. The reason for his place in history was a singularly dirty campaign he waged in 1950 when he succeeded in
unhorsing incumbent Democratic Sen. Claude Pepper in the
primary. His attack has passed into the folklore of the gothic
politics of the South, in particular this passage: "Are you aware
that Claude Pepper is known all over Washington as a shameless
extrovert? Not only that, but this man is reliably reported to
practice nepotism with his sister-in-law, and he has a sister who
was once a thespian in wicked New York."

Still on the phone from the Seaview, Humphrey had better
luck in reaching Cannon and Bartlett. But despite his skill at
salesmanship he could get no firm commitment one way or another from either of them.

James Pearson pleaded with his more conservative Kansas colleague, Frank Carlson, to vote "aye" on Monday. Carlson promised to pray over his decision and then said, "If it becomes
absolutely necessary to give you my vote, I'll do it. But I expect
to catch a lot of hell from the real estate people back home."

Jack Miller was a difficult problem. His vote could be had, but
at a price—the adoption of a series of amendments, some pica-
yune, others substantial. Miller had a deserved reputation as a
bore. The saintly Phil Hart spent five hours bargaining with
Miller and then went out to a pizza parlor for a break. To his unpleasant surprise, Miller turned up there, and so Hart had to
spend two more hours with him. Later, Hart's colleagues suggested he should be canonized.

The end of the era of white racism in U.S. politics: September 6, 1977. Strom Thurmond, former Dixiecrat, walks daughter, Nancy, 6, to an integrated school in Columbia, S.C.

*Congressman John B. Anderson,
Illinois, broke with fellow Republican
leaders to smash the log-jam
threatening passage of the open
housing civil-rights bill. Black
discontent which led to the rioting,
the burning and looting in the
nation's capital, right, compelled
Anderson to act. "I decided," he said
later, "we had to break with the past.
I asked myself whether we wanted a
society . . . like this."*

In the Senate, the bearded, gentle-mannered, soft-spoken Phil Hart of Michigan, whom many associates called "a saint," organized enough colleagues to break a Southern filibuster that threatened the bill. Victory seemed doubtful until the last vote, which decided the issue. Often called "the conscience of the Senate," Hart died of cancer. The newest Senate Office Building has been named after him.

Just before the roll call started, Cannon decided to vote for cloture, a difficult vote for anyone from a sparsely settled state dependent upon federal expenditures which, in turn, were controlled by Southerners on the Senate Appropriations Committee. During the course of the roll call, Ed Brooke "converted" Jack Miller by promising to vote for all Miller amendments if Miller voted against the filibuster.

The key vote now was Bartlett's. He kept his own counsel and agonized as the names were called. He did not cast his vote on the first go-round of the tally. Just before the gavel fell to end the roll call, his Alaska colleague, Ernest Gruening, said, "Bob, for God's sake, vote 'aye.' It's the last chance to save the bill." His was the last vote cast. It produced an audible "whew" and tension-breaking applause in the public galleries. Afterwards, Bartlett told me, "I had to vote that way. It was a matter of conscience. But what in God's name are they going to do to me in the Appropriations Committee?"

As far as could be determined, the Southerners on the committee took no reprisal against him. The late Bob Bartlett, who was elected to the Senate when Alaska achieved statehood, was soft-spoken, gentle, and kind. He was one of the best-liked members in recent history. Only Phil Hart could be said to have a firmer place in the affections of his colleagues. After Hart's death, a new Senate office building was named after him.

The filibuster was broken. To ensure final passage without further filibusters, the Senate adopted anti-riot amendments stipulating criminal penalties for traveling across state lines with the intent of inciting or participating in a riot. But the bill was still in peril, for it would have to be reconciled with an entirely different measure passed by the House the previous year—a measure that contained nothing about open housing. The House bill was just six pages long; the Senate measure, fifty pages.

In the House, a coalition of Republicans and Southern Democrats planned to bury the bill in a Senate-House conference despite the continuing threat of civil disorder. It was a threat that was quickly transformed into frightening reality. Nineteen days after the Senate passed the bill, Martin Luther King, Jr., was assassinated, and smoke darkened the skies over America's cities.

Instead of helping the bill's embattled fortunes, the curfew in the nation's capital, the erection of police blockades, and the presence of troops on the plaza of the Capitol itself—the spot where presidents are inaugurated—were operating against enactment. Members were reluctant to legislate—as one put it—"with a gun at our heads."

The Democratic leadership in the House saw the threat inherent in a conference on the two bills. Weeks, even months, could be consumed. Then the conference agreement would be subject to a vote in the Senate and a certain filibuster. Meanwhile, the real estate lobby, which exercises genuine power in virtually every congressional district, would have time and momentum to build up fatal resistance. There was only one way out of the dilemma: a special rule from the House Rules Committee allowing the House to vote on taking the Senate version and sending it directly to the White House.

The conscience of one man finally made this hazardous ploy possible. The man: forty-six-year-old John B. Anderson of Rockford, Illinois, a handsome, prematurely gray-haired Harvard Law School graduate; a former state's attorney of Winnebago County; a father of four; a member of the American Legion and a trustee of the First Evangelical Free Church of Rockford. Until this moment, he was a relatively obscure, four-term congressman. A Republican, his conscience forced him to use his wit and extraordinary oratorical ability to pit himself against the Republican hierarchy of the House which had made a deal to join the Southern Democrats in sabotaging the measure.

The situation was complicated by the failure of the Democratic leadership in the House. It had effectively lost control of the Rules Committee which is supposed to serve as the instrument of the leadership. Theoretically, it was impossible to lose control, since the committee was stacked ten to five for the Democrats. But the chairman, Mississippi's William Colmer, remained hostile to any civil rights bill. James Delaney, of Queens, New York, turned suddenly hostile to blacks when some of them picketed his house on a wholly unrelated issue at a time his wife was gravely ill with cancer. And a third Democrat, B. F. Sisk of Fresno, California, succumbed to the real estate lobby in his district.

The five Republicans were expected to follow blindly the bidding of the Republican leadership. (Their leader: Gerald Ford of Michigan, a future, though accidental, president of the United States.) This meant that in a showdown vote, the effort for a special rule sought by the Democratic leadership would fail, seven to eight. In fact, on a test vote on March 17, the committee vot-

ed eight to seven to delay further committee action until April
9—just two days short of a scheduled two-week Easter recess.

In voting with his Republican colleagues, Anderson was a
troubled man. A few days earlier, he had been back in his district attending a municipal meeting where an open housing or-
dinance was being debated. Among the witnesses were a young
black high school teacher and his wife. They had responded to
103 real estate ads in the local press and had been turned down
103 times.

The night of the King assassination, Anderson left his office
late and drove home through Rock Creek Park. He was stopped
twice at police barricades. The next day he read through the
Kerner Report, reading, as he put it, "every one of its 425 dou-
ble-column pages." He told me:

> The police barricades were a vivid example of the kind of society
> we must live in, unless we're willing to have a reconciliation between
> white and black. I asked myself whether we wanted a society where
> we must go through checkpoints like this. That night, as I was trying
> to fall asleep, I thought of the fact that twenty-two percent of our
> forces in Vietnam are blacks. They'll come back, look for decent
> homes, and be turned away. We could not live with such a blot on our
> moral escutcheon. I decided we had to break with the past.

Anderson broke with his leadership. The Rules Committee voted out a rule by a one-vote margin allowing the House to vote to
send the Senate bill to the president. The House vote was 229 to
195. The bill was signed into law one week after King's death.
After two decades in the House, Anderson announced his retirement as of the close of the Congress expiring on January 3, 1981.
At the same time, he plunged into the presidential race in the
full knowledge of the odds against him. Though elected and reelected to the third highest Republican leadership post in the
House, Anderson had to keep fighting for his post. He was too
"progressive" for his conservative colleagues.

There was one more civil rights legislative crisis, we hope the
last one in our history, to be surmounted. The Voting Rights Act
of 1965 was to expire in August 1970. It had been singularly effective: over one million black citizens had been registered to
vote under its provisions. Since the job was not yet completed, a
five-year extension was sought by civil rights advocates. Without
it, the accomplishments of the past five years could be undone.

Meanwhile, there had been a steady acquisition of political power by blacks accompanied by a diminution in civil disorder. It was difficult to escape the conclusion there was a linkage. This was why Father Theodore M. Hesburgh of Notre Dame University, the chairman of the Civil Rights Commission, called the 1965 act "the most effective civil rights law ever enacted."

And now President Richard Nixon, abetted by Attorney General John M. Mitchell, set out in the year of the law's expiration to scuttle the measure in the pursuit of the "Southern strategy" to turn the GOP into a majority party by wooing conservatives of all parties to the Republican standard. Nixon and Mitchell proposed not just an extension, but a wholesale revision of the law. It would apply not only to those Southern states that still required special federal scrutiny but to the entire nation, thus diluting and imperiling enforcement of its provisions. There was even a graver danger in their proposal to delete the provision in the law requiring prior federal approval of changes in voting simply by adopting new procedures and laws rendering black votes ineffective.

With the all-out backing of the Nixon administration, the conservative coalition in the House succeeded in passing the revised version by 234 to 179. It was the high point of the effort to gut the voting rights law. However, through the bipartisan leadership of Democratic leader Mike Mansfield of Montana and Republican leader Hugh Scott of Pennsylvania in the Senate, there were more than enough votes to extend the existing law.

Then a new and wholly unanticipated situation developed— among Senate liberals, of all people—that appeared to imperil the bill: a proposed amendment to lower the voting age to eighteen. In the long run, it helped get the Senate bill through the House and to a president who signed it with obvious distaste. But at the time, it was profoundly disturbing to some of the civil rights forces.

On February 23, almost six months before the final enactment of the extension of the law, Ted Kennedy circulated a memorandum among his colleagues. In eight legal-sized pages of single-spaced typing, it set forth a novel legal proposition: that the voting age could be lowered to eighteen by statute. Proposals to lower the voting age by constitutional amendment had been kicking around Congress for thirty years, and it seemed likely that it would take another three decades to get anywhere. Ted didn't know whether it should be offered as an amendment to the Voting Rights Act. He was of two minds about it. Civil rights advocates were against it for fear it would jeopardize the Senate measure when it got back to the House. As with the 1968 open housing measure, the only way the Voting Rights Act could be extended without gutting it was to get the House to agree to accept the Senate bill without going to conference. The danger of appending an amendment reducing the voting age was the increased likelihood that the House would insist on a conference.

On March 1, Teddy left for a visit to Ireland, his mind still not made up. On the eve of his departure, Mike Mansfield—who in his capacity as majority leader had an elegant, long, black Cadillac limousine equipped with telephone and uniformed chauffeur—offered Democratic Sen. Warren E. Magnuson of Washington a lift to his apartment in the Shoreham. During the ride through Rock Creek Park, Magnuson said to Mansfield, "You know, Mike, Teddy's got a pretty good idea there. I was a member of the state legislature in Washington in 1933, and I introduced a bill permitting eighteen-year-olds to vote. I couldn't get it to the floor for a vote. It still hasn't passed. Ted's going to Ireland. Suppose you introduce the amendment." Magnuson knew that such an amendment offered by the majority leader would have greater impact than if it were offered by Ted Kennedy. "I'll think it over, Maggie," Mike said.

Mansfield, who succeeded Lyndon Johnson as majority leader, possessed a leadership style 180 degrees removed from that of his predecessor. He refused to whip or cajole a colleague into line. He seldom said more than, "If you can see your way clear to do so, I would appreciate your vote on this." Mansfield stated frequently—and meant it—that every senator was equal to his colleagues. His effectiveness was a direct result of his moral authority. After retiring from the Senate, he was appointed ambassador to Japan by President Carter.

The next morning, Mansfield saw Magnuson and said, "I think your idea is a good one. I'll introduce the amendment." With Mansfield's prestige behind it, the amendment was adopted in the Senate by sixty-four to seventeen (including the vote of Barry Goldwater, who provided strong support). The top-heavy vote came despite the outspoken opposition of the Nixon administration, which condemned the procedure as unconstitutional.

Many civil rights advocates continued to fear it would mean the bill's death.

The genesis of the statutory route was a June 1966 U.S. Supreme Court decision in *Katzenbach* v. *Morgan*. The issue was a challenge to a section of the voting rights law, authored by the two New York senators, Javits and Bob Kennedy, which overrode a New York State law denying the ballot to anyone who couldn't pass even the simplest literacy test in English. It was aimed at Spanish-speaking Puerto Ricans. By a vote of seven to two, the Court sustained the constitutionality of the law on the ground that Congress had the authority to enforce the equal protection clause of the Fourteenth Amendment—authority which overrides any state constitution denying equal protection of the laws. The Court's decision was a startling one because the Constitution grants to the states the sole power to set voting qualifications.

Archibald Cox, a Harvard law professor who was U.S. solicitor general at the time the case was decided, saw the implications of the decision. In the November 1966 issue of the *Harvard Law Review,* he published an article which held that Congress now had the power to grant the vote to eighteen-year-olds by statute. All Congress had to do was to make a finding that disenfranchisement of these young men and women was, on the face of it, unfair treatment outweighing any legitimate state's rights. At the time of the Morgan case, a young lawyer, Carey Parker, was a Supreme Court clerk. After joining Ted Kennedy's staff, he began proselytizing his boss to support the idea. Teddy's mind was made up when another Harvard law professor told him the age of maturity was fixed at twenty-one in the eleventh century because that was the age at which it was thought that a young man would be capable of wearing armor.

Though the proposal caught fire with Mansfield and Goldwater, it didn't with a key figure in the House—Emanuel Celler of New York, the aging chairman of the House Judiciary Committee. "Manny" Celler was against lowering the voting age because, he said, the youth of Germany was responsible for the elevation of Adolf Hitler. Youth was too suggestible to be given the vote.

But Manny was in a bind. He knew the House had to take the Senate bill or there would be no voting rights law. The consequent disenfranchisement of the blacks who had been added to

the voting rolls would lead to civil disorder of unimaginable pro-
portions. In addition, Speaker John McCormack wanted the voting age lowered in this, his last year in Congress. He wanted to
cap his career. McCormack called Manny into his office and told
him, "Manny, times are changing, and we have got to change
with them."

Manny capitulated. On April 8, he made a speech expressing
his reservations about lowering the voting age but said he would
support the proposal. Accused of inconsistency, Manny responded to his hecklers with, "Consistency is the hobgoblin of little
minds." Manny was misquoting Ralph Waldo Emerson who actually said, "A foolish consistency is the hobgoblin of little
minds." Meanwhile, Jerry Ford was collaring members and
pointing out the dangers of the lowered voting age. If found unconstitutional, he said, bond issues and sewer projects for which
people would be voting could be thrown out as invalid.

In a voice trembling with emotion, McCormack delivered his
swan song: "I shall not be back here next year. Nothing would
make John McCormack happier than to see this resolution
adopted."

The final vote was 272 to 132, and the bill was sent to the
White House.

What has been the impact of the Voting Rights Act? In 1978,
there were 4,503 blacks holding elective office, including the
mayoralty of several of the nation's greatest cities. Birmingham,
Alabama, once known as the most segregated large city in
America, was added to the list in 1979. The South continues to
lead all the other regions in the number of black elected officials
at the local, county, and state levels.

In the 1976 election, Jimmy Carter was the overwhelming
choice of black voters, garnering an estimated 5,206,400 votes
or ninety percent of all black votes cast. In thirteen states moni-
tored by the Joint Center for Political Studies, black votes for
Carter exceeded his margin of victory. These states accounted
for 216 electoral votes; Carter won by 56 electoral votes.

In September 1978, the former Dixiecrat candidate for the
presidency, seeking another Senate term—Strom Thurmond of
South Carolina—made a point of being photographed taking his
little girl to an integrated school. The era of white racism in
American politics was over.

CHAPTER 8

"The Only Thing My Father Ever Asked of Me"

———————

The Senate is a club. It is a self-consciously exclusive club, shaped as much by unwritten as by written rules. It is a place where the role of personality and interpersonal relationships often outweighs political imperatives.

Few personalities in recent decades have so fascinated his colleagues as well as the public as Edward Moore Kennedy, the youngest of the Kennedy brothers. In addition to his relationship to a martyred president, there is what one might call the factor of "the inevitability of Teddy."

I first became aware of this phenomenon at lunch with a Kennedy aide, David Burke, in the halcyon days before Chappaquiddick upset the steady forward thrust of Teddy's career. I asked Burke whether Teddy would go for the presidency in 1972. His reply: "I really don't know, and I don't believe he knows. But what difference does that make? In 1972, he'll be forty years old. In 1976, he'll be forty-four. In 1980, he'll be forty-eight. In 1984, he'll be fifty-two. In 1988, he'll be fifty-six. In 1992, he'll be sixty. In 1996, he'll be sixty-four. And in the year 2000, he'll be only sixty-eight. It's bound to happen one of those years."

Chappaquiddick convinced some observers there was nothing "inevitable" about "the inevitability of Teddy." An early by-product of that mishap was his loss of a Senate leadership post to another man, one totally lacking in national stature. Since Teddy is not a quick man on his feet in the give and take of floor debate, he was probably lucky to lose that contest.

Whether or not the memory of Chappaquiddick is fading with the passage of time, there is that intangible aspect of Teddy's personality which stirs in even the flintiest of hearts the capacity for forgiveness. On the eve of his election to the Senate in 1962, he himself revealed he had cheated in college by getting a fellow student at Harvard to take his Spanish test for him. The reaction of the Massachusetts voters: "a youthful escapade."

Similarly, anyone else's Senate career would have been severely damaged by something like the Morrissey case. Teddy came out of it unscarred, in part because he drew back from the brink of folly just in time.

In 1961, when he signed a bill creating seventy-three new federal judgeships, President Kennedy had said:

> I want to take this opportunity to say that for our federal courts I shall choose men and women of unquestioned ability. I want for our courts individuals with respected professional skill, incorruptible character, firm judicial temperament, the rare inner quality to know when to temper justice with mercy, and the intellectual capacity to protect and illuminate the Constitution and our historic values in the context of a society evidencing profound and rapid change.

These admirable sentiments were recited word for word four years later by officials of the American Bar Association before the Senate Judiciary Committee in a context their author never anticipated. They were stated as the very reason why the Senate should reject, on the grounds of gross and manifest professional incompetence, Boston Municipal Judge Francis X. Morrissey, who was being sponsored for the federal bench in Massachusetts by the late president's brother, Teddy. Because the short, dumpy, florid-faced Morrissey was found unqualified four years earlier by the A.B.A., the Massachusetts Bar Association, and the Boston Bar Association, Jack Kennedy had not been able to bring himself to nominate the family friend and retainer.

The fifty-five-year-old nominee, one of twelve children of a longshoreman, was a social worker in the Boston Welfare Department when he was hired by the "founding father," Joseph

Kennedy, to keep a watchful eye on his three growing sons, Jack, Bobby, and Teddy. Busy with financial affairs in New York City and elsewhere, Joe Kennedy would receive periodic reports and occasional emergency calls from Morrissey. If a Kennedy was traveling in New England, no matter what the hour of day or night, Morrissey was at the airport or railroad station with an automobile and reservations for overnight accommodations.

In 1946, when Jack Kennedy entered politics as a candidate for the House, Morrissey was a constant traveling companion and counselor for the shy youth. Later he served in the same capacity for Teddy. By this time, Morrissey was widely known as Joe Kennedy's "man in Boston." He developed close ties with Richard Cardinal Cushing and, thanks to Joe Kennedy's influence, a private audience with Pope Paul VI was even set up.

After Lyndon Johnson succeeded Jack Kennedy, Joe Kennedy urged Ted to press for Morrissey's nomination. Ted told the president why he wanted Morrissey for the federal bench. "It's the only thing my father ever asked of me." Because he was being the dutiful son, Ted Kennedy risked damaging a promising Senate career. Even if he succeeded in persuading enough of his colleagues to vote for Morrissey's confirmation, his credibility would be scarred and his fellow senators indignant for feeling obligated to vote for an incompetent nominee because of senatorial courtesy.

Senatorial courtesy is not to be underestimated, even though its rules are unwritten. Nominees sponsored by senators for federal positions in their own states are almost always approved unless there is great cause to the contrary. Without such a rule, the Senate would become a jungle, and such nominations would be imperiled because of political faction. A senator can kill any unsponsored presidential nomination from his state for a post in his state by stating that he finds the nominee "personally offensive" or "personally obnoxious." The formula has been resorted to many times in history and has never failed.

The principal witness in opposition to the Morrissey nomination was Albert E. Jenner, a slender Chicago attorney with awesome credentials on Capitol Hill. He was then chairman of the A.B.A.'s Committee on the Federal Judiciary, which investigates potential judicial nominees at the request of the Department of Justice. Earlier, he had served as senior counsel with the Warren

Commission investigating the assassination of President Kennedy. Subsequently, he was the minority counsel for the House Judiciary Committee when it was weighing the impeachment of President Nixon.

Jenner told the senators that his committee considered the following factors in making its assessment: intellectual capacity, scholarship in law school, knowledge of the law, industry and diligence, broad legal experience, trial experience, judicial temperament, and good health. Judge Morrissey, he said, "is blessed with very good health." He did not, however, measure up to any of the other factors. Morrissey flunked his bar examination twice, Jenner went on; took sixteen years to go through law school, twelve years to become a member of the Massachusetts bar, and became a member of the Georgia bar by getting a certificate from a diploma mill which shut down as soon as the peach state tightened up the qualifications for practicing law.

Teddy had anticipated such an adverse report, however. To offset it, he went to great effort to submerge Jenner as well as hostile editorials on the nomination under a mountain of accolades from obliging friends in Massachusetts. The Massachusetts Bar Association, which had once found Morrissey unqualified, was persuaded to reverse itself. A resolution endorsing Morrissey was whipped through the Massachusetts House of Representatives. On the eve of the hearings, statements in favor of Morrissey from thirty-eight of the state's most prominent judges, lawyers, and business tycoons were rushed to the Senate press galleries. The New England papers were loaded with favorable stories about Morrissey.

Even before the proceedings began at 10:30 A.M., the high-ceilinged, walnut-paneled hearing room in the New Senate Office Building was jammed with newsmen, Morrissey's friends from Boston, and curious spectators. On the horseshoe-shaped dais sat members of the ad hoc subcommittee selected for the preliminary examination: Chairman Thomas Dodd of Connecticut, Quentin Burdick of North Dakota, and Everett M. Dirksen. Other members of the Judiciary Committee moved in and out of the room. Before the Morrissey matter came to a climax, virtually the entire Judiciary Committee was involved.

Because of Teddy's popularity with his committee colleagues, he was allowed to suggest the makeup of the ad hoc group. He passed over other Republicans and picked Dirksen as the most friendly. As it turned out, Teddy's choice was as unfortunate as his continued sponsorship of Morrissey.

Teddy was the first witness. Elbowing his way through the crowded room, he sat at the witness table below the dais, and in a firm, clear voice reminiscent in its overtones of Jack Kennedy's, read a statement that would have done justice to such judicial titans as Benjamin Cardozo or Charles Evans Hughes.

> I would like to put in the record [he said] a list of more than fifty judges in the Commonwealth of Massachusetts who have asked to be recorded in favor of Judge Morrissey's appointment.... If the attorneys who try before Judge Morrissey, the district attorneys who prosecute before him, the judges who sit with him, and the people who work with him think he can do the job, this, to me, is very convincing evidence of his professional qualifications, for these are the judgments of those who know him best.
>
> All of us who sit in the Senate take very seriously our responsibility to recommend persons for the federal judiciary. I have tried to do so in this case. I have known Judge Morrissey for many years. I have worked with him closely where the measure of a man can be taken. He understands the law, and thus he can make the law an instrument of justice.

Then followed a string of witnesses, none more eloquent than Walter H. McLaughlin, president of the Massachusetts Bar Association, who testified about his group's endorsement. McLaughlin failed to mention that it had, not just once, but twice, found Morrissey unqualified. Speaking in the voice of a trained, after-dinner speaker, McLaughlin inveighed against the criticism of the nominee because of Morrissey's activity in Boston Democratic politics.

> Since 1789 [he said] the vast majority of our judges, state and federal, have won their judicial spurs because of a political affiliation with the appointing power ... but on this appointment, it suddenly becomes a national disgrace, and the press and news media have made it their prime target of attack upon this decent citizen of Massachusetts.

But even McLaughlin's advocacy did not extend to Morrissey's qualifications as a lawyer and a judge. In his peroration, he said,

> I bring to you, gentlemen, the judgment of the Bar of Massachu-setts that there is room within that black robe of judicial office for a warm and understanding heart. Brilliance alone can never be its sub-stitute; and although Frank Morrissey's instructions to the jury can never be memorialized as gems of the law, plain and simple justice will flow from his courtroom.

At this, there were some snickers from the press table, and Dodd gently rapped for order.

Speaker John McCormack came over from the House to make one of his rare appearances as a committee witness during his 38 years in Congress. To McCormack, the fact that Morrissey had twice flunked his bar exams was something to be proud of. "I think it's to his credit. It is evidence of his determination, his courage, and his devotion to the law." As for Morrissey's friend-ship with the Kennedys: "I like a man who is loyal. We all do. Loyalty is an attribute to be commended. He has been loyal to the Kennedys. They're all dear friends of mine."

Outside in the corridor, McCormack stopped before the TV cameras set up there. Roger Mudd of CBS asked, "You don't re-gard, then, this nomination as a political payoff to an old friend of the Kennedys?"

"Why, no," McCormack replied. "Of course not." There was a long pause as he pondered his next words. "Furthermore, what's wrong with taking care of your friends when they're qualified? I do. This is not a political payoff, but if I have an opportunity to help someone and there's two or more persons qualified, cer-tainly I'm going to give some consideration to the one who's been my supporter for many years. Nothing wrong with that in American life."

John McCormack was almost the last of a dying breed of poli-tician in America. He never cultivated the press in furtherance of his ambitions. He never overcame his suspicion of the press. He saw no need to pander to the television tube. His strength flowed from his intimate knowledge of his fellow Irish Catholic voters in South Boston. The cigar-chomping McCormack (the cheaper the cigar the more he liked it) had his last hurrah in 1970 when he retired after forty-five years in the House.

Bernard Segal, a prominent Philadelphia attorney who formerly held Jenner's A.B.A. post, and who had appeared many times before the Judiciary Committee and was always received with deference, did not persuade the panel one whit when he said, "From the standpoint of legal ability and legal learning and legal experience, we have not had any case where those elements are less adequate than in the case of Judge Morrissey, and I say that with deep regret." Both Jenner and Segal testified that Morrissey could not even tell them what case, if any, he had ever tried as a lawyer. But the panel was clearly sticking with the nominee.

Outside the committee room, away from the oppressive Senate club atmosphere inside, Jenner was a little more unbuttoned. "You should have seen what he put in his biography that he submitted to the A.B.A." he said to me. "When he listed his seven children, he identified one as the godchild of Joe Kennedy, another as the godchild of President Kennedy, and then he informed us that Richard Cushing Morrissey was 'the first child ever baptized by a cardinal on live television.'" (Richard Cardinal Cushing, the Kennedys' close friend, had delivered the invocation at the Kennedy inauguration. Carried away by the occasion, he delivered a twenty-minute invocation, perhaps the longest in the history of inaugurals. It was interrupted only briefly by a fire that broke out in the heating device beneath the lectern and by Speaker Sam Rayburn's sister's refusal to stand that long with head bowed. She sat down and said in an audible voice, "That man should be shot.")

Inside the committee room, after the public had left for the lunch break and the members were filing out, Quentin Burdick told his colleagues, "I'll vote to confirm. After all, he seems to meet the minimum qualifications." Dodd said, "Look, what am I going to do? I'm just going to take the stance that if any colleague of mine in the Senate says his nominee is qualified, that is prima-facie evidence of his qualification." That evening, at a dinner party at the home of Sen. Vance Hartke of Indiana, Dodd said, "I wish Morrissey had been nominated instead for a seat on the appellate bench. Then he could have a bright young law student write his opinions for him, and not be confronted with the need to make decisions from the bench during a trial."

Despite his "minimum qualifications," Morrissey might have

escaped trouble in the Senate had it not been for a curious episode in his youth. While attending the Suffolk University Law
School in Boston—an uncredited law school at that time, Jenner
reminded the panel—he took the bar exam and flunked it. At
the suggestion of a classmate, he went to Athens, Georgia, in
June 1933, where he "enrolled" in what Jenner described as a
"diploma mill," the Southern Law School. In September, he got
a law degree and on motion of the "dean" of the three-man faculty, was admitted to the bar of Georgia, after swearing he was a
resident of that state. Then Morrissey entrained immediately for
Boston, where he was soon to run unsuccessfully for the state
legislature as a resident of Massachusetts.

Throughout the morning and afternoon sessions of the committee, Morrissey was seated in the front spectator row. He
looked unusually natty in a black suit and a conservative tie. Listening to the favorable testimony, he looked very composed and
pleased. During the unfavorable testimony, his sober demeanor
was replaced by a malevolent glare at the A.B.A. witnesses. By
the time he took the stand in his own defense late in the day, he
looked rumpled. His voice rose to a shout. He waved his hands
as he defended himself, admitting he had shown "poor judgment and immaturity" in the Georgia episode. "I did not have
the proper capacity to make a proper judgment at that time,"
he said, "nor did I have anyone to guide me or to advise me. I
have my weaknesses. My weaknesses have been stated here
very clearly and I admit they are weaknesses." Dirksen then
had to leave for the Senate floor. Aside from a few perfunctory
questions about the Georgia episode, there was no cross-exami-
nation. After less than half an hour, Morrissey left the stand and
the hearing was over.

The next morning, the full committee met behind closed
doors. Most of the senators present, in the best Senate club tradition, were prepared to vote for the nomination. Dirksen said
he wasn't satisfied about the apparent discrepancy in Morrissey's testimony. He wanted to know how Morrissey could have
sworn in the Georgia courts that he was a resident of that state
when he went right back to Boston to live. "There's an ugly
word for that," Dirksen said. "It's called perjury." "Oh, hell,
Ev," said Dodd, trying to mollify him, "that episode took place
back in the thirties. He was a kid then. We all make mistakes."

Boston Municipal Judge
Francis X. Morrissey, left,
was sponsored for the Federal
bench in Mass. by young
Senator Ted Kennedy. The
Morrissey nomination proved
embarrassing for Kennedy,
and he risked a promising
Senate career when the
Senate firmly rejected
Morrissey as being grossly
and manifestly incompetent.
Below, Morrissey and family,
with Ted Kennedy standing
in background.

(The white-haired Dodd was to be censured by his colleagues in another two years for misuse of political funds and for double-billing for official and private travel.)

Teddy Kennedy chimed in, "When you're just twenty-three, you do things you wouldn't do when you're older." Teddy didn't mention the Harvard episode of his youth. "What is important is what his record has been in the past ten years, and I submit it has been good. You don't think fifty Massachusetts judges would endorse him if it wasn't a good record."

But Dirksen remained unconvinced. It was decided to hold another closed door meeting, this time in Ev's Republican leadership office near the Senate floor, at 5 P.M. that day. Morrissey was instructed to be present.

I have already described the room, its 1814 Jefferson chandelier, and the marvelous view of the Mall. Though the room was comfortably air-conditioned, Morrissey was sweating. Shortly after the secret hearing started, Sen. Hugh Scott, a member of the committee, rushed in. He saw the short, rumpled figure of Judge Morrissey and thought he was someone's chauffeur. "Where the hell is the witness?" he asked. Morrissey didn't think it was funny.

Dirksen began grilling Morrissey about his Georgia experience. "Who were your sponsors for admission to the Georgia trial bar?" he asked. When Morrissey said he didn't remember, Dirksen answered for him. "I'll tell you who they were. They were the dean of the diploma mill and two other members of the faculty."

Because of Morrissey's hazy memory, there was no way of resolving the question of how long he had remained in Georgia and whether he really had been a resident of that state, as he swore when he was admitted to the Georgia bar. Far rougher and more effective was Dirksen's grilling about Morrissey's courtroom experience before he went onto the Boston municipal bench. The grilling ended when Morrissey was compelled to admit that he had never made a living as a lawyer.

Nevertheless, the vote was six to three for Morrissey's confirmation. Voting against confirmation were Dirksen, Scott, and Democratic Sen. Sam Ervin, Jr., of North Carolina, a former member of the bench in that state. Ervin explained, "I can't vote to put a man of that limited experience on a court of that importance." Ervin, with his homely Southern wit, keen intelligence, and highly mobile eyebrows, was to achieve national renown and respect as chairman of the Watergate committee hearings which helped bring down Richard Nixon.

When Scott got home that evening, he told his wife, "Marian, today I listened to the most incompetent man ever nominated for the federal bench." The ordeal was far from over, not only for Morrissey but for Teddy. "You've got to keep in mind," Scott told me the next day, "that the Kennedys have become identified in the public mind with the pursuit of excellence. The kindest thing you can say for Morrissey is that he's not a national disaster."

Republican Sen. Leverett Saltonstall, Teddy's Massachusetts colleague and the very avatar of New England Protestant aristocracy, was deeply in political debt to the Kennedys. They had assured his reelection in 1960 by refusing to help his Democratic opponent, Gov. Foster Furcolo. Initially, Saltonstall said he had "no objection" to the nomination. He later withdrew that limited endorsement and called for a further investigation after the revelation that Morrissey had sworn he was a resident of Georgia before taking off for Boston to run for state office in Massachusetts. With that, Dirksen felt he was free to lead an all-out fight against Morrissey.

To head off mounting disaster, Teddy asked his friend, Attorney General Nicholas Katzenbach, to order a quick FBI investigation of the Georgia incident. When Bobby Kennedy had left the Justice Department to run for the Senate, he had persuaded President Johnson to install Katzenbach as his successor.

After receiving the FBI report, Katzenbach wrote to the Judiciary Committee indicating that Morrissey had been cleared of any wrongdoing. "I conclude that there is no basis whatsoever to question either Judge Morrissey's credibility or his recollection of the events surrounding his studies in Georgia." The letter failed to impress the doubting senators. It was a curious document, for it failed to clear up the question of Morrissey's candidacy for the Massachusetts legislature. The Massachusetts constitution requires a year's residence before taking office.

But the FBI "clearance" was enough to unleash both Teddy and Bobby into frenetic action. On the Senate floor, Teddy could be seen buttonholing colleagues, putting his arm around

the shoulders of some of them. One Republican senator, thus
embraced, told me a few minutes later, "I'm afraid Teddy has
set back the Irish three generations by pushing for this nomination." Bobby was not so gentle in his buttonholing. When Teddy
was turned down by a colleague, he would politely express his
regrets. Bobby put senatorial backs up by demanding reasons.
One senator told Bobby angrily, "I don't want to argue about
it."

Next, Teddy sent every senator a two-page, closely typed,
eight-paragraph letter which bore down on the A.B.A. as the villain in the controversy. It was referred to in Senate cloakrooms
as "the last Brandeis letter" because the A.B.A., to its everlasting
shame, had also found the late, great Supreme Court justice unqualified. "The ABA," wrote Teddy, ". . . set itself up as a prosecutor. It impugned the integrity of a man who is a judge of an
important court in my state. . . . The ABA's procedures in this
case have been such as to create serious doubt in my mind that
its position on this nominee should be respected or relied upon."
Then, referring to the possibility that someone might try to recommit the nomination to committee for further study—a gentle means of burying it—Teddy wrote: "A vote to recommit
Judge Morrissey's nomination would be a vote to leave his integrity in question for the next several months. This would be
extremely unjust. We cannot permit the Senate's role in confirming judicial appointees to be turned into an instrument of
character assassination of decent and able men." In the light of
what was to take place a little more than twenty-four hours later, this paragraph takes on more than passing interest.

Teddy then followed up his letter with telephone calls to
nearly every member of the Senate. The responses were dis-
heartening. Tom Dodd, who had chaired the ad hoc committee
at Teddy's request, hinted that Teddy abandon the struggle.
"I'm not concerned about Morrissey," he told him. "I'm concerned about Ted Kennedy. I don't want to see you hurt."

I was in the office of Sen. Ernest Gruening of Alaska when
Teddy's call came through. Gruening said, "I'm sorry, Teddy.
I'm going to vote against the nomination. The man simply is unqualified. I consider it one of the sacred duties of the Senate to
maintain the prestige of the judiciary. When the judiciary is
tampered with, a body blow is struck at everything we stand for.

I couldn't vote for him if my own brother asked me to. I should like to offer you this advice: consider withdrawing the nomination."

Teddy thanked him for his candor and said, "I respect your convictions." (Ernest Gruening, who along with Bartlett was one of the first senators elected from the forty-ninth state, was Alaska's last territorial governor and the author of its standard history. He and Sen. Wayne Morse of Oregon originally stood alone in opposition to U.S. involvement in Vietnam.)

The harshest blow came when Teddy discussed the nomination with a Kennedy protegé. Joseph Tydings of Maryland owed much of his Senate victory to Kennedy support. Tydings went to Teddy's office before Teddy could call him, and pointed to his long record as a fighter for improvement of the Maryland bench. In the Senate, he was chairman of the subcommittee on improving the judiciary. "I couldn't hold my head up in Maryland if I fudged on this nomination, Teddy," Tydings said. "I'll tell you this, my vote against Judge Morrissey will be the hardest one of my life."

Young Tydings, the son of the late Millard Tydings whose surprise defeat occurred during the height of the McCarthy terror, was genuinely pained over deserting Teddy on the Morrissey matter. He was defeated after one term in the Senate and now practices law in Washington.

By this time, President Johnson had become aware of the trouble facing the nomination. After all, it was *his* nomination made in his capacity as president of the United States. Everyone in the controversy had forgotten that, but Johnson knew it would be recalled later. Johnson never liked to lose, even though in this instance he had nominated Morrissey only as a favor to Teddy, whom he liked.

Johnson called Vice President Hubert Humphrey and told him to do some lobbying for the besieged nomination. While Bobby waited in the nearby Senate Reception Room, puffing on a slim cigar, Teddy was conferring with Humphrey in the vice presidential office just behind the Senate rostrum.

"I'm going to do everything I can to help you," Humphrey promised. He soon found out, however, that he wasn't able to deliver. He went back into the Senate, mounted the rostrum to preside, spotted Sen. Walter "Fritz" Mondale of Minnesota—his protegé who had been appointed to Humphrey's seat in the Senate when Humphrey became vice president—and wrote a note which he sent to Mondale by Senate page. The note read, "I hope you will be in the fold on the Morrissey vote." Mondale wrote on the reverse side of the note, snapped his fingers for a page, and sent it back to Humphrey. It read, "Addressee unknown."

Humphrey then saw Democratic Sen. Fred Harris of Oklahoma enter the chamber and summoned him to the rostrum by hand signal. Humphrey whispered, "I hope I'm going to be able to tell the president that you are solid on the Morrissey nomination." Harris replied, "Don't tell him that, Hubert. I guess you better tell him I'm shaky."

Humphrey next summoned Eugene McCarthy of Minnesota, whom Humphrey had helped win the hot primary fight that led to McCarthy's eventual Senate victory. McCarthy owed much to Humphrey, but he felt compelled to tell him that he had "to protect Fritz's flank" and would vote the way Mondale did. Gene McCarthy's challenge to President Johnson, a factor in LBJ's decision in 1968 not to seek a second term, was still in the future. But even at this date, McCarthy was harboring resentment over LBJ's choice of Humphrey instead of himself for vice president.

Mike Manatos, the White House liaison aide for the Senate, recalled a conversation with one senator whose vote he was soliciting, after the president had become concerned:

The senator: "Look, Mike, I know you're telling me that the president wants Morrissey confirmed, but he's not really serious about this, is he?"

Manatos: "Yes, Senator. The president has made a commitment, and he's going to see it through. After all, Senator, this isn't such a bad appointment. I've seen a lot worse stiffs than this in my life."

Meanwhile, Dirksen, now committed to Morrissey's defeat, was also working hard. Going over the list of possible absentees in Republican ranks, he manned the phone day and night ordering absentees to return for the vote. "I had to phone all over hell's half-acre to get them to come back," Dirksen told me. "I got ahold of John Sherman Cooper in Kentucky. He said he had to make a speech. I told him, 'I don't care what speech you have to make. You get on a plane and get back here. I need you.' I reached all the way to Denver and told Gordon Allott (senator from Colorado) and Hugh Scott to cancel their joint appearance and get back. I said, 'This is an order.' " (When the showdown came, all thirty-two Republicans were present. There were fourteen Democratic absentees.)

The day before the vote, Dirksen sent a message to Bobby Kennedy asking Bobby to see him in his Capitol chambers. It was an unpleasant scene. Dirksen told Bobby he had some information on Morrissey that "wasn't pretty." He hinted broadly that he was prepared to use it unless the nomination was withdrawn. Visitors in the outer office heard the exchange of shouts through the closed door. Bobby said he had heard of such allegations, and that they had been disproved by the FBI's investigation. Though Dirksen told some of his colleagues he was going to use "the bombshell," he began to have doubts as he left the Capitol late that evening. He told me, "I'm going to sleep on it. There is such a thing as senatorial courtesy." The "bombshell" concerned the tax troubles of an Italian gangster who lived in Boston and for whom Morrissey might or might not have gone to bat.

At 7 P.M. Teddy and Bobby went into the office of Majority Leader Mike Mansfield just off the Senate floor. There, over coffee and cigars, they sat around a marble-topped coffee table in soft leather chairs and discussed the situation. Mansfield said he had been informed by Dirksen that he was contemplating making a sensational charge on the Senate floor, but he didn't think "Ev would do it." The real problem, said Mansfield, was whether to insist on a vote on confirmation. Mansfield's aides had polled senators and he was inclined to agree with the Kennedy brothers that they could beat a recommittal motion by four or five votes. But, Mansfield went on, some of the votes that Teddy got would be very reluctant ones. This had become a hot issue in many areas with the newspaper editorials unanimous in their condemnation of the nomination. "Yes, I know," said Teddy glumly. "I've already gotten five editorials in the *New York Times* on this one."

At 8:30 P.M., with no final decision reached, the meeting broke up. Teddy and Bobby returned to Teddy's office in the Old Senate Office Building. In a room decorated with Kennedy memorabilia, including a large photograph of Joe Kennedy with six-year-old Teddy at his side, the two pondered their next move.

By 10 P.M., Teddy reached his decision. He would ask Mansfield to call up the nomination the next day. He would make a speech defending the integrity and qualifications of Judge Morrissey—and then ask unanimous consent to recommit the nomination for further study because of the questions remaining in the minds of his colleagues.

Teddy and his speechwriters went to work writing a fourteen-minute speech. The next morning, Teddy called Dodd and told him what he planned to do. Dodd sighed and said he was doing the right thing. Then he called Morrissey in Boston and told him his plan. He said he had concluded that further debate would be damaging to Morrissey's career on the federal bench, with nearly half the Senate voting against him as unqualified.

Dirksen slept on his own problem and awoke with the decision to withhold his "bombshell." He would take his chances on beating Morrissey even though he believed he lacked the votes. Senatorial courtesy prevailed.

The Senate convened at 9:30 A.M. The Morrissey nomination would be taken up around an hour later. At 11:04 A.M., during a quorum call, Teddy went up to Dirksen on the Senate floor, put his arm around his shoulder, and told him what he planned to do as soon as the quorum call was over.

"Teddy," Dirksen said, "I think that is a wise and courageous thing to do." Teddy then told Mansfield. Aside from Tom Dodd and the members of the Kennedy clan in the galleries, no one else knew.

At 11:11 A.M. Teddy began speaking. His voice was clear and resonant. There was a healthy glow on his cheeks. His hair was freshly barbered. He had the look of a man who had made a difficult decision and was relieved that the tension was over.

> This is a controversial nomination [he said] the most controversial before the Senate this year. . . . I wish at the outset to state what is clearly not at issue: first, Judge Morrissey's integrity and character— his moral fitness for this solemn post—are not at issue. . . . Second, with the exception of one small group of witnesses, Judge Morrissey's legal qualifications and ability are accepted.

Teddy said that Morrissey's qualifications had been found "perfectly adequate" by fifty fellow judges in Massachusetts. "They are satisfied," he said, "as the president is satisfied, and as I am satisfied, that Francis Morrissey will fulfill the high tradition of the U.S. District Court in Massachusetts."

Teddy explained why Morrissey went to Georgia. "Simply stated, the answer is that he was young and he was poor—one of twelve children, his father a dockworker, the family living in a home without gas, electricity, or heat in the bedrooms; their shoes held together with wooden pegs their father made." At this point there was a frog in his voice. The resonance vanished. Teddy tried clearing his throat. Then he paused to drink from a glass of water placed on his desk. His voice cleared up, and he continued without pause to the end. It wasn't until he neared the very end that Teddy disclosed to the Senate that he himself was going to move to recommit the nomination for further study.

The gratitude of Teddy's colleagues was so overwhelming that, by this one gesture, he seemed to have wiped the slate clean. Quentin Burdick turned to a colleague and said, "Well, I'll be damned. And to think that I bled for Morrissey in the committee. But he's doing the right thing." Afterwards, Dirksen told me, "It took a lot of courage to do that. Younger men find it more difficult to subdue their pride. I ought to know. By the time you reach my age, the pride is a bit more flexible."

At 6 P.M., Teddy took off for a two-week trip to Southeast Asia, including Vietnam, a trip he had delayed for several days to fight for Morrissey. As he left, he knew his decision had brought him back into the club.

CHAPTER 9

"Kicked in the Head
by a Horse"

Senatorial courtesy can be appreciated if understood in strictly institutional terms. It comes into force not only when a popular member such as Ted Kennedy finds himself in difficulty. Under proper conditions, it surfaces even in the case of those members who are thoroughly detested by many of their colleagues. It is the centripetal force that holds together a body made up of men—and an occasional woman—who view themselves as ambassadors from disparate, sovereign states.

A senator may despise another, but on the floor of the Senate he will address that despised colleague as "able" and "distinguished." It is an almost unforgivable sin for one senator to address another in the second person. It must always be in the third person. It may sound silly, but it contributes much to civility.

Even in the more unruly House there are governing rules, written and unwritten, contributing to civility. Third person usage is mandatory, and the formula varies only slightly from the Senate. A senator will address another directly as, say, "the distinguished Senator from Oklahoma"; in the House, it will be "the distinguished gentleman (or gentlewoman) from Oklahoma."

The absence of deference from outsiders can be devastating

for those outsiders. Charlie Wilson, as we have seen, got into trouble with members of the Senate Armed Services Committee by addressing them as "you men."

When Richard Nixon was elected in 1968 along with a Democratic Congress, the Democrats on the Interior Committee were eager to go after Nixon's nominee for secretary of the interior, Walter Hickel of Alaska. Hickel had made some comments in an offhand fashion that disturbed environmentalists, who feared he would be eager to hand over natural resources to private industry.

I breakfasted in the Senate dining room with Kenneth Be-Lieu, Nixon's liaison aide with the Senate, on the day before Hickel's appearance for his confirmation hearings. BeLieu feared Hickel's rejection; it would be a sorry way for a new administration to begin.

"Have you any suggestion?" he asked me. "I've got to write Hickel's opening statement for him."

"Yes," I replied. "Be sure that in every sentence he speaks of 'the Senate in its wisdom' or 'the committee in its wisdom' and that he always addresses the members as 'distinguished senators.'"

The statement was a model of sycophancy—and it worked. He came in for fulsome praise from the committee members, and his confirmation sailed through.

The best example of the operation of senatorial courtesy on behalf of an unpopular member came in the case of one of the most strong-minded, bullheaded, feared, and disliked senators of modern times—Wayne Morse of Oregon.

Dean and professor of law at the University of Oregon, the lean, nimble, wiry, mustachioed six-footer was elected to the Senate in 1944 and served four terms until the people of Oregon finally wearied of his eccentricities and violent temper and turned him out of office after twenty-four years. A genuine loner in the Senate, he will be remembered longer for his feuds than for his legislative accomplishments; the first were monumental, the latter minuscule. He liked the nickname voiced in Senate cloakrooms where he was often called "Tiger," but never to his face. Because of a strong streak of paranoia in his makeup, Morse suspected that the tea and orange juice he sipped during a filibuster might be poisoned. Instead of allowing the Senate dining room staff to prepare his beverages, he had two trusted aides brew the tea, examine each orange, the knife that sliced it, the squeezer that squeezed it, and the glass into which the juice was poured.

In an arena noted for the stamina of its denizens, Morse stood out. He broke all records in 1953 with an oration against a bill to give the tidelands title to coastal states, speaking for twenty-two hours and twenty-six minutes. After his speech, he held a press conference, went to his office where he dilated on his feat, and then—only then—went casually to his private toilet. His explanation for such inhuman stamina: clean living.

He was elected as a Republican. During the 1952 Eisenhower campaign, he soured on the general, feeling that Ike had caved in to the conservative wing of the party led by Sen. Robert A. Taft. He was revolted by Ike's failure to condemn Joe McCarthy. When Congress convened in 1953, he called himself an independent and arrived on opening day carrying a metal folding chair which he said he was prepared to place in the center aisle apart from either party's side. He was persuaded to take a desk with the Republicans, who then proceeded to oust him from the Armed Services and Labor committees and consign him to the wasteland of the District of Columbia Committee.

The next Congress, elected in November 1954, produced a Democratic House and an evenly divided Senate. By his vote, Morse could give either party the control of the Senate and its committees. He could make Lyndon B. Johnson either majority or minority leader. He voted with the Democrats, was given a coveted seat on the Foreign Relations Committee, and was restored to the Labor Committee. He was reelected as a Democrat in 1956.

Morse never mellowed. With the passage of the years, his voice became raspier and his invective even more finely honed. The only senator who ever succeeded in humbling Morse, however briefly, was Barry Goldwater of Arizona. Goldwater's speech took a month to research and write. The most difficult part was devising a speech which would hold Morse up to scorn without violating Senate Rule XIX, Clause 2, which states: "No Senator in debate shall, directly or indirectly, by any form of words impute to another Senator any conduct or motive unworthy or unbecoming a Senator."

Goldwater solved the ticklish problem by quoting copiously from Morse's vitriolic attacks upon presidents Herbert Hoover, Harry S. Truman, and Dwight D. Eisenhower; cabinet officers John Foster Dulles and Douglas McKay, Ike's Interior Secretary, FDR's Interior Secretary Harold Ickes, Charles E. Wilson, and Ike's H.E.W. Secretary Mrs. Oveta Culp Hobby; and fellow senators Irving Ives of New York, William Knowland of California, Leverett Saltonstall of Massachusetts, and even Morse's own protegé and colleague, Richard Neuberger of Oregon. Then he said that he was "gravely concerned" about the "low esteem" into which the Senate had fallen here and abroad and expressed regret that it might have been caused by the kind of invective and name-calling indulged in by Morse. Goldwater said,

> It is sufficient to say that when I hear such words and phrases as: cowardly, untrustworthy, amoral, deceit, trickery, disloyal, snide, sanctimonious, disrespect, gutless, mediocre, mental difficulties, lack of veracity, lack of intellectual honesty, disgraceful, contemptible, reactionary, class-conscious, corrupt machine politics, malfeasance, totalitarian, lacking in political morality, the most dangerous man who was ever in the White House, political hypocrisy, maladministration, slave to big business, fascist, big lie technique, political mush, half-truths, immorality, dangling and dancing from puppet strings jerked by evil and reactionary forces, demagoguery, evil, bent on war, gross incompetency, enemy of the people, enemy of democracy, dishonest, unreliable, unstable, a subversive character, police state tactic, a tool of the oil interests, a stooge for American business, et al, all of which have been used by the senior senator from Oregon to describe various individuals in public life, the senator from Arizona is in disagreement.

With a plea for the restoration of the dignity and reputation of the Senate, Goldwater concluded, "As the senior senator of Oregon so succinctly stated on June 30, 1954: 'The issue is whether the Senate of the United States is going to countenance political thuggery in American politics.'"

Throughout Goldwater's speech, Morse sat still, resting his cheek on his hand and occasionally smiling sardonically. His reply was surprisingly gentle and brief. He was willing to be judged by his record in the Senate; he was never going to be afraid to call a spade a spade, and that if there was anything that concerned him less than the criticism of the distinguished senator from Arizona he didn't know what it was.

None felt the full force of Morse's invective more than his younger colleague, Dick Neuberger. The feud between them became one of the hottest in Senate history. Neuberger, who was a dozen years younger than Morse, was as different from Morse as a balmy breeze from a hurricane. Dick Neuberger was universally liked in the Senate. He was gregarious, gentle, thoughtful, kind, and easily hurt. He was an ardent nature lover and explorer, the Northwest correspondent for the *New York Times* for fifteen years, and the author of seven books, including one on the Lewis and Clark expedition.

Once he and Morse were so close that they were known collectively as "The Morseburger." The bitterness that developed between them turned the Democratic party back home into a shambles and contributed to the election of a Republican governor in 1958 in the face of a national Democratic tide.

In 1954, Morse, who had only just switched his party allegiance, campaigned all over the state for Neuberger. The two had met twenty years earlier when Neuberger was editor of the student paper at the University of Oregon and Morse, the law school dean. Neuberger became an author, a correspondent for the *New York Times,* and then went into state politics, serving five years in the state senate. Morse's campaigning helped elect Neuberger, who became Oregon's first elected Democratic senator since 1914. Morse's political apostasy and Neuberger's surprise victory produced the narrow Democratic majority in the Senate, and confronted President Eisenhower with the first of three successive Congresses controlled by the opposition party.

The friendship first began to turn sour during the 1957 debate on civil rights legislation. Morse, a self-styled "strict constitutionalist," voted with the Southern bloc to send the House-passed measure to the Senate Judiciary Committee before it reached the Senate floor. Neuberger voted with the dominant liberal coalition which feared, correctly, that the bill would die in a committee controlled by James O. Eastland of Mississippi.

Morse voted against the bill on final passage because he felt it had been amended into a state of futility. Neuberger voted for it as a step in the right direction. Morse lost no time in telling his constituents that he thought Senate liberals, including his colleague, had been "sucked in" by the Southerners.

The rift widened during the fight the following year over the administration's proposal to increase first class mail rates from three to five cents (oh, halcyon days!). Neuberger said he was convinced by the evidence presented. He supplied the vote that brought the bill out of the Senate Post Office Committee over Democratic objections. Morse was indignant. Publicly, he said the postal increase meant shifting a greater burden onto "the little people." Privately, he said that Neuberger, a prolific writer of articles, was reluctant to press for an increase in the postal rate for newspapers and magazines.

The blow-up finally came in August 1958 over a minor bill. Neuberger and Congressman Charles Porter of Oregon were the authors of a measure that would allow the government to release some surplus federal real estate to the city of Roseburg, Oregon, for a municipal historical museum. The bill passed the House. In the rush for adjournment, the bill's only chance for final passage lay in its enactment by the Senate through unanimous consent. Just one objection would kill the bill. Morse voiced that objection on the ground that the bill was contrary to the so-called "Morse formula" by which the municipality should pay part of the cost of the land. (Morse was the only senator who promoted or believed in the "Morse formula.")

From this point on, Morse and Neuberger confined their discussions to a series of letters which, for sheer vituperation, should earn them some measure of immortality in any collection of political correspondence.

On August 5, the day after Morse raised his fatal objection, Neuberger dispatched a letter of protest from his office—Room 348 in the Old Senate Office Building—to his senior colleague—in Room 417 on the floor above. This letter and all those that followed were written to "Dear Wayne" and closed with the words "With best wishes, Sincerely yours." Morse's letters started coldly with "Dear Neuberger" and concluded with "Very truly yours." "You may recall," Neuberger wrote,

> your letter of July 11 which stated irrespective of any differences that might exist between us: "I shall continue to offer to work with you at all times on any matter or problem that involves the welfare of our state and our senatorial duties in representing the people of the state and of the nation in the Senate." I regret that you evidently did not feel this applied to the bill to transfer the Lilly Moore property to the city of Roseburg before that bill reached the floor yesterday there to be met by your objection to its enactment....

*In happier days before her flap with
Morse, Clare Booth Luce,
Ambassador to Italy and the most
handsomely accoutered member of
the U.S. diplomatic corps. Here, her
mink jacket matches her trim gray
suit and her long-handled, tight-
furled umbrella is wine-red to go
with her small hat and scarf.*

currence, not mine. I do not concede, as you do, having engaged in any personal attacks. . . . You have accused me without specification of "undercutting" and "character assassination". . . . It has been your letters, not mine, that have contained the terms "disloyal," "untrustworthy," "amoral," "cowardly" and "snide." It has been your letters, not mine, that have hurled accusations of "trickery" and "deceit."

I shall gladly concede, without contest, your pre-eminence in the use of personal invective and imprecations. If you now wish to call a halt on your part to this kind of thing, I shall be only too pleased.

This led to Morse's final outburst on August 13.

I am amused by your letter of August 12 which reflects again your sanctimonious holier than thou attitude. . . . When you were a student of mine, I found you amoral. I had hoped over the years that you would mature and develop a character of moral responsibility. Your relations with me in the Senate have proven that I was mistaken in placing that hope in you.

My disrespect for you is so complete that I think it is perfectly clear in light of your August 12 letter that there is no basis left for any personal relationship. . . . My criticism of you for untrustworthy and cowardly attacks and amoral conduct . . . was based on the totality of your record in your relations with me. . . .

I fully expect that you will continue to write me letters as long as I answer yours. I wish to notify you that this is the last personal letter you will receive from me.*

This correspondence soon became public. I dropped in on Wayne Morse one afternoon to ask him whether there was any truth to cloakroom reports that he and his colleague were no longer speaking to one another. He confirmed the report. When I asked why, he said, "Because Neuberger is disloyal." Then he insisted on showing me his display of blue ribbons he had won for the prize palominos and polled Devon cattle he raised on his farm in Poolesville, Maryland.

I interrupted the talk of animal husbandry to ask how he communicated with Neuberger on Oregon problems. By correspon-

---

* In December, Neuberger, age forty-six, learned that he had testicular cancer. He died fifteen months later. Morse delivered the eulogy in the Senate: "Oregon and the nation have lost a courageous leader, one whose voice and pen will be sorely missed in this time of national and international crisis." He concluded, "We will all be lonesome because this fallen leader is no more in mortal flesh, but his record will live on as his monument."

dence, he replied. I went upstairs one flight and asked Neuberger whether this was true.

"Oh, yes," he said. "Would you like to see the letters?" And he handed me the correspondence file.

Even case-hardened members of the Senate were shocked. Yet in the following April, the Senate rose to *defend* Wayne Morse, almost in a hysterical fury, because he had been attacked by someone outside the club. The one who caused the furor was a woman with a tongue as sharp as Wayne Morse's: Mrs. Clare Booth Luce.

In a colorful and eventful life—a life that included one marriage to a wealthy Wall Street broker and another to a wealthy and powerful magazine publisher; the editorship of sophisticated magazines and the authorship of successful Broadway plays; a successful political career that embraced two terms in Congress and was crowned by her designation as America's first woman ambassador to Italy—Mrs. Luce has been noted for her acid wit as well as her beauty. Many have been the victims of that wit and even more, the targets of her barbed criticism. Included among her victims were two Democratic presidents, Franklin D. Roosevelt and Harry S. Truman. Mrs. Luce is a Republican.

When Ike nominated her for ambassador to Brazil, no problems were expected. The Senate Foreign Relations Committee, in a secret session, confirmed the nomination without even bothering to call her in for testimony. Chairman J. William Fulbright felt she was so qualified that it was unnecessary to call her in. Among those agreeing was Wayne Morse, who seconded the nomination. Then, by ironic happenstance, her husband's magazine came out with an article quoting a State Department official as saying Bolivia should be carved up among its neighbors. The story led to grave riots in Bolivia, and special protection had to be provided for some seven hundred Americans there. Max Ascoli, the late publisher of the now defunct magazine, *The Reporter*, rushed to Washington from New York to tell Morse Mrs. Luce was the source of the Bolivian quote. He showed Morse an article the magazine had run some time back sharply criticizing Mrs. Luce's record as ambassador to Italy. Then Morse, on his own, dug up a 1944 quote by Mrs. Luce in which she said FDR had "lied us into war."

At Morse's demand—since the committee's action was still unofficial—Fulbright reopened the nomination and summoned her to testify in open session. Mrs. Luce appeared before the committee wearing a severe navy blue tailored suit and carrying a brown mink stole over her arm. She wore jeweled earrings and several gold and silver bracelets on her left wrist. Her carefully waved hair was no longer blonde but white and silver.

Through most of the hearing, she handled herself like a gracious hostess with an iron will who would not let any domestic crisis shatter her calm or courtesy. To the sharpest questions she gave polite replies in her mellifluous voice. Only an occasional flashing of her piercing blue eyes betrayed her suppressed anger. Until the questioning got hot, she sat still in her chair, with her carefully manicured hands—the nails colored a bright cerise—folded primly in her lap.

As the tension in the room mounted, she began chain-smoking thin Italian cigarettes which she carried in a Japanese lacquered case. It was apparent that, aside from the question dealing with the Bolivian incident, Mrs. Luce was totally unprepared for what she would run into. She handled the Bolivian question with disarming candor:

> When I first read the news of the Bolivian incident in the newspapers, and that is where I saw it first, since I am not the editor of *Time* magazine, certainly not the South American edition, and since, I regret to say, I don't always read it every week, I saw it in the newspapers first, I promptly telephoned Secretary Herter and assured him that if the incident would in any way embarrass the department or the administration, my own great desire to continue with my mission to Brazil must be left completely out [of consideration].
>
> He thanked me very much and said that he would look into the matter. Since that time it turned out that the Brazilians themselves, or let us say, Brazilian public opinion sees no reason whatsoever why it should prejudice my mission. As one Brazilian newspaper put it, I am not Mr. Luce, and I am not the editor of *Time*, and I am being sent as an ambassador to Brazil, and not to Bolivia.

She was unprepared for what followed.

"Do you still believe," Fulbright asked her, "that mortal enemies of the United States are growing and thriving in the organism of the Democratic party?"

"I don't really know what you are referring to, Senator," she replied.

Fulbright then quoted a statement she had made over a national hookup on September 30, 1952: "For twenty years mortal enemies of ours have been growing and thriving in the organism of the Democratic party. There is only one way to dislodge them. We must shake them out. Yes, the tree of government must be shaken hard. Then these rotten apples, these mortal enemies, will fall out from the top branches."

Fulbright asked, "Who did that refer to—'in the top branches'? It must have referred to President Truman. You don't subscribe to that doctrine, that he was a traitor to this country, do you?"

"I never said that the president was a traitor," she replied.

Fulbright's next question: "In light of events that have happened in recent years, would you still assert that the only American president who ever lied us into a war, because he did not have the political courage to lead us into it, was Franklin Roosevelt?"

She asked Fulbright to repeat the question while she reached for her first cigarette, then said, "I do not believe, and I think history proves it, that we were told the truth."

Fulbright, pressing: "You think he lied us into a war?"

"I stand by my statement," she said, crushing out her first cigarette and lighting another.

Fulbright, in his most avuncular manner, said, "I was hoping that time had mellowed your judgment a bit, but it hasn't. That is quite clear."

She replied, "Time has mellowed my language, and I hope, my judgment: but the accuracy, historical accuracy, I must stand by."

Morse then said he couldn't vote for her unless she documented her charge. If undocumented, he said, he would consider it "subversive."

She protested, "I was a private citizen, expressing a private opinion." Morse pointed out she was not a private citizen when she made the statement on October 11, 1944, but a member of Congress.

To get her off the hook, George Aiken of Vermont pointed out that Germany and Japan had been completely forgiven for what happened fifteen years ago, and that Mrs. Luce should not be held "fully responsible" for what she had said in the heat of an election campaign.

The edge was taken off the Fulbright-Morse attacks by Sen. John F. Kennedy who announced he intended to vote for her nomination. Sen. Hubert H. Humphrey stepped down from the dais to grip her hand. Both were then presidential aspirants who did not want to antagonize the Luce publishing empire.

Committee confirmation came quickly, and the Senate approved with relatively little fuss, especially after Democratic leader Mike Mansfield offered the most compelling argument yet advanced in support of the nomination: "Granted that Mrs. Luce made mistakes; granted that along with thousands of others, Mrs. Luce made intemperate statements in the heat of political campaigns ten or fifteen years ago. Are these in themselves reasons for disqualification of a presidential nomination of this kind? What counts is not what Mrs. Luce said fifteen years ago, but what she will do now and in the days ahead."

She was confirmed by a vote of seventy-nine to eleven.

Then she committed a real blunder. When the news of her confirmation was relayed to her by an AP reporter in New York City, she could not resist hitting back at Wayne Morse. "I am grateful for the overwhelming vote of confirmation in the Senate. We must now wait until the dirt settles. My difficulties, of course, go some years back and began when Senator Wayne Morse was kicked in the head by a horse."

In August 1951, after he had won the championship at a two-day horse show at Orkney Springs, Virginia, Morse was walking behind a mare named Missy when the horse suddenly kicked up her heels and hit him on the chin. He suffered a compound fracture of the jaw and lost thirteen teeth. As soon as the report reached the Senate, Sen. William Jenner of Indiana, who disliked Morse intensely, took up a collection among his colleagues to buy hay for the horse. He picked up $40 in pledges in a few minutes in the Republican cloakroom.

Morse was in the anteroom behind the Senate chamber when Mrs. Luce's comment was printed on the AP news ticker there. Tearing off the dispatch, he showed it to Sen. Paul Douglas and chuckled, "That explains me, but what accounts for her?" Morse had good reason to chuckle. In just three sentences, she had (1) delivered a gratuitous assault upon former Secretary of State Dean Acheson by paraphrasing his comment on the China problem—"Let's wait for the dust to settle"; (2) implied that Morse was mentally unbalanced because of a head injury; (3) made a laughingstock out of the senators who had urged her confirmation because time had mellowed her language and judgment; and (4) raised grave doubts in the minds of some of her supporters as to her ability to function as a diplomat in South America where anti-American tensions not long ago had erupted in a serious threat upon the life of Vice President Nixon.

She had played into Morse's hands and he knew it. He walked onto the Senate floor, gained recognition, and said, "I rise to a point of personal privilege." With a smile on his face, he said, "I have in my hand a very interesting news release. I happen to be one of those politicians who can take it as well as dish it out. . . . I hope my colleagues who voted against me a few minutes ago will pardon my chuckle at their expense. I say that because not so soon did I expect that those of us who voted against the nomination of Clare Boothe Luce would be proved so right." He then read the item and said, "This is an old, old pattern of emotional instability on the part of this slanderer. . . . I promise to the nation that each night in my prayers I will pray for God's guidance to this lady so that she will be more stable in her ambassadorial duties than she was when she issued this press release this afternoon." A wave of anger swept the Senate. A Senate tally clerk told me later, "The Senate can be like a woman in changeability of its moods. One minute it will be rocked with laughter; the next, it will be in a passion of rage." Democratic Sen. Frank Lausche of Ohio rose to make a very emotional speech. On the verge of tears of indignation and regret, he said: "I think the statement she made following the Senate's confirmation of her nomination indicates an absence of rationality so serious that if she made such a statement before the vote was taken, I would not have voted in her favor." Ralph Yarborough of Texas said, "We are sending to one of the largest nations in Latin America an ambassador who is apparently more skilled in invective than in diplomacy. If I now had the opportunity to do so, I would join the senator from Ohio in voting against confirmation."

Sen. Gale McGee of Wyoming said, "I not only regret my vote, but I urge that the proper authorities in this administration now give due weight to this intemperate remark and possibly reconsider the appointment. . . . What is to prevent this ambassadress from making the same kind of a comment in a release south of the border? What is to prevent her touching off another kind of intemperate series of incidents such as those I noted published in her husband's magazine not many weeks ago?" Then Dennis Chavez of New Mexico, who also had voted for confirmation, said, "I feel in my heart if Brazil had known that Mrs. Luce had made this kind of statement, Brazil would have notified the State Department she would not be received as ambassador."

Morse was not the only Washington official watching the news ticker after the confirmation vote. Mrs. Luce's bumptious victory statement was seen by presidential aide Bryce Harlow who took it at once to Ike. The president was upset and told Harlow to get Mrs. Luce on the telephone immediately to find out whether she had been correctly quoted. Ike did not get on the phone. The conversation between Harlow and Mrs. Luce took place in his presence, however. Harlow said the president wanted to know whether she had been correctly quoted and whether she had been speaking for publication. She admitted the accuracy of the quote and did not deny she intended it for publication. She explained that she had had plenty of provocation. She was upset, she said, by the information that she had received from her doctor who told her that Wayne Morse had telephoned him to ask whether she had ever had psychiatric treatment. She told Harlow to tell the president she had never had such treatment.

Ike commented to Harlow that she was "only human after all" and told him to call Dirksen in the Senate cloakroom. When Dirksen came on the phone, Harlow told him the president had just seen the quotes on the ticker from Sen. Lausche and others. Ike wanted to know whether the Senate planned to push through a resolution calling upon him to return the nomination before the oath of office was administered. Dirksen said there was some cloakroom talk, but he didn't think the resolution would get anywhere. By this time, Henry Luce got into the act. He issued a statement to the press in which he said he had advised her to resign because her mission to Brazil had been "profoundly compromised" by "a few angry men who intended at her expense and at the expense of our Latin American relations to settle their little grievances at *Time*."

Three days later, a tremulous Clare Luce emerged from the White House to announce her resignation because "the climate of good will was poisoned by thousands of words of extraordinarily ugly charges against my person" by a senator whose "natural course" would be "a continuing harassment of my mission with a view to making his own charges stick."

But she got little sympathy. The *Washington Post* said, "It is time she learned that the kind of acid which is funny in *The Women* [a successful play she wrote about a group of bitchy women] sears when it is sprayed in public." Even worse—for one so sophisticated about Washington—she had broken the rules of the Senate club.

CHAPTER 10

Interlude:
Three Nominees &
a Bogus Romanoff

⌇⌇⌇⌇⌇

Some stories, trivial in themselves, are worth preserving for the light they throw upon the operations of Congress when it is functioning in a mood of comparative benignity.

If the circumstances are just right—a brief era of good feeling while a new team takes over the White House, or if old and congenial friends and colleagues are involved—a situation that should produce tension, righteous reproof, or even hostility is transmuted into heavenly concord or into an aw-shucks-fellows-let's-not-let-it-happen-again at worst.

The scene was the prestigious Senate Committee on Foreign Relations. Established in 1816, it is one of the oldest committees in Congress. On this day, January 15, 1969, just five days short of the inauguration of Richard M. Nixon as the thirty-seventh president, it was meeting in its old-fashioned, ornate room in the Senate wing of the Capitol. The room, decorated with nineteenth-century chandeliers and sconces, is taken up almost completely by a huge, oval, green-baize-covered mahogany table, leaving room for only a handful of spectator seats.

What was scheduled to be a very routine hearing on the qualifications and opinions of the man designated to be the new undersecretary of state turned into a mutually embarrassing inquiry into the nominee's auto driving record and whether he

155

was—to use his own pejorative—a "lush." It was certainly not
what the small handful of newsmen who drifted into the room
expected. They had come hoping to hear a discussion of our
commitments to Vietnam and the outlook for the peace negotia-
tions in Paris.

The witness was Elliott Richardson, attorney general for the
Commonwealth of Massachusetts. His hair carefully groomed as
always, the trim of his dark blue pin-striped suit impeccable, he
was in manner and voice the very embodiment of Back Bay Boston and Ivy League. He was a perfect type cast for the part. A
cum laude graduate of Harvard University Law School where
he had been editor-in-chief of the Harvard Law School *Journal,*
Richardson had been law clerk for Judge Learned Hand and Justice Felix Frankfurter before joining prestigious law firms and
then moving into a distinguished public career. Up to this time,
he had served under President Eisenhower as assistant secretary
of health, education and welfare and had twice been elected in
Massachusetts to serve as its lieutenant governor and attorney
general.

He was to become the "Mr. Clean" of the Nixon administration, serving successively as undersecretary of state, secretary of
HEW, secretary of defense, and finally as attorney general of
the scandal-ridden Department of Justice which Congress expected him to depoliticize and remove from the tarnish of Watergate. Under President Ford he was to serve as ambassador to
the Court of St. James and secretary of commerce. Angering
Boston Democratic machine politicians, including Speaker of
the House Thomas "Tip" O'Neill, President Jimmy Carter appointed Republican Richardson as his ambassador-at-large and
special representative to the Law of the Sea Conference. They
had nothing against Richardson personally; they wanted the
prestigious post to go to a "deserving" Democrat.

Most of all of this lay in the future on the day Richardson appeared seeking confirmation as undersecretary of state. "I wel-
come and appreciate," Richardson told the committee in a
cultivated voice, "the committee's granting of an opportunity to
me to appear before you in open session so that I could respond
to the questions that have been raised about my driving record." With the exception of Chairman J. William Fulbright,
who knew what was coming, the committee members acted as
though they had not heard the witness correctly.

Richardson then proceeded to read from a sheet of paper listing ten driving violations. Shaking his head with puzzlement, Sen. Jacob K. Javits of New York said, "Would the chair mind—I would like for myself, Mr. Richardson—I know you well and I have great faith in you, but I do think you ought to explain why this congenital series of traffic and other violations for motorists. I am much older than you, and I do not think I have had nearly as many. What is the reason for that?" If Javits's syntax was fumbling, it was because he was flabbergasted. Javits has never had to fumble for words.

Richardson asked that he be given the opportunity "to get the facts on the record in more or less chronological order."

> There are two significant violations involved [Richardson said]. The others, I think, could fairly be characterized as minor traffic violations, although I think Senator Javits raised a fair question as to their number.
>
> The first of the significant violations occurred on May 8, 1939. I was then eighteen years of age, a sophomore in college. I drove from Cambridge into Boston, ran into a traffic island, blew out a tire, was approached by a police officer who observed that I was plainly under the influence of alcoholic beverages, and I was duly escorted to the nearest police station. I pleaded guilty the following day without, I might add, seeking representation of counsel, and paid $75 in fines and my driving license was suspended for a year.
>
> In that instance, the only extenuation I can offer is that I had been at a party at one of the Harvard houses where they had one of these rum fruit punches whose lethal character was well disguised by the fruit.

Twelve years later, on May 11, 1951, "at an early hour in the morning," Richardson went on, he turned a corner of a back street in his own town of Brookline, drove up on the sidewalk, and knocked down a traffic sign. He pleaded guilty to "the charge of driving to endanger." Suddenly remembering that he had skipped a bit of the chronology, Richardson said:

> I should have stated earlier, in 1939, where there were two charges in fact at the time, one driving to endanger and the other driving under the influence. In this instance of one charge of driving to endanger for which I paid a $200 fine and lost my license for four months, although no charge of driving under the influence was made at the time, I admitted to the police officer that I had had a few drinks during the course of the evening.

> Massachusetts records also show between 1938 and 1952 speeding
> offenses with total fines of $15, one violation involving two charges of
> not slowing down, total fines of $15, and one charge of failure to ob-
> serve a traffic sign, $2 cost paid.

Javits was about to turn to another topic, one dealing with foreign policy, when Richardson suddenly went on, "I have lived in
Washington for a total of six years." Puzzled, Javits asked, "What
were those years?"

Richardson replied, "1948, 1949, I was a law clerk for Mr. Justice Frankfurter, 1953 and 1954 as assistant to Senator Saltonstall, and late 1956 through late 1959 as assistant secretary of
HEW; and during those years I was stopped twice for speeding,
once in 1949 and once in 1957; charged with going forty miles
an hour in a thirty-mile zone; and I was stopped three times during those six years for failure to observe traffic signs. None of
these instances required court action, and the violations techni-
cally do not constitute convictions. I forfeited collateral of $5
and two $15 in each case. The 1949 speeding charge was fol-
lowed by a thirty-day suspension."

Javits, looking as though he wished he'd never started this
gambit, asked, "When was the last charge?"

"The last charge of all," said Richardson, "the only recent one
was the last of the Washington charges in 1957."

"And nothing after that?" asked Javits, confident now the
weary recital was at an end. But it wasn't.

"The only thing after that," said Richardson patiently—
though by now he was looking as embarrassed as Javits—"is a
speeding charge in New Hampshire on January 24, 1964. This
was a situation of entering a small town with a posted lower rate
of speed in the town and I didn't, simply did not, slow down
soon enough or rapidly enough."

Javits asked, "Do you consider this succession of events unusual or are you just unlucky?"

"I think it is in degree unusual," Richardson said. "I certainly
do not particularly, having served as a law enforcement officer
myself, want to sound as if I thought these violations were matters of no concern, and I am by no means proud of them, but I
think it is always fair to say that I have never concealed them."
By this time, Richardson decided he should say something in his

own defense. "There is one further point. . . . I have seen the text of a nationally syndicated column which was mailed out, I believe, yesterday, at least received yesterday by subscribing newspapers. It recites many of the circumstances which I have described to you, but it couples this with the assertion, or at least the plain inference, that I am an alcoholic, and I think it is quite important to hit that inference squarely and directly. It is absolutely without foundation."

Suddenly, everything fell into context. Until then, the dismal recital of the squalid events more properly would have belonged in a meeting of the gospel union mission and not the Senate Committee on Foreign Relations.

Two days before the committee meeting, the late Drew Pearson had sent out his *Washington Merry-Go-Round* column for release on January 16, the day after the scheduled hearing. Pearson charged that Fulbright was planning to hold a closed-door hearing on the Richardson nomination probably to conceal Richardson's "alcoholism." "One point in the career of Elliott Richardson," the column read, "is unfortunate and could be a reason for Chairman Fulbright's secret hearings. . . . He has a good record in government—except for alcoholism."

Fulbright had planned a closed hearing, but for a different reason. He wanted both Secretary of State-designate William Rogers and Richardson to be able to answer committee questions on delicate foreign policy matters with candor—something Fulbright felt they could not do at an open hearing before they were confirmed by the Senate. However, Rogers and Richardson obtained an advance copy of the Pearson column. Rogers conferred with Fulbright, and both agreed it was best that Richardson testify at an open hearing.

The remaining questions were gentle and routine. Karl E. Mundt of South Dakota said, "I would almost assume, since the secretary of state gets a limousine and a car and a driver, maybe that would happen to you."

"I hope so," Richardson replied.

Sen. John Sherman Cooper of Kentucky pressed the point. "You will have a driver in the next administration?"

Richardson: "I hope so."

As for Vietnam, NATO, the Nuclear Non-Proliferation Treaty, the issue of national commitments—not a word was uttered by anyone. There was a passing reference to what Fulbright called "the perennial question of the reorganization of the State Department" which Nixon had promised during the campaign. Richardson's unilluminating response was, "I can only say that I regard this whole problem as of key importance to the ability of this administration ... to develop and carry out policy, and I would hope that I will be able to make a useful contribution to identifying the opportunities for improving the effectiveness of the system."

In the previous Truman administration, the Senate Judiciary Committee had had to wrestle with the problem of a presidential nomination for the federal bench in which drinking was the least of the dilemmas presented by the nominee. The committee could not turn its collective back on the nominee. He was a fellow member of Congress.

Ever since he first went to Congress in 1937 as representative from Pittsburgh's Golden Triangle, the city's shopping and business district, Herman P. Eberharter, a self-styled "100 percent New Dealer," had voted with almost unfailing regularity precisely the way the administration wanted him to. He received the reward of regularity—Harry S. Truman nominated him for a federal judgeship in the Western District of Pennsylvania. But if the president believed that unswerving devotion to New Deal principles was qualification enough for the bench, the judiciary committee of the American Bar Association thought differently.

The bar committee chairman, John G. Buchanan, told the senators that Eberharter was unfit to serve on the bench because of "drunkenness" and "criminal" offenses, including the "cruel and barbarous" beating of his first wife. He then proceeded to read into the record a long list of Eberharter's brushes with the law. Among them: In 1919, Eberharter was charged with larceny in the theft of twenty phonograph records valued at $17. The case was nolle prossed upon payment of costs. In 1922, he was arrested for "manufacturing, selling, transporting, and possessing alcoholic beverages." He pleaded not guilty and was released after paying costs. In 1928, he was convicted of disorderly conduct, but the conviction was reversed on appeal. Buchanan testified also that Eberharter had violated the law while a member of Congress by representing for a fee a firm that had business with the government.

Another witness, a Red Bank, New Jersey, lawyer, testified that Eberharter had been arrested in May 1945, on a disorderly conduct charge when he "attempted to pick fights with passengers, especially men in uniform," while aboard a train bound from Washington to New York.

A few days later, Eberharter had his day before the Senate committee.

Item: He admitted he had been charged in 1919 with the larceny of twenty Victrola records valued at 85 cents each. The case was quashed. The charge, he said, resulted from a fight between the woman he later married and her sister. His wife-to-be had given him the records to hold for her; the sister claimed the records were her property. The unfortunate Eberharter apparently was caught in the middle.

Item: He admitted he was indicted in April 1922 on a charge of possessing intoxicating beverages. He was standing on a street corner. A policeman asked him what he had on his hip. A pint of moonshine, said Eberharter. He was hauled into court and made to pay a small fine.

Item: He admitted he had crossed the center white line of a street in Pittsburgh while driving his car some years later. "I had the smell of alcohol on my breath, but I wasn't drunk," he told the committee.

Item: He admitted he had crashed into a car in Pittsburgh while driving on the Boulevard of Allies, but denied he had been drinking. "I dozed off and ran into the car," he said. "If the police had smelled any liquor, they would have had me examined."

Item: He admitted his first wife had obtained a divorce from him in 1923 on an allegation of "cruel and barbarous treatment," but denied the accusation. Nearly all divorces in Pennsylvania, he said, were granted on those grounds. It simply was not true that neighbors had to come in and separate him and his wife while he was "beating and choking her."

Item: "I had a few drinks, yes, but I certainly wasn't intoxicated," said Eberharter in commenting on the "Newark incident." On May 14, 1945, he was removed from a Pennsylvania Railroad train bound from New York to Washington at the Newark station after threatening to fight several of the railroad cops. Eberharter explained he was angry because he saw a uniformed

Restauratuer, bon vivant, intimate of such Hollywood stars as Edward G. Robinson, left, Mike Romanoff was a bogus Russian prince who wrote a fortune in bad checks. Congress helped him become a citizen after endorsements from then Vice-President Nixon and J. Edgar Hoover.

Proper Bostonian Elliott Richardson, just nominated for Undersecretary of State, explains drunk driving record to Senate Committee. Below, Frank Shakespeare, who was nominated to head the U.S. Information Office, apologizes to same committee for resorting to Madison Avenue prose.

Pennsy employee sitting down in a crowded train while women and children stood. He agreed he might have told one of the policemen, "the hell with you and the Pennsylvania Railroad," but he wasn't drunk, no sir.

The balding, bespectacled Eberharter chain-smoked nervously as he testified in a low, almost quavering voice. At one point, Chairman Pat McCarran of Nevada, who always wore silver dollars mounted as cufflinks, broke in and assumed an avuncular tone toward his besieged colleague.

MCCARRAN: "When, if at all, did you first commence the use of alcoholic liquor?"

EBERHARTER: "Well, when I was quite a child, or maybe ten or twelve years old, my father used to get beer by the keg. He used to give me a glass of beer once in a while."

MCCARRAN: "How continuous has it been since then?"

EBERHARTER: "There are many times I have not drank [sic] for a long time."

MCCARRAN, picking up the grammatical solecism: "Are there many times when you have not drank for a long time? Is that your answer?"

EBERHARTER: "Oh, yes. Many times I have not drank for three or four years at a time."

MCCARRAN: "Let us be frank with this committee now. You have been under the influence of liquor pretty heavily at times, have you not? So let us be frank."

EBERHARTER: "Senator, I have at times drank more than I should."

MCCARRAN: "If this committee would confirm you, and you would thereafter indulge in the excessive use of alcoholic liquor to such an extent as to disgrace yourself, this committee would be responsible. I want you to be frank with this committee and tell us whether or not in the event that this committee saw fit to confirm you, assuming that in the past you may have been guilty of excessive use of alcoholic liquor, have you got control of yourself so that it will not occur again?"

EBERHARTER: "I definitely think I have control of myself, Senator."

Congress adjourned soon after this exchange and the nomination died in committee. No effort was ever made to revive it. Eberharter continued to serve in Congress until his death on September 9, 1958, a good nine years later.

The story of another nomination should be related here. It did not involve drinking, but it did involve a nominee from the world of advertising who was intoxicated on Madison Avenue prose. Were it not for the fact that his name was submitted to the Senate for confirmation during the early Nixon honeymoon period, his nomination might have been rejected or, at the very least, buried.

Frank Shakespeare's mistake was to write his own statement. He couched it in the overblown, Madison Avenue prose suitable for a TV documentary. Elegant words rich in generalities and meager on specifics appeared to contain sentiments more congenial to the philosophy of former Secretary of State Dean Rusk, with whom Fulbright quarreled, than that of his successor.

Fulbright's mellowness vanished as he listened to Shakespeare's extended speech of which the following paragraphs were typical examples:

> We live in a time when men are restless, when all is questioned, when the most sacred institutions can no longer take acceptance for granted, when new ideas whirl the globe and every society is questioning itself. It is a time of opportunity and a time of danger.
>
> The opportunity is that men, from out of the ferment, may find new ways to progress themselves and be brothers. The danger is that in the urgency of the quest for the new, men may fail to see what has worked in the past.
>
> In such a world, the story of America must ring clear.... Indeed, our material success has intertwined the fate of other free nations with our own to the extent that we now bear special and immense responsibilities which we did not seek but must not shirk.... Our mark upon these times will depend on the course set for the nation by the President and the Congress, dependent on their judgment and God's grace.

Peering first at the press table to make certain the bored reporters were alert to what was about to take place, and then peering quizzically at Shakespeare over his Benjamin Franklin glasses, Fulbright, in his lilting Arkansas twang, started to give the witness the business. "That was a very eloquent statement," said Fulbright with mild sarcasm. "I would be interested if you would just expand a bit on what you had in mind when you wrote: 'We now bear special and immense responsibilities which we did not seek, but must not shirk.' Responsibility to do what and to whom? Those words are fraught with meaning that I don't quite grasp and I wondered if you would make it a little clearer to me."

"I think," said Shakespeare, "in that sense we are by far the strongest nation among those on the side of freedom, that much of what we do and what we say is going to be tied intimately in the course of history with whether freedom survives or not."

Fulbright leaned forward, put his hand to his ear, and asked: "I didn't hear. With what?"

Shakespeare, beginning to show his nervousness, replied: "I think that the way we conduct ourselves will have much to do with whether or not freedom survives."

"Well," drawled Fulbright, "I may be a little slow this morning, on Monday morning, but what is that responsibility? This idea of responsibility, what brought it to my mind is not so long ago we had public speeches by prominent officials that we were going to take the Great Society to all of Asia and so on. Is this the kind of responsibility you have in mind, that we are going to take the Great Society to Asia?"

As Shakespeare ducked a direct answer, Fulbright pursued his prey. "It does worry me a little. It is a broad phrase that we 'bear special and immense responsibilities which we did not seek, but must not shirk.' It is a full, rounded phrase, and I am bothered by what it means. Surely you have something in mind. The responsibility to do what? Couldn't you give me a little more specific idea? Shall we form more treaties, should we have greater military commitments, greater, more NATOs, or what do you have in mind?"

Shakespeare: "Senator, I don't think that I should speak to the point of what the policy of—"

Fulbright, breaking in: "But these are *your* words. You said we have special and immense responsibilities. These are not just words. They mean something to you. They don't mean anything to me until you tell me what you had in mind. You should have something. Even senators have something in mind usually when we use words. This is going to be your business to use words to all the world, and you shouldn't use words that you have no conception of what they mean."

Shakespeare, leaning forward and looking decidedly uncomfortable, gave it a try. "I think the United States is the central economic force in the free world. I think this puts us in a position of central leadership of the Western world, whether we would choose it or not. I think that the world is in struggle between conflicting ideologies and we are the leader of one of those camps, in my view."

Fulbright: "Have we been elected the leader?"

Shakespeare: "No, sir."

Democratic Sen. W. Stuart Symington of Missouri took up the needling: "I notice you say: 'Americans are free to worship, to speak, to choose their leaders, and work out their destinies as they see fit in a land of unparalleled abundance.' You agree that other countries are free to worship, to speak, to choose their leaders, and work out their destinies as they see fit, do you not?"

Shakespeare: "Not all of the countries. Some of the countries."

When Symington asked him whether he would include Vietnam, Shakespeare said he wouldn't want to comment on Vietnam.

"What," asked Fulbright, "do you think about a country like Brazil? Is it working out its destiny in freedom?"

Shakespeare: "Yes, within reasonable freedom I think it is."

Fulbright, raising his eyebrows: "Is Paraguay?"

Shakespeare: "I am less familiar with Paraguay."

"Is Argentina?"

"Yes."

"Is Spain [note: Franco's Spain]?"

"Yes."

"What," Fulbright pursued, "is your distinction between a military dictatorship that is in South America and a dictatorship of the proletariat?"

"I don't think this is a generalized distinction. I think you have to take it on a case by case basis."

Republican Sen. Clifford Case of New Jersey tried to get Shakespeare off the hook by pointing out that the USIA role is nothing more than telling the American story abroad. Shakespeare was so grateful that he forgot himself and quickly slipped into Madison Avenue-ese: "If I were to put that in merchandise terms, I agree exactly with what you are saying. We have a sensational product and the more familiar the people of the world become with the product, the more successful we will be."

Shakespeare's nomination was confirmed. It was too trivial to wage a battle about, especially at the start of a new administration. But it was a long time before he erased the unfortunate impression he had made on the committee. In a cloakroom conversation a little later, George Aiken of Vermont said, "I wonder if the president took him on because CBS wanted to dump him." He thought a moment and then went on, "I've known it to happen, sometimes the worst witness turns out to be a good administrator." But he confessed he wasn't too certain if it would happen in this case. It didn't.

A singular act of beneficence was performed by Congress and approved by President Eisenhower midway through his second administration when enabling legislation was enacted to pave the way for U.S. citizenship for one of the most engaging fraudulent characters of the twentieth century.

A restaurateur, bon vivant, and intimate of Hollywood stars, Michael Romanoff was a self-styled Russian prince. He was born Harry F. Gerguson, but no one ever knew just where, whether in this country or, more likely, in Russia. In later years, he assumed the title of Prince Dmitri Michael Obelensky-Romanoff, using that name to write a fortune in bad checks.

In and out of jail and in and out of deportation proceedings throughout the 1930s, he nevertheless wound up owning exclusive restaurants in Beverly Hills, Palm Springs, and San Francisco, and in Hollywood's golden years, Romanoff's was a place for celebrities to be seen. When Romanoff presided over the laying of a cornerstone at one restaurant, the guests on hand included actors Clark Gable, Ronald Colman, Joseph Cotten, and David Niven. He finally closed up shop and retired in 1962. He died nine years later while shopping in Beverly Hills.

Congress was fully aware of Romanoff-Gerguson's history when it enacted the legislation. The report of the House Judiciary Committee accompanying the measure stated in part:

> The beneficiary, Michael Romanoff (also known as Harry Gerguson) is the husband of a U.S. citizen. His exact age, which appears to be between 65 and 68 [this was in 1958], and his place of birth are unknown.
>
> The first immigration record identified in his case is in 1922 when he sought admission as a United States citizen after arriving in New York as a passenger from Europe on November 29 of that year. He was excluded and ordered deported but escaped from custody and was again apprehended in 1924.

There was a seven-year hiatus in the record. He next applied for admission to the U.S. on April 19, 1932, after arriving as a stowaway on the *Ile de France*. He said he had unintentionally departed from the U.S. in April, when he had gone to see some friends embark and remained aboard. He was excluded as a stowaway and deported to France. Later that year, he was caught in New York City and ordered deported again, after claiming that he had entered from Canada. Actually, he had entered by stowing away on the *Europa*.

The report concluded: "The Department of Justice has been unable to prove that Mr. Romanoff was born outside of the United States and he has been unable to prove birth in this country. The enactment of this legislation will resolve that dilemma."

There was additional information available to the House committee from the files of the Immigration Department. "Romanoff," the files stated, "said that he has attended school only a short time, but he considers himself to have education equal to that of a university graduate, having successfully passed the entrance examination to Oxford University in England in 1913." This same source disclosed that when Romanoff came into this country in 1922, he told Immigration officials that he had been "imprisoned in Germany for several years for having killed a man in a duel." The memorandum goes on: "Romanoff was found to be insane in Liverpool, England, in 1915, following an arrest for false pretenses." Five years later, he was sentenced to six months when he was convicted for the same offense on which he had been locked up earlier as insane.

The last item stated that he was imprisoned for ninety days following a perjury conviction in New York City on April 5, 1933. A memorandum submitted to the committee by Republican Congressman Donald L. Jackson of Santa Monica, California, adds one other conviction: a $200 fine in 1930 for paying a Cleveland, Ohio, hotel bill with a check that bounced. "Since 1933, Romanoff's record," stated Jackson, "is without blemish." How could a man with such a record obtain American citizenship with the aid of Congress and President Dwight D. Eisenhower?

One clue: Letters praising Romanoff were listed in the House committee report from J. Edgar Hoover and Hollywood producers Leland Hayward and Darryl F. Zanuck. The Zanuck letter stated in part, "Mr. J. Edgar Hoover has told me on more than one occasion that he considers Mr. Romanoff a fine American. I could go on and add many names to this list of important people with whom I've discussed Mr. Romanoff. This list would include Vice President Richard Nixon, Senator William Knowland, Mr. Leonard Firestone, etc."

Incidentally, there is no mention in any of the Immigration or congressional files concerning Romanoff's relationship with the imperial Russian family.

CHAPTER 11

Chappaquiddick II

———

Perhaps no politician in American history has experienced such violent swings in fortune as Ted Kennedy. Now that "the inevitability of Teddy" has begun once again to fire the imagination of his fellow Democrats, one forgets that only a few years ago—in January 1971—he suffered the incredible humiliation of being booted out of a high leadership post in the Senate by his Democratic colleagues.

And the man who beat him, to the astonishment not only of Teddy but of even those senators who voted to unseat him—Robert Carlyle Byrd—was so obscure on the national scene that David Brinkley, the NBC newscaster, dubbed him after his victory "the widely unknown senator from West Virginia." In the graph of Teddy's career, this humiliation occurred during one of the downward dips. Even so, Byrd could not have toppled Teddy if a dying senator, half a dozen miles away in Walter Reed Hospital, had cast off his mortal coil four hours earlier. Dying of lung cancer and emphysema and in a deep coma at the time, Richard Russell of Georgia lived just long enough for his proxy vote, prepared in advance, to be cast for Byrd and swing the tide against Teddy.

Thus the sheerest happenstance enabled Byrd to become the assistant majority leader, and when Majority Leader Mike Mansfield retired six years later, it was easy for Byrd to move up to one of the most powerful and influential posts in the national government.

The majority leader of the Senate is the man who decides what bills come to the floor for action and when. Thus, his decisions can mean life or death for legislation. He presides over the Democratic Policy Committee, which advises on the order and priority of legislation. He presides over the Steering Committee, which makes committee assignments, thus placing senators in his debt.

When these powers are wielded by a strong, ruthless leader, as in the case of Lyndon B. Johnson, every law enacted has his personal stamp upon it. When a leader such as Mansfield refuses to exercise the power potential, the Senate becomes a more freewheeling and less predictable body.

Byrd has steered a course midway between those of his two predecessors.

The contrast between Kennedy and Byrd could not be wider—the first born to wealth and sharing in the charisma of the Kennedy clan; the latter born in poverty in a poor mining town, placed by his father after his mother's death, and raised as a foster child. Moreover, he was utterly lacking in charisma then and now.

Byrd and Teddy did have something in common—a youthful episode which both succeeded in living down: Teddy, the Spanish test taken by proxy, and Byrd, a membership, at age twenty-four, in the Ku Klux Klan. As Byrd has explained innumerable times, "It is something I have to live with. It was a youthful mistake." The revelation of Klan membership occurred in 1952 in his first race for Congress. He won anyway and went on to serve six undistinguished years in the House before being elected to the Senate in 1958. His victories then and since have been little short of astonishing in their magnitude. He won fifty-nine percent of the vote the first time; sixty-eight percent six years later; seventy-eight percent in 1970 when he carried all the fifty-five counties of the state; and in 1976 he ran without opposition!

Lacking a smiling personality and a magnetic presence, Byrd overcame such obstacles easily by making himself one of the best political fence-menders in Congress. He makes fifteen hundred phone calls a year to people back home "to see how they're doing"; faithfully answers constituent mail; returns to the state "to stop along the streets and talk to people" at least twenty-five times a year; and provides weekly columns to seventy newspapers and taped messages about what he is doing for West Virginia to its sixty-three radio stations. Byrd attended law school at night at American University, graduating summa cum laude and becoming the only member in Senate history to obtain a law degree while serving in that body.

In 1967, Byrd began his ascent in the Senate hierarchy with his election to the highly insignificant post of secretary of the Democratic Conference, the body of all Senate Democrats. But he did something no predecessor had ever done: he worked at it. Whatever tasks were necessary for fellow senators—reminding them when a bill or an amendment was of importance to them or "protecting their flanks" when they had to be absent— they were performed by Byrd. After such favors, no matter how small, Byrd would send notes to his colleagues saying he had enjoyed working with them and was looking forward to being of assistance in the future. In the Senate, it is called "piling up chits" against the day when a big favor is sought in return. By the time Byrd was preparing to defeat Teddy for the assistant leadership, he had accumulated what was possibly the biggest pile of chits in Senate history.

Teddy was elected assistant majority leader (the post is also known as Whip) in January 1968 by defeating Russell Long of Louisiana. An unhappy marriage, finally ending in divorce, had driven Long to drink. Occasionally, he appeared on the Senate floor in a clear state of intoxication. He neglected his leadership duties and Byrd moved into the vacuum, thus making something of his insignificant leadership post.

Kennedy was not an effective leader. He was not quick on his feet, and without a prepared text and especially when tangling with a skillful old-timer, Teddy could be made to look foolish. A typical instance was an exchange with that sly old fox, Republican Sen. John Williams of Delaware. Teddy rose to challenge a statement Williams had made on a fiscal matter on which Williams, the senior member of the Senate Finance Committee, was an expert. Williams replied that he did not have time "to educate the senator from Massachusetts on the floor," but that if Kennedy wanted to see him in his office, he would gladly receive him. His face flushed, Teddy sat down.

Chappaquiddick took place in mid-July 1969, and after that,

Teddy's clout in the Senate diminished sharply, and his appearance on the floor became a sometime thing. Once again, Byrd moved into the vacuum of "protecting the rights" of his colleagues: remaining on the floor every minute of the session, seeing that his colleagues' pet bills would come up as scheduled, and that they were called to the floor to defend those bills or make a long-scheduled speech at the first available moment.

There was sympathy for Teddy in the Senate because of the Martha's Vineyard tragedy, but it was diluted by a rather transparent device Teddy resorted to which irked members of the club. Teddy would not allow Byrd to offer adjournment motions if he—Teddy—was in town and Mansfield was unavailable. Teddy had informed Byrd that if it was time to adjourn the Senate, Byrd must first make a point of no quorum, and while the roll was being called, Teddy would be summoned to the floor where he would call off the quorum call and move to adjourn the Senate. Teddy might be absent the entire day but would then rush in at the last moment so that the *Congressional Record* would show that he had adjourned the Senate.

One day, while Democratic Sen. Harrison "Pete" Williams of New Jersey was making a speech to a virtually deserted Senate, Mansfield whispered to Byrd that he had to leave, and said: "Bob, fold it up." When Williams finished, Byrd said, "Mr. President, if there be no further business to come before the Senate—" He was interrupted. As he rose to offer the motion, a Kennedy aide rushed from the back of the chamber into the Democratic cloakroom to tell Kennedy what was happening. Kennedy then came rushing through the door, shouting for recognition. "Mr. President, Mr. President. If there be no further business to come before the Senate, I move, in accordance with the previous order, and pursuant to Senate resolution 481, as a further mark of respect for General Charles de Gaulle, former president of France, that the Senate now adjourn."

In the course of Senate business, occasions occur when routine resolutions must be processed. So routine are they that they are usually muttered, and the presiding officer announces, "Since there's no objection, the resolution is passed."

On such occasions, the resolutions are divided up. The presiding officer will be handed a list of senators to be recognized for the purpose. On one such occasion, Byrd went to the presiding officer's desk to see when it would be his turn to be recognized for that purpose. Teddy had drawn a penciled line through his name. At the time—it was in October 1970—Byrd grumbled to me, "Sometimes I can't even make a routine motion. This has been going on for two years. I just sit there and have to take it. It's frustrating." And that's when the notion occurred to Byrd to challenge Teddy for the leadership post when the next Congress convened in January 1971. About the same time, several of Byrd's colleagues urged him to run. They knew of Byrd's frustrations, but they were even more annoyed at Teddy's inept handling of his duties.

In mid-November, when Mansfield happened to be off the floor, Teddy moved, without the usually customary notice to anyone on his side of the aisle, to bring up the highly controversial Consumer Protection Act of 1970. This brought on a real flap. The only other senator on the floor, Republican Marlow Cook of Kentucky, at the quick nudging of an alert aide, demanded a "live quorum," where a majority of the senators must appear to answer their names. This allowed time for interested senators to come to the floor to protest. Assistant Republican leader Robert Griffin said indignantly, "I would like to make it abundantly clear that particularly when it comes to controversial measures, the minority expects and wants some notice about the scheduling."

Alerted to the crisis, Mansfield rushed to the floor from his office and apologized to the Senate. "Interested senators were apparently not consulted and for that I apologize. It should not have been done." The bill was temporarily withdrawn. Teddy flushed with embarrassment. Byrd, sitting in the rear of the chamber, smiled.

During the election recess of Congress, Byrd and his wife went to the Greenbrier Hotel in Greenbrier, West Virginia, for a rest. It was the evening of the day they arrived when Byrd received a telephone call from Teddy in Massachusetts. "Say, Bob," said Kennedy, "a newspaperman just called me and said you were considering running for the Whip job. I want to know if you are, so we can get our ducks in a row."

"Oh, that's pure speculation, Ted," Byrd replied. "I've given it some thought, but it's premature. We have work to do. We've got a rump session coming up, and we're going to be pretty busy. The election for the Whip job is two months off."

The story Kennedy was referring to appeared the next morn-

Ted Kennedy, who was to challenge an incumbent President, Jimmy Carter, for failing to provide "leadership," was booted out of his Senate leadership post in 1971 by a majority of his colleagues, because he failed to provide leadership. He was replaced by "the widely unknown" Robert C. Byrd, West Virginia, who became an excellent leader, rivaling his skill as a country fiddler. To win, Byrd desperately needed the proxy vote of Richard Russell of Georgia who was dying in Walter Reed Hospital in Washington. His last act was to sign the proxy letter just before slipping into a coma and dying four hours later.

RICHARD B. RUSSELL, GA., CHAIRMAN

ALLEN J. ELLENDER, LA.   MILTON R. YOUNG, N. DAK.
JOHN L. MCCLELLAN, ARK.   KARL E. MUNDT, S. DAK.
WARREN G. MAGNUSON, WASH. MARGARET CHASE SMITH, MAINE
SPESSARD L. HOLLAND, FLA.   ROMAN L. HRUSKA, NEBR.
JOHN C. STENNIS, MISS.   GORDON ALLOTT, COLO.
JOHN O. PASTORE, R.I.   NORRIS COTTON, N.H.
ALAN BIBLE, NEV.   CLIFFORD P. CASE, N.J.
ROBERT C. BYRD, W.VA.   HIRAM L. FONG, HAWAII
GALE W. MCGEE, WYO.   J. CALEB BOGGS, DEL.
MIKE MANSFIELD, MONT.   JAMES B. PEARSON, KANS.
WILLIAM PROXMIRE, WIS.
RALPH YARBOROUGH, TEX.
JOSEPH M. MONTOYA, N. MEX.

THOMAS J. SCOTT, CHIEF CLERK
WM. W. WOODRUFF, COUNSEL

United States Senate

COMMITTEE ON APPROPRIATIONS

WASHINGTON, D.C. 20510

January 18, 1971

Honorable Mike Mansfield
Majority Leader
United States Senate
Washington, D. C.

Dear Senator Mansfield:

In the event it is not possible for me to be present when the Senate Democrats caucus for the opening of the 92nd Congress, I hereby tender my proxy in favor of Senator Robert C. Byrd of West Virginia if he is a candidate for the position of Assistant Majority Leader.

With best wishes, I am

Sincerely

Richard B. Russell

ing in the *Boston Globe*, written by a newsman close to Kennedy. Since Byrd had by no means decided at the time to make the challenge because of its riskiness, he concluded Teddy had given the story to the *Globe* to smoke him out.

"Well, Bob," Teddy went on, "I'm about to take off for a NATO parliamentarians' meeting in Brussels tomorrow morning. If you have any intention of running, I may not go. If you can assure me you'll make no moves, I'll go to Belgium."

"Ted, I can't make any kind of assurance," Byrd said. "All I can tell you is that it's premature."

"Sure, you can do it. You can tell me whether you'll run or not." Teddy's voice sounded testy.

"Well, I won't," Byrd snapped.

By now, Byrd's back was up. He told his wife he was returning to Washington the next morning. He didn't like Teddy's effort, as he told her, "to lay down the rules for me." Teddy went on to Belgium.

In Washington, Byrd made a series of phone calls, first to Mansfield and then to the first half-dozen senators whom he could reach, including some he knew he could not win over. He told each one the same thing: "I want to alert you to the possibility that there may be a Whip's race in January. I'll talk with you about it later." Byrd asked for no commitments. He wanted to alert his colleagues to the possibility of a race so that they could avoid making commitments to Teddy or anyone else. Though Teddy was in Belgium, Byrd judged—and judged correctly—that Teddy's aides would be busy drumming up support in his absence.

When the Congress resumed its labors in mid-November after a month's layoff, Byrd decided there was only one way to beat Teddy—and he was far from certain that it could be done—and that was by establishing a low profile. If it became clear that Byrd was going to challenge him, Teddy would really go to work, and Byrd would probably be beaten.

As Byrd saw it, Teddy had a "national constituency," and if Teddy appealed to it, there would be greater pressures upon uncommitted senators. "If each senator was left to his own judgment," Byrd told me, "I felt I had a chance. I felt I had to deal with a man, not with his national constituency, if I was to have that chance."

To avoid stirring up that "national constituency," Byrd spoke only with those colleagues who "appeared promising." Congress finally adjourned on January 2, 1971, its constitutional deadline, and the new Ninety-second Congress was convening late, on January 21. The Senate Democratic caucus, the meeting at which the members elect their leaders, was scheduled for January 18.

During much of that time, Teddy was sunning himself in Montego Bay, Jamaica. Byrd was in Washington telephoning senators. There was one senator who could not be present, the dying Richard Russell. Another, Warren Magnuson of Washington, wasn't certain the weather would permit him to arrive in time. Byrd asked him to mail in his proxy. Then he asked Russell's Georgia colleague, Herman Talmadge, if he would try to get a proxy from Russell at Walter Reed Hospital.

On Monday morning—the crucial caucus was to be Thursday—Talmadge brought the proxy letter to Russell for his signature. The letter, which Talmadge wrote for him, read: "In the event it is not possible for me to be present when the Senate Democrats caucus for the opening of the 92nd Congress, I hereby tender my proxy in favor of Senator Robert C. Byrd, of West Virginia, if he is a candidate for the position of assistant majority leader." Russell read the proxy message slowly, and then, with obvious difficulty, signed his name. It was Richard Russell's last official act as senator and—as it turned out—it sealed Teddy's defeat.

In the forty-eight hours before the crucial Thursday morning caucus, Byrd went into action, even dialing the sacrosanct extension—56148—to get senators out of the Senate baths to discuss the situation with them. "Look," Byrd said, "I'm making a final check. I don't know yet whether I'm going to run. I don't want to be slaughtered. If you can't vote for me, please tell me now."

Byrd had reason to be cautious and worried. Teddy was not only making calls and asking for commitments but was urging several of his colleagues to consider announcing for Byrd's leadership post. He succeeded in persuading Frank Moss of Utah to enter the race. Teddy's staff put out the word to Boston newsmen about the strategy. As one of them stated it, "Teddy wants to do more than just beat Byrd. He wants to destroy him by getting him out of the leadership lineup entirely."

At 1:45 A.M., Thursday, the day of the caucus, Byrd sat down at the desk in his modest home just across the Potomac River in Virginia and went over his list for the umpteenth time. To win, he needed twenty-eight votes. His list showed twenty-eight, and the fate of one of those was, as Byrd put it, "in the hands of the Lord." The failure of Russell to live until the proxy could be cast; the inclemency of the weather that might prevent a supporter from flying to Washington or landing there in time; the last-moment change of mind of any senator—and Byrd was done for.

"I always told myself," Byrd later recounted to me, "that I would not announce for the post if I had only twenty-eight votes. I felt I should have a margin of one or two votes for safety. I went to bed that night without knowing what I was going to do." He woke at 5 A.M. and still didn't know. He was at his Capitol Hill office at 6 A.M. and went over the list again and again. He began calling Senate offices. One of the first to arrive, Herman Talmadge, came in at 7:30 A.M. Talmadge said he was going to call Walter Reed Hospital and get the latest word on Russell's condition.

Byrd reached his West Virginia colleague, Jennings Randolph, who had offered to make the nominating speech. "I don't know yet, Jennings," Byrd said. "I'll give you a signal at the caucus. If I nod my head, go ahead and place my name in nomination. If I don't, then don't do anything." Then Byrd placed telephone calls to eighteen senators to whom he had not spoken before because he felt it would be futile. Nevertheless, he felt he had nothing to lose, and he just might pick up one or two. He reached all eighteen—and drew eighteen blanks.

At 9:50 A.M., ten minutes before the scheduled caucus, he left his office, telling his secretary: "I don't know what I am going to do." Only moments earlier he had heard from Talmadge, who gave him the distressing news that he had not been able to get through to Russell's doctors. Talmadge told Byrd he had instructed an aide, Charles Campbell, to keep trying and to stand outside the closed doors of the caucus room to give Byrd the latest information if Byrd should step out of the room and request it.

On his way to the Senate underground trolley, Byrd ran into Russell Long of Louisiana, who was on his way to the caucus. "What are you going to do, Bob?" Long asked.

"I don't know, Russ," Byrd replied. "If Dick dies, I'm not going to run."

Long then took his own list out of his coat pocket and compared it with Byrd's. Long had also been buttonholing senators. He wanted Teddy, who had knocked him out of the leadership post two years earlier, humiliated in the same way. He had not hesitated to use his clout as chairman of the Senate Finance Committee, where he was in a position to help senators with special tax bills, on Byrd's behalf. In addition, his top aide, Robert Hunter, a pious Roman Catholic, had not only spent the night working over aides to other senators, but interspersed his efforts with prayers for Byrd.

At 10:35 A.M., Byrd got up from his chair in the caucus and went out one of the rear doors where he saw Campbell, who told him he had finally gotten through to one of Russell's doctors and been told that Russell was still alive. Quietly, Byrd went back into the room, sat in his chair, turned to Randolph, and nodded his head. Byrd gave the nod just as Hawaii's Dan Inouye was nominating Ted Kennedy for another term as assistant majority leader.

When Randolph stood up and placed Byrd's name in nomination, there was a hubbub. One senator was heard to exclaim, "I'll be goddamned. Bob Byrd's got it." With his reputation as a careful counter, the senators felt that Byrd would not have allowed Randolph to nominate him unless he had the votes.

As it turned out, to Byrd's surprise and to Teddy's clear distress, Byrd had more than enough. Byrd thought Russell's proxy would give him just the bare majority to make the gamble. The announcement by Mansfield, after the counting of the secret ballots, that Byrd had won by thirty-one to twenty-four stunned everyone—especially Teddy, who ended up with two less than the "solid" twenty-six commitments he had thought he had.

The vote was secret and the ballots were burned immediately in the fireplace. At once the suspicion arose that Teddy had been double-crossed by the half-dozen other presidential hopefuls in the Democratic ranks.

To this day, Teddy doesn't know who let him down, though he has his suspicions. There's no question that at least two of his "solid" supporters lied to him when they pledged their vote. Suspicion has fastened, and I believe accurately, on Hubert H. Humphrey, the man with the best reason to vote for Byrd. He owed him a great political debt. Byrd had campaigned for Humphrey all over West Virginia during the 1960 primary race there. Humphrey lost that race—which knocked him out of the presidential race—to Jack Kennedy, thereby virtually nailing down his nomination. It was a dirty race. The Kennedy forces had brought in Franklin Roosevelt, Jr., who intimated that Humphrey, who had not served in World War II, was a draft dodger. Also Humphrey, who ran out of funds early, complained bitterly later to intimates that the Kennedys had "bought" the state.

The other defector very probably was Birch Bayh of Indiana, who had strong presidential ambitions at the time.

But these alone could not explain the Byrd margin of victory. Two votes—those of Henry Jackson and Warren Magnuson— were cast for Byrd because he had fought for federal financing of the supersonic transport plane which meant much to the state of Washington and which had opposed Ted Kennedy.

One thing is certain: Byrd could not have gotten 31 votes unless they came from other parts of the country aside from the South and border states and unless they came from unvarnished liberals.

Unless one is close to the Senate, it is difficult to understand how its members look upon that body as a great *institution* and how a man's conduct is viewed not just ideologically, but institutionally. The veteran Connecticut senator, Abe Ribicoff, a long-time supporter of the Kennedys, explained:

> Bob Byrd would do even the smallest chores for senators. You must realize that Ted Kennedy, whom I liked, never bothered. There were a lot of people in the Senate who were jealous of the Kennedys. As they saw it, he could get on page one or on the TV tube with a proposal he's advancing, and another senator with the same idea would be lucky to get near the classified ads.
>
> There was another factor. Almost everybody feels Teddy wants to be president. They figure that he'll stay back, use the leadership post as a "bully pulpit," and everybody else would knock their brains out. So they said to themselves: "Let's clip his wings." I know Teddy, and I can tell you he didn't expect to lose. He was caught flat-footed.

Still, Teddy would never have been challenged by Byrd if the breath of life had not still remained in Richard Russell.

After Teddy's defeat, the word in the Senate cloakrooms was that he had suffered "Chappaquiddick II" and some senators were convinced this had hurt his chances for the presidency even more than Chappaquiddick I.

How, it was asked, could any man seek the leadership of his party and the nation if he was rejected by his colleagues as assistant leader of the Senate? It might have been accidental, but just three days later, the newly sworn-in Sen. John Tunney of California—once Teddy's roommate at Harvard and a man who embarked on his race for the Senate as a Kennedy protegé—somehow failed to see Teddy's outstretched hand as he walked back from the rostrum to his rear Senate desk after taking the oath of office. Yet there appeared to be something symbolic about that episode. Teddy must have known it. His face was flushed.

Today, however, if one were to say Chappaquiddick II, he would be met with a stare of incomprehension. One should never underestimate the resilience of the Kennedys.

CHAPTER 12

The Movie Star
& the Cabinet Officer

~~~~~~

Parallel lines converge in politics as they do in the graphic arts. Movie star Jimmy Stewart wanted a brigadier general's star in the Air Force Reserve. President Dwight D. Eisenhower wanted Lewis L. Strauss as his secretary of commerce. Stewart got his star, but only after two years' delay and at a price. The Air Force Reserve, which wanted the advancement to go through for publicity purposes, had to undergo a congressional investigation of its promotion practices and change them. After a memorable Senate battle, Ike's nomination of Strauss was defeated. Strauss was the first cabinet nominee to be rejected in thirty-four years, and the first ever because a powerful senator just didn't like him—a dislike that was monumental and towering.

The fates of the two men converged; the humiliation of the first was to become inextricably intertwined with the defeat of the second.

Tall, graying, but debonair as ever, Jimmy Stewart arrived at the Westover, Massachusetts, Air Force base in March 1959 to record the commentary for a TV documentary film with the intriguing title of *Cowboy 57*, the code designation for the B-52 crew which starred in the film.

In the press conference that followed his arrival, Stewart was asked whether Sen. Margaret Chase Smith of Maine was going to hold up his promotion to brigadier general. Stewart, a colonel in the Air Force Reserve, replied with a singular absence of tact, "I don't know. When you ask me that, you are asking me to prognosticate the actions of a woman."

Stewart couldn't have committed a more egregious error in making a remark now recognized as sexist. Margaret Smith wasn't just another "woman" but one of the toughest politicians ever to appear on the senatorial scene. Her slim grace and invariably gentle manner fooled people who didn't know her well.

White House aides soon learned they could not approach her as they were accustomed to do with other senators. The mere act of asking how she intended to vote on a given amendment or bill would be enough to make her vote the opposite way. Neither Republican nor Democratic leaders would dare ask her to vote a certain way. In advance of a vote—especially an important vote—senatorial leaders, through their aides, could mark their tally sheets with good indications of the probable outcome. Alongside Margaret Smith's name, they could at best place a question mark.

Any newspaper reporter who made a factual error, no matter how minuscule, in a story involving Senator Smith, would soon be overwhelmed in correspondence by a mountain of data underlining the mistake.

Other Democratic senators, who were ready to go into any state in the Union to campaign for fellow Democrats, stayed away from Maine, knowing she would never forget or forgive such outside interference. At some point, they knew, they would need her vote. (Her Democratic colleague from Maine, Ed Muskie, ventured to help her opponent, William D. Hathaway, in 1972 only when he sensed that Senator Smith, then seventy-four, would finally be defeated after twenty-four years in the Senate on the age issue and her failure to campaign all-out this time.)

At the 1964 Republican presidential nominating convention, she was seriously proposed for the nomination. The nominating speech was made by George Aiken. By July 1968, when she had to go into the hospital for hip surgery, she had established an all-time record for consecutive roll-call votes—2,941. (It has since been surpassed by Wisconsin's William Proxmire.)

The *Congressional Directory,* published semi-annually with

each new Congress, contains biographies written by the members themselves. These go into great detail about their lives and careers, including such minutiae as their membership in the local American Legion post or the board of directors of the state's mental health association. This is her entry, and it was never changed: "Margaret Chase Smith, Republican." And this was the personage Jimmy Stewart was ready to dismiss as "a woman." Two years earlier, Stewart's promotion had been stopped dead in its tracks by Senator Smith when she charged that he wasn't qualified for promotion to flag rank over the heads of 1,900 other reserve colonels. She did more than make a charge—she proved it to the satisfaction of her colleagues on the Senate Armed Services Committee which voted thirteen to nothing to reject the promotion.

Two weeks before Stewart's arrival at Westover, President Eisenhower resubmitted Stewart's promotion along with a dozen other names. Eight of these were for promotion to flag rank, and five, from brigadier to major general. At first glance, it looked as though Stewart would have no trouble. The Air Force caved in to the Armed Services Committee and, after some resistance, downgraded his mobilization assignment from deputy operations chief of the Strategic Air Command to chief of staff of the 15th Air Force. He had also been checked out on SAC bombers, as the committee demanded. However, the resubmission of Stewart's nomination stirred up protests from Air Force reservists all over the nation who complained, in letters to senators, that his promotion was a body blow to the morale of reservists.

So Senator Smith took a second, then a third look at his record, and decided the Air Force was trying to put something over on the committee again. She found that Stewart, at the time the nomination was sent up, had not done his minimum fifteen days active duty in the current fiscal year. He had done only eight days. Smith then asked the Pentagon why he hadn't completed the minimum and was told "the press of business" had interfered. She didn't find that explanation adequate after learning that Stewart had been hunting tigers in India for the past three months. Then she discovered that though Stewart was rated as a pilot of a combat plane, he was not in a "qualified" status. He had not been checked out in a combat plane recently enough to be "qualified" under Air Force regulations. To hold a command position of any flying group, be it a squadron or wing, one must be "qualified." This would certainly apply to the chief of staff for the 15th Air Force.

This wasn't all she found. Stewart, she learned, was in the very lowest training category in the Air Force Reserve, category D. And she began asking why a reserve officer in such a training category should be promoted at all. In category D, at that time, the reservist had to train only fifteen days a year. In category A, for example, he had to put in at least sixty-three days. Furthermore, reservists were placed in category D for two reasons only: (1) when the mobilization assignment closely paralleled the civilian occupation which, in Jimmy Stewart's case, happened to be that of movie actor, and (2) when the reservist had just come off extended active duty—and Stewart had not been on extended active duty for fourteen years.

A sharp look at the other nominations sent up along with Stewart's showed that seven of the thirteen were not qualified. For example, there was the case of Charles Blair, Jr., a transatlantic airline pilot whom the president had nominated for brigadier. Blair never had a day's combat duty in any war and had received no decorations or awards. He served for twenty years in the naval reserve, advancing from ensign to lieutenant, j.g., in all that time. He resigned in 1952 and joined the Air Force Reserve as a colonel in 1953.

So far as the senator was concerned, it was clear that the Air Force was promoting its friends in the civil aviation field and in the motion picture industry. Finally, she shot off 150 questions to the Pentagon—after clearing them with Armed Services Committee Chairman Richard Russell—in which she asked the identity of the selection board members, the standards used in selecting these names over 1,900 others, and the amount of time given to the consideration of each choice. By now she was not alone in the crusade. She was joined by Democratic senators Clair Engle of California and Howard Cannon of Nevada—the latter a qualified Air Force jet pilot himself—who had been hearing from Air Force reservists back home.

Finally, in July 1959, after a six month tug-of-war between the Armed Ser. ices Committee and the Pentagon, Jimmy Stewart got his promotion. But both Stewart and the Air Force had to pay a price.

At the very last moment, the Air Force agreed to downgrade Jimmy Stewart's M-Day (or mobilization) assignment from chief of staff of the 15th Air Force to public relations. And the Armed Services Committee ordered "an intensive and sweeping" congressional investigation of the promotion system employed in all the services to upgrade reservists to flag rank. When the promotion was originally pigeonholed, Russell had passed the word informally to the Air Force to downgrade Stewart's M-Day assignment and make him do his minimum active reserve duty if they planned to try again for the promotion.

When the name was resubmitted on Lincoln's Birthday, the Air Force yielded on the latter stipulation but fudged on the assignment by changing it from chief of staff to SAC to the 15th Air Force. Russell took aside the senior Republican on the committee, Leverett Saltonstall of Massachusetts, and told him to tell the Air Force that it simply had to downgrade the M-Day assignment to something "more realistic," such as public relations. An embarrassed Saltonstall went to an anteroom and telephoned Air Force Secretary James H. Douglas. In a few moments, he returned and told the committee he had just been informed by Secretary Douglas that Stewart's M-Day assignment had been changed to "Public Information, Headquarters, United States Air Force, Washington, D.C." An official letter, he added, was being sent to the committee confirming Stewart's new assignment.

At Russell's direction, the committee then did something unprecedented: it voted to confirm the promotion on the condition that the Air Force make a public announcement within a week of the change of Stewart's M-Day assignment. If it failed to do so, the promotion would not be sent to the Senate. And then the committee unanimously voted the sweeping investigation of the promotion-selection system employed by all services in advancing reservists to flag rank.

It was at this point that the destinies of the movie actor and the Cabinet nominee converged.

Lewis Strauss (who pronounced his name as if it were spelled "straws") was no stranger to Washington or to the Senate. He had been in public service for forty-two years. Three times, in earlier years, he had been confirmed by the Senate—as a rear admiral during World War II, as a member of the Atomic Ener-

gy Commission in 1947, and as AEC chairman in 1953. He held
a recess appointment as secretary of commerce, and now his
name was before the Senate for confirmation in that post.

Rejection of a cabinet nominee is a rare thing in American
history, as mentioned earlier. Cabinet officers are considered
part of a president's "official family" and doubts are nearly always resolved in the president's favor. Only seven times before
had such nominees been rejected, and it has taken a clear showing of gross incompetence or turpitude to overcome traditional
senatorial reluctance to withhold confirmation.

There was nothing approaching this in the current case. A
year earlier, President Eisenhower had pinned on the proud
chest of Lewis Strauss the Medal of Freedom, the highest civilian award this government can bestow. He was the fifteenth
man to receive this honor. His citation read, in part:

> He was an effective supporter of the development of thermonucle-
> ar technology at a time when a less determined and imaginative
> course might have resulted in severe damage in our security and that
> of the free world. He initiated a long-range detection system for
> atomic explosions which adds both to our safety and to our hopes for
> successful disarmament.... Through his wisdom and foresight, his
> country enjoys greater security today and greater hopes for genuine
> peace in the years ahead.

On March 10 of the following year, Rear Adm. Hyman Rickover, the "father of the atomic sub," wrote to Strauss from the
U.S.S. *Skipjack*, the first nuclear-powered, streamlined, single-
screw attack submarine. Writing while the ship was submerged,
Rickover told Strauss, "The ship successfully met all her trials,
surfaced and submerged, and attained highest speed ever made
by any submarine.... I want you to know that your understanding and help were just as significant in creating this revolutionary submarine as the efforts of the designers and builders."

Yet on June 18—at 10:40 P.M. to be exact—Democrat Wayne
Morse of Oregon rose in the Senate to deliver a fifty-minute ti-
rade against Lewis Strauss as "an enemy of the people." At
12:33 A.M., the Senate rejected his nomination, by a vote of for-
ty-nine to forty-six.

In 170 years, thirty-three American presidents have submitted 450 cabinet nominations to the Senate. Lewis Strauss be-

came the eighth to be rejected. Historians examining his career and the 1,128 pages of the printed record of the sixteen-day hearing before the Senate Commerce Committee will wonder how and why the Senate rejected him.

His opponents said the printed record revealed Strauss as a "liar," a man who dealt in "half-truths," who "preferred to mislead Congress rather than admit error," and who deserved the near-traitorous appellation of "enemy of the people." And yet the record fails to substantiate any one of these charges. I read every single page of the hearings and had to agree with the judgment of Democratic Sen. Thomas J. Dodd of Connecticut who told the Senate just before the vote, "The charges against him remain unclear and are unresolved matters of contention. If I could briefly summarize all the charges made against Strauss, I would divide them into three groups: accusations that are grave but not proved; accusations that are proved but not grave; accusations that are both grave and proved but which, in my judgment, reflect credit and not discredit upon Admiral Strauss."

The defeat of Lewis Strauss can be understood only within the context of the bitter enmity of one powerful senator and the presidential ambitions of another. The bitter enmity was nursed by Sen. Clinton P. Anderson of New Mexico, the chairman of the Joint Atomic Energy Committee. The presidential ambitions, which he tried desperately to conceal, were those of Lyndon B. Johnson, the majority leader of the Senate and, after the president himself, perhaps the most powerful political figure in the nation.

The Anderson feud with Strauss was a nasty one, verging on pathology. He called him unbearably arrogant and deceitful and accused him of withholding information from Congress. And he vowed to block the confirmation. Originally the hatred was rooted less in ideological differences than in the personality conflicts of two proud men. In fairness to Anderson, it must be admitted that Strauss struck many others as arrogant and overbearing—though not bad enough to merit the treatment he received from the Senate.

It didn't take long, once the battle was joined, for the conflict to take on an ideological coloration. As an agent of the Eisenhower administration, Strauss resisted further expansion of the TVA and fought for the Dixon-Yates proposal which would have

After twenty-four years in the Senate and still going strong at 82, lecturing on college campuses, Margaret Chase Smith's lady-like demeanor conceals a will of steel that awed Presidents and fellow Senators alike. She condemned McCarthy when most of the Senate was too intimidated to speak out. Movie Actor Jimmy Stewart tangled with her to his regret.

After dismissing her as just "a woman," Jimmy Stewart had to wait months for his brigadier general's star and suffer humiliation. Caught in the middle of this epic struggle was Commerce Secretary Nominee Lewis L. Strauss, left. Mrs. Smith's utterly surprising "no" vote sank him, making Strauss the eighth cabinet nominee in U.S. history to be rejected. The price of Strauss's defeat: a Senate investigation of Air Force promotions, especially Stewart's.

brought private power into an area the public power zealots
looked upon as sacrosanct. Again, acting as an agent of the administration, Strauss resisted Democratic efforts to push for
greater governmental development of nuclear power for peaceful purposes. The administration wanted private industry to
play the greater role. So he gradually became a symbol to the
left wing of the Democratic party—a symbol of Wall Street, of
arch-conservatism.

When Ike gave Strauss the recess appointment to the commerce post the previous November 13, the consensus even
among Strauss's opponents on Capitol Hill was that he would be
confirmed after some harsh words had been uttered for the record. But when Clinton Anderson decided to wage an all-out
fight, the left-wing Democratic image of Strauss became vitally
important. For during the course of the struggle over Strauss,
this idea emerged: no Democrat who hoped for the presidential
nomination in July 1960 had a chance unless he voted against
Lewis Strauss. This vote became a badge of respectability, of acceptance, of belonging in the liberal wing of the party—the
wing which was going to dominate the Democratic Convention.

Anderson was one of the first men in the Senate to hail Lyndon Johnson publicly as the man best qualified to be the party's
nominee. Johnson knew he had to consolidate his position with
the liberal wing of the party, where he was weakest, if he was to
have a chance for the nomination. Also, Anderson would be in
control of the New Mexico delegation and would deliver those
delegates and perhaps more in the Southwest to Johnson if the
majority leader played his cards right.

Yet Johnson had to play a Machiavellian game. He could not
come out against Strauss too early and seek his defeat in the
light of day without alienating his conservative support in Texas.
Furthermore, Johnson knew there was a risk that the defeat of
the only Jewish member of the cabinet could hurt the Democrats in November 1960. Also, he had to continue pretending he
was not a presidential aspirant. Johnson tried to make the best of
a tortuous situation by having his aides pass the word to undecided Democrats that "the leadership position was adverse to
Strauss."

But when Arthur Krock of the *New York Times* wrote that
Johnson's vote would be "decisive," Johnson took to the Senate

floor to deny the validity of the thesis. The Strauss nomination, he said, was *not* a party matter. Each senator was to vote his conscience on the basis of the record. He himself would reach no conclusion until he had studied that record. In fact, he wouldn't tell how he intended to vote until just before the roll call. But the men in the Senate closest to Johnson knew of his decision to vote against Strauss after Clinton Anderson decided to wage an all-out fight. Each of the four presidential hopefuls in the Senate—Johnson, Hubert H. Humphrey, John F. Kennedy, and Stuart Symington—knew that the others were going to vote against Strauss.

Lyndon had the votes to defeat Strauss—if he was determined to achieve that result. But there was doubt and suspense right up to the end of the roll call. He would vote against Strauss, but would he work to defeat the nomination? Democratic Sen. Mike Monroney of Oklahoma told this writer only an hour before the roll call, "I'm going to vote against Strauss, but I hope and pray he will be confirmed by a small margin. The Democratic party is going to be hurt and hurt badly by the defeat. Right now a lot of people are saying that Lewis Strauss invented the hydrogen bomb and kept this country ahead of the Russians. If he is defeated, the Republicans will have people believing next year that Lewis Strauss could also walk on water."

Lyndon squirmed as pro-Strauss pressures were brought to bear. The Texas oil industry, operating through Lyndon's friend, Treasury Secretary Robert Anderson, had been pushing for Strauss. He was also worried about the religious issue. Clergymen of all faiths wrote to their senators urging confirmation of Strauss, who was not only a prominent Jewish layman but was co-chairman of the National Conference of Christians and Jews.

Republican Sen. Hugh Scott gave serious consideration to speaking out on the Senate floor on "the intolerance and bigotry" involved in the fight against Strauss. He told Democratic Sen. Vance Hartke of Indiana, in a corridor chat, that "anyone representing a state like Indiana which has large Jewish communities should think twice before voting to reject Strauss." Hartke called one of the Lyndon aides and told him about the conversation. Something had to be done, he said, to scotch the religious issue. The aide went to Democratic Sen. Richard Neuberger of Oregon and urged him to make a Senate speech against Strauss.

Such a speech coming from a senator of the Jewish faith would remove the issue at once. Neuberger regretfully begged off. He said he had just received a telephone call from his father in Oregon who said that Strauss had once done a favor for him and urged him to vote for Strauss. Neuberger said he intended to vote against Strauss if his vote was needed to defeat him, but he did not want to make a speech in view of his father's request.

Lyndon, through his aides, first worked for Strauss's defeat; next, shrank back into his shell after the *Times* column; and finally, moved into action to defeat the nominee. If he failed to achieve the defeat of Lewis Strauss when he had the power to do so, Anderson would know that Lyndon had let him down— and there would go Anderson's support for the presidential nomination.

For three days running, the Republicans, who felt they could win, pressed for a vote. Lyndon held them off until he was certain he had not only the vote, but the right "mix"; and when he did, he set down the date for the tally. It gave Johnson sardonic satisfaction to know that by pressing for a vote on that day, he was compelling Sen. Thruston Morton of Kentucky, the chairman of the Republican National Committee, to return from Denver an hour before he was to keynote the meeting of the Young Republicans. He grinned at the thought that Vice President Richard Nixon, who was scheduled to address that convention the next day, had to remain in Washington in case his vote was needed to break a tie.

By noon on the day before the vote, Democratic Sen. Harry F. Byrd, Sr., of Virginia, a friend and supporter of Lewis Strauss, came to Senate Republican leader Everett M. Dirksen and gave him the bad news. There had been a shift in the vote, he said. As it stood now, it was close to a tie. Dirksen had better get every absent Republican back to Washington.

Five Republicans were away from the Senate. Two of them were in the Bethesda Naval Hospital in nearby Maryland for a checkup. These presented no problem; they could be in the Senate with an hour's notice. The other three absentees presented real logistical problems. Senator Morton was due in the Brown Palace Hotel in Denver around 11 A.M. The night before he had been the speaker at a Republican fund-raising dinner in Salt Lake City. If Morton arrived in time, he could get back to the Denver airport in time to catch the 11:30 A.M. plane, bringing him to Washington by 8:08 P.M. Morton got to the Brown Palace at 11:10 A.M., left a brief message to explain his failure to keynote the Young Republican convention, and took off in time to catch the plane.

That left two absentees. Sen. Wallace Bennett of Utah was in Salt Lake City. When Dirksen reached him, it was too late for him to return to Washington by commercial plane. Dirksen would have to provide a military jet to get him back. Sen. Milton Young of North Dakota was in Devil's Lake, North Dakota, for an encampment of the National Guard which was celebrating "Milton Young Day." Only a military jet could get him back in time, too.

Dirksen telephoned Ike's congressional liaison aide, Wilton B. Persons, and told him he needed some jets to get his absent senators back. Persons hesitated. There were only two military jet planes for civilian transport, he explained, and neither one was immediately available. Of course, he went on, there were plenty of jets—trainers and cargo planes—available at Air Force bases near the absent senators, but they would require some pre-flight instruction and checking out. They would have to be instructed especially on the use of the oxygen mask.

A Senate colleague of Dirksen's, overhearing Dirksen's end of the conversation, slipped out of Dirksen's office and put in a call to Strauss at the Commerce Department. "If you want to be confirmed as Secretary of Commerce," he said, "you better build a fire under the White House. You call Jerry Persons right now and tell him to provide some jets and get Milt Young and Wallace Bennett back here in time or you're finished. That's how close the vote is. We need every goddamn, single vote."

The White House swung into action. Bennett received a call from the Hill Air Force base in Ogden, Utah. A jet trainer was being dispatched. He would receive some pre-flight instruction, he was told, but no oxygen problems were anticipated since the trainer would fly as low as possible. The trainer stopped once in Kansas City to refuel, giving Bennett time to get a sandwich.

The Young problem was not so easily solved. He was not going to walk out on the Milton Young Day celebration before it was over—which would be 7 P.M. Washington time. Furthermore, he was not going to ride in any jet trainer. The Air Force instead provided him with a jet cargo transport. He would not be back in Washington until about 3 A.M.

The Republicans filibustered until most of the absentees arrived. They couldn't hold out for Milt Young, so Dirksen sought and obtained a "live" pair: Mike Mansfield, the assistant Democratic leader, agreed to withhold his own vote. When the roll call started at 12:13 A.M., Dirksen did not know what the outcome would be. He received some unpleasant shocks as the votes were announced. He didn't expect conservative Democrat Allen Frear of Delaware to vote against Strauss. Frear had sat in on pro-Strauss strategy meetings. Now Dirksen realized he had been Lyndon Johnson's "double agent." Dirksen also thought he had had the vote of Jennings Randolph of West Virginia. And only that morning, Dodd of Connecticut had told him that Democratic Sen. Harrison Williams of New Jersey would vote for Strauss.

But then came the real shocker, and Dirksen knew Strauss was going down to defeat. When her name was called, Margaret Chase Smith of Maine said, "No." Barry Goldwater looked up from his tally sheet and cast her a look of cold hatred. The next day Goldwater, who was chairman of the money-raising Senate Republican Campaign Committee, swore that she "would never get a dime" from his committee when she ran for reelection. (She did, though. Passions cool off in the Senate.)

Her negative vote was vital to Lyndon Johnson. He could have won without it, but he did not want Lewis Strauss defeated on a straight party-line vote. True, he had the vote of another Republican, William Langer of North Dakota, but Langer was such a maverick that he didn't count. Margaret Smith was a "regular."

Now this was where the Jimmy Stewart and Lewis Strauss destinies became intertwined. Senator Smith was a heroine to the disaffected Air Force reservists. But she was getting abuse from Jimmy Stewart's fans all over the nation—and all over Maine—who felt he was being unjustly harassed. She wanted an investigation of the promotion policies of the armed forces reserves. The man who could give it to her was Lyndon B. Johnson, who just happened to be chairman of the investigating arm of the Armed Services Committee, the preparedness subcommittee.

On Monday, September 21, the preparedness subcommittee

issued a unanimous report blasting all the services and confirming the worst fears of the parent Armed Services Committee which, at Johnson's request, had authorized the inquiry. A sample study of recent flag promotions showed that these had been awarded to many "whose records of reserve participation as 'weekend warriors' were less than adequate at the time of being selected for promotion." The report went on:

> Two of the nominees were overage for promotion while two others had resigned their commissions from the regular military service to accept better paying jobs with industry. They were given high ranks as reservists and were recommended for promotion over other reservists of longer standing in the reserves.
>
> Another nominee, who had not participated in reserve activities for more than four years, was called up from the retired reserve and shortly thereafter was recommended for promotion, while still another nominee was given a mobilization day assignment diametrically opposed to any relationship to his civilian occupation.

The last one was Jimmy Stewart, though the report named no names. The report reached these concusions:

> There was some evidence that these promotions have been conferred without reference to the nation's needs, to any known military requirement, or to the capability of the individual.
>
> There appeared to be no systematic order or logic in the selection of officers for promotion to these ranks.
>
> There appeared to be a disturbing trend to use the reserve component as an instrumentality of some benefit for regular officers who resign their commissions to accept better paying jobs with industry.

In his letter of transmittal of the report to Armed Services Committee Chairman Russell, Lyndon Johnson wrote: "I also wish to compliment Senator Margaret Chase Smith of Maine for her diligent and untiring efforts in promoting a more effective and vigorous military reserve for the nation."

CHAPTER 13

A Tragic Case

―――――

It is idle but fascinating to speculate about the "mute inglorious Miltons" born in the wrong milieu and at the wrong time. Would a genius like Johann Sebastian Bach or Ludwig van Beethoven have been able to flourish if born in the Congo in the eighteenth century, or a Napoleon if he grew up in Costa Rica in the twentieth?

But in the case of Richard Brevard Russell of Georgia, speculation no longer is idle. As his life and career demonstrated, the late, great senator from Georgia, by the testimony of his own colleagues, could and should have been president—but he was born in the wrong place and at the wrong time.

He was not only one of the greatest men ever to grace the Senate, but in many ways one of the most tragic. For it was his misfortune to be branded a sectional leader when he actually possessed all the attributes of character and intelligence of a national leader. He came on the stage of history at a time when the nation was still struggling to resolve the racial injustices that existed at the foundation of the Republic and were to erupt in civil war just seventy-four years later.

The Aristotelian concept of tragedy did not apply to Russell. The tragic flaw was not in him, but in the geography of his birth and career and in the times. The late President Harry S. Truman wrote in his memoirs, "If Russell had been from Indiana or Missouri or Kentucky, he may very well have been President of the United States."

He was not alone in his assessment. When Lyndon B. Johnson was vice president, I had a chat with him in his Capitol Hill office one day about Russell. Johnson told me, "If the members of the Senate were to cast a secret vote on the man they believed best qualified to be president of the United States, they would choose Richard Russell."

The courtly Georgian, who remained a bachelor all his life, was the only senator in American history to serve more than half his life in the Senate. He entered it on January 12, 1933, after a term as the nation's youngest governor. Before his death, he was first in seniority and thus was chosen president pro tem, putting him third in line of succession to the presidency. He was also chairman of the most powerful of committees, Appropriations, after having served as chairman of the Armed Services Committee for fifteen years.

When Ted Kennedy was first elected to the Senate, at age thirty, he paid a courtesy call upon Russell. "You were young, too, when you were elected to the Senate," said Kennedy. With an avuncular smile, Russell said, "Yes, I was. But by that time I had been governor of Georgia, and before that, Speaker of the Georgia House of Representatives for four years." Kennedy changed the subject.

He held one other post, the leadership of the Southern bloc, which was his not by virtue of seniority but by sheer ability. Russell was not a racist. He was not one of those who achieved leadership among his fellow Southerners by shouting "nigger, nigger" on the hustings. Master of the art of filibuster, he did not blemish the device of unlimited debate by reciting "pot likker" recipes or resorting to other clownish devices to prevent a debatable issue from being resolved.

Possessing one of the finest minds ever to grace the Senate scene, Russell knew the complex rules governing that body better than anyone else. But even more, he knew better than anyone else how to use those rules to achieve or frustrate a specific legislative goal. Beyond this was Russell's extraordinary knowledge of the political and geographical problems of other senators. "If I were representing your state," he would suggest to senators who were opposing him or asking his advice, "I would. . . ." He'd then outline a course of action which they would follow to their profit or ignore to their loss.

He was a vastly cultivated man, deeply read in history (he had read Gibbon's *Decline and Fall of the Roman Empire* several times) and philosophy. He also possessed an extraordinary knowledge of foreign affairs. In 1956, to cite a typical example, he was attending a NATO parliamentarians' conference in Paris when Soviet troops invaded Hungary. A young foreign service officer from the State Department gave Russell a proposed resolution condemning the Soviet invasion and asked him to introduce it at the meeting and seek its passage. Russell, polite as always, looked at the resolution and told the State Department man, "That's a fine resolution, young man, but do you really think an American delegate should introduce it? Wouldn't it come better from a delegate representing a labor or socialistic government?"

Then, in his gentle, Southern, and quiet musical drawl, Russell spoke for fifteen minutes to his fellow American delegates about the internal politics of the various European nations at the conference. One of those present later described it as nothing short of virtuosic. At the end, Russell told the State Department official, "Young man, why don't you take that resolution over to one of the Belgian delegates and just ask for his comments." The Belgian did more than comment. He asked permission to introduce the resolution and it was unanimously adopted.

Despite his leadership of the Southern bloc in the steadily losing battle over civil rights legislation, Russell knew all along that, as he put it privately, "the Southern way of life was doomed." He was realistic, and those closest to him said he knew the legislative proposals he was fighting would, in one form or another, become law one day. One source close to him in those struggles told me,

> What Dick Russell wanted was to prevent a kicking and screaming match between the South and the rest of the nation. He knew the changes were coming, but he wanted them to come more slowly than some of the others in the Senate. He didn't want guerrilla warfare and armed conflict. Russell was a man who believed there would be change, but also believed that the people would react badly to too rapid change.

An example of Russell's extraordinary floor leadership on civil rights legislation came during the impassioned struggle over the proposed Civil Rights Act of 1957. When enacted, it became the first major civil rights bill to pass in eighty-two years. It was also the first so-called voting rights bill; it gave federal courts the authority to order local registrars to permit blacks to vote. Subsequent laws plugged some of the loopholes in this historic "first."

Russell knew that restricting proposals to aid blacks denied their franchise was not an easy task for a national leader to undertake even though he was a Southerner. But he felt that the proposal as presented to the Senate was too drastic a remedy at that time of our history, and that it was necessary, by his lights, to force compromises before the bill could be allowed to come to a vote.

He was particularly concerned about one section of the bill, soon to receive national prominence as Part III, which gave the Justice Department sweeping authority to seek injunctions in virtually any instance of the denial of civil rights. So strongly were national passions aroused that Part III became *the* issue; passage of the bill without it would be deemed a betrayal by civil rights advocates. On the other hand, the Southerners who knew deep down it was wrong to deny the franchise by trick, nevertheless felt virtuous about denouncing Part III.

By close examination of the way in which Part III was written, Russell made a dramatic discovery: the section of the bill was poorly drafted. It embraced a number of other statutes already on the books—including some that were adopted in Reconstruction days and afterwards allowed to become dead letters as post-Civil War passions died down. Nevertheless, passage of Part III would inject new life into ancient laws. So Russell rose to his feet and made a relatively short but explosive speech, in which he pointed out that passage of Part III would give the federal government the authority to declare martial law and install military government in any section of the nation.

President Eisenhower quickly renounced support of Part III, and on the motion of an ardent civil rights advocate, Clinton Anderson of New Mexico, it was deleted from the bill by the Senate. Then Russell forced another compromise—to grant the right of jury trial in cases of criminal contempt. Having achieved these ends, Russell allowed the bill to come to a vote,

Two Presidents, Harry S. Truman and Lyndon B. Johnson, agreed the man best qualified to be President was Senator Richard B. Russell of Georgia. His tragedy was that he had to waste his tremendous talents fighting what he knew was a rear-guard battle against civil rights. Six years after his death, another Georgian, Jimmy Carter, made it to the White House.

and the first of a great series of bills to establish genuine civil
rights for blacks went onto the law books.

Russell was a great stabilizing influence in the Senate. Without his skill, the three-quarters of the nation outside the South
would have ridden roughshod over the South. Perhaps it should
have; this is an iffy proposition. But Russell's view must be respected. He did not say "no" to change but tried to regulate the
pace of change to prevent the disorder he believed would follow upon change forced down the throats of one-fourth of the
nation by a stronger three-fourths.

In this connection, it should be noted parenthetically that it
took two decades to enact federal aid to education because of
the unresolved conflicts involving federal aid to parochial
schools. It took as long to enact Medicare because of the fear of
the nation's doctors that it would "socialize" their profession.
The virtue of two decades of debate was that the irreconcilable
was reconciled; the insoluble was solved. Revolutionary laws
were passed by a people finally prepared to accept them after
twenty years of debate ranging from the grass roots to the halls
of Congress. The sad history of Prohibition reveals the consequences of enacting a law, however "noble in purpose" (as Herbert Hoover called it), which the people cannot accept. It's the
Lecky Principle in practice.

Russell's essential reasonableness in this prickly area of national debate where race was pitted against race and region
against region was not shared by all the other members of the
Southern bloc. And as Russell's vigor declined and as the political power of the blacks increased as a result of laws placed on
the books, there were elements in the Southern Senate bloc
which became troublesome.

The prime example was Strom Thurmond of South Carolina
(who finally saw the light in another fifteen years). At one point,
in 1960, just when Russell had achieved all the compromises
possible on the civil rights bill that year and had won the plau-
dits of his colleagues and the press whom he convinced that the
South did have some logic in its opposing stances, Thurmond
violated a gentleman's agreement by fellow Southerners not to
filibuster. He staged an all-day and all-night, record-breaking,
headline-making—and totally useless—filibuster. Still, as long as
Russell maintained his physical vigor and as long as civil rights

battles were still to be waged, there was no replacement in the Southern caucus for him. Even such naysayers as Thurmond had no alternative but to follow Russell's leadership.

In retrospect, it is sad that such admittedly great talents had to be employed in causes that had no end but defeat, though Russell could make them honorable defeats. The struggle left its mark upon the man, too, in a subtle psychological way.

Russell ran for the Democratic presidential nomination in 1952. Intellectually, he knew that at this time of the nation's life, a Southerner could not be nominated. But it is one thing to know something intellectually and quite another to reject it emotionally.

The nation was very much in need of fresh leadership, and the available talent seemed thinly spread. Russell made his presidential bid and moved North in search of delegates. In New Jersey, the horrible truth of his situation was brought home to him in secret discussions with potential delegates. He was told bluntly that (1) he was by far the ablest candidate on the horizon and (2) he couldn't possibly get the nomination because he was a Southerner. Russell continued in his doomed struggle for the nomination right up to the moment it went to Adlai Stevenson. But he came out of the battle honorably; he was able to say to his fellow Southerners that he had been able to make a fair fight for the prize, and he felt he could in good conscience campaign for the Democratic ticket in the South.

Dwight Eisenhower carried only four Southern states, and one of them, Texas, perhaps went Republican because of the tidelands oil issue and not for sectional reasons. Had Russell not made the fight and subsequent campaign, the Southern rejection of the Democratic ticket might have been catastrophic in scope.

But something happened internally to Russell after the 1952 campaign. It was his realization that he had been rejected by his party not because he wasn't equipped for the job, but because he was born and reared in the South. Russell soon lost some of his zest for legislative battles. In fact, one reason for the emergence of Lyndon Johnson as one of the most powerful legislative leaders in American history was the slow but ineluctable abdication of Russell's leadership in many areas to LBJ, whom Russell had hand-picked for the party leadership role in the Senate.

The stabilizing force that Russell represented in the Senate was not totally limited to the civil rights struggles. And had it not been for those inevitable struggles, his power and prestige would have been employed for other and worthier purposes. They were certainly so employed at a moment of great crisis in American history when President Truman fired Gen. Douglas MacArthur for insubordination. The country was deeply divided over the issue, it was as close to a state of national hysteria as it had ever been in its history. At stake was nothing less than the basic American principle of civil supremacy over the military.

To preserve not only the principle of civilian supremacy but his presidency, Truman had no choice but to recall MacArthur as United Nations military commander in the Far East. His announcement came on April 11, 1951, at 1 A.M. He was firing MacArthur because the general was "unable to give his whole-hearted support to policies of the United States government and the United Nations in matters pertaining to his official duties."

Both the State Department and the Pentagon felt the time was propitious for proposing a truce to the Communists. Aggression against South Korea had been repelled; the North Koreans were pushed back into their land; and every effort should be made "to prevent the spread of hostilities and to avoid the prolongation of the misery and the loss of life." (The quote is from a carefully worded statement sent to each of America's U.N. allies for approval three weeks earlier.) The U.N. was therefore "prepared to enter into arrangements which would conclude the fighting and ensure against its resumption." MacArthur was opposed to the peace initiative.

So intense was the national reaction against the dismissal that Truman took his case to the country in a radio address that evening. "The cause of world peace," he said, "is more important than any individual." He said that by following suggestions that U.N. forces bomb China or permit Chinese Nationalists to attack the mainland "we would be running a very grave risk of starting a general war." The entire basis for the U.S. participation in the Korean War was action to avert just that.

The speech did not ease the hysteria in the country or the indignation—especially Republican indignation—in the Congress. Just eight days after he was stripped of his command, MacArthur made his memorable address, at congressional invitation, to an overflow joint meeting of the House and Senate. He closed his speech by praising the men he had commanded and referred to himself as an old soldier who would not die but simply fade away. "I now close my military career ... an old soldier who tried to do his duty as God gave him the light to see that duty. Good-bye."

Congress was overcome by emotion. Republicans talked of impeaching the president. With hindsight, one can see that MacArthur really peaked at that moment; from then on it would be downhill. Republicans selected him as their keynote speaker for that summer's presidential nominating convention, and MacArthur, seized with presidential ambitions himself, hoped that with an Eisenhower–Taft deadlock, the Republicans would turn to him as their standard bearer. It didn't turn out that way; in fact, his keynote address was as great a flop as his address to Congress was a singular, though brief, triumph.

But after that moving address, the country's anger could be appeased by nothing short of a full-scale investigation of the dismissal. How to handle this without exacerbating the situation called for the most skillful of legislative craftsmen. The Democratic leadership in both houses agreed the investigation should be made jointly by the Senate Armed Services and Foreign Relations committees. Russell, chairman of Armed Services, was selected to preside over the joint inquiry.

To keep passions in hand, Russell held the inquiry behind closed doors. To keep the public fully informed, he arranged for transcripts to be made available to newsmen as soon as they could be physically processed by stenographers and "sanitized" by Pentagon censors who were constantly present in the Capitol. Reporters could get the testimony within hours, sometimes minutes, of its utterance. On the other hand, such emotional stimulants as lights and cameras were absent.

Russell handled the inquiry so evenhandedly that no one could complain. When, at long last, the hearing, which began May 3, ended on June 25, no final report was felt necessary. Russell made a comment to the effect that all the participants were patriotically motivated. As one of the insiders reported later, "When the dust settled, MacArthur was no longer the national leader outrageously ousted in the performance of his duties; he was now just an executive with the Remington-Rand Company."

Russell played a role, though not so central, in another great task that had to be performed to heal the wounds of a distracted nation. He was named to the Warren Commission after the assassination of President Kennedy. His presence on that panel gave the inquiry its credibility and made its findings, however disputed by some, acceptable to the many. A beloved president had been killed by a lone sociopath, not by a fingerman for a vicious national or international conspiracy. However history may ultimately deal with that inquiry, its immediate results were unquestionably salutary and helped the nation over a spot as rough as that brought on by the ouster of Douglas MacArthur.

It will be a long time before there is another man like Richard Russell in the Senate. Perhaps it will be a long time before such a man will be needed on the national stage. But should the time come and the man not be available, it will indeed be a sad time for the nation.

His tragedy lay in the fact that his unusual gifts couldn't be used—except in certain exceptional instances—for national rather than regional ends, and that that very regionalism kept one of the ablest Americans of this century from attaining the White House. Yet such is the whirligig of time and so unpredictable its operations that no one at the time of Russell's death would have predicted that six years later, almost to the day, another Georgian would take the oath of office as the thirty-ninth president of the United States.

CHAPTER 14

"Larger than Life"

———— ∿ ————

It was a scene that Lyndon Baines Johnson would have loved. There was his flag-draped coffin in the center of the vast rotunda of the Capitol where, for so many years, he had by the great force of personality and a political gift amounting to sheer genius, dominated the legislative scene for so many years.

Surrounding the coffin in a tightly packed circle were some 1,600 men and women, many of whom had shared his triumphs and failures. In one quadrant there was the entire diplomatic corps; in a second, present and former members of the Senate; in a third, the present and former members of the House of Representatives.

There were men who had served in his cabinet: former Health, Education and Welfare Secretary John Gardner—one of the few present who actually shed tears during the obsequies— and former Interior Secretary Stewart Udall, whose son had become a permanent resident of Canada, a fugitive from military conscription because of his quarrel with LBJ's war in Vietnam.

There was Hubert H. Humphrey in a somber suit and black tie, his lined face beginning to show the ravages of age. LBJ's vice president, he had hoped to be chosen by the electorate as Johnson's successor. LBJ's failures had been Humphrey's misfor-

211

tune too, for it had been LBJ's escalation of the war that cost
Humphrey the presidency.

There was Van Cliburn, the tall, stringy concert pianist, who
had come into President Johnson's orbit with an invitation to
the White House after winning an international piano competition in Moscow—and who brought a touch of warmth into the
cold war. And there was Bobby Baker, once Majority Leader
Lyndon B. Johnson's trusted Senate aide, who stained that relationship with scandal and who still bore traces of his prison pal-
lor. "It's a sad day," he said.

Hovering on the edge of the crowd was a former Democratic
congressman from New York, Allard Lowenstein, who had initiated the "dump Johnson" movement because of his fierce opposition to the Vietnam War, and whose activities had finally met
with success when LBJ announced his retirement. He had flown
down from New York City, not to gloat, but to pay his respects.

"Why have you come?" I asked him.

Lowenstein was at a loss for words. After groping awhile, he
said, "I wanted to pay my respect to a massive man. He cared
massively, he worked massively, and he erred massively. I just
wanted to slip in and say good-bye. When a man dies, if you
don't find in that moment the things you cherished together, I
don't know when you can."

For five solemn minutes, the vast crowd was utterly still as the
color guard stood stiffly at attention by the casket. Then the air
shook as distant cannon gave off a twenty-one-gun salute. President Nixon, who had escorted a brave, wanly smiling Lady Bird
Johnson, stepped forward and placed a wreath of red carnations,
white chrysanthemums, and tiny baby's breath blossoms in front
of the casket. Pinned to it was a card with just the words "The
President," inscribed in black ink.

To each side of the presidential wreath were placed similar
wreaths, each with a broad diagonal ribbon, one reading, "The
House of Representatives" and the other, "United States Senate." Over a thirty-year span of his life, LBJ had served in both.

Former Secretary of State Dean Rusk delivered a brief, moving eulogy: "In simpler and more robust days a thousand years
ago, he might have been known as Lyndon the Liberator, who
tried to free men from their bondage. For he was determined to
free our people in body, mind, and spirit. He was a man of
peace, and he would have welcomed the development of the

peace that is now before us." Then Rusk paid tribute to what he termed Johnson's "finest single message"—the speech Johnson delivered to a joint session of Congress calling for enactment of a strong civil rights bill and ending with the memorable words: "We shall overcome."

The sadness of the occasion was intensified further by the thoughts of lost opportunities. Those who had known him at first hand shared the conviction that he was an authentic legislative genius, "a man larger than life"—a phrase uttered over and over again when news of his death reached the Capitol—whose contribution to the enactment of the greatest outpouring of domestic legislation in American history had been vitiated by the Vietnam War.

Had he lived another forty-eight hours, he would have seen the end of the war.

Few present failed to note the irony of the fact that LBJ's successor, who had entered the rotunda with Lady Bird on his right arm and who, in his message to Congress had paid Johnson such a moving tribute—"It was there [in the House and Senate] that he first became a legend and there that he began to influence our destiny as a great nation"—was in the midst of dismantling LBJ's Great Society. Consider these headlines, all on page one of the *Washington Post* that morning, Wednesday, January 24, 1973:

"Pact to End War Reached; Cease-Fire, U.S. Pullout Set."

"Nation Mourns LBJ: Body to Lie in State at Capitol."

"Administration to Propose Dismantling of OEO." (The Office of Economic Opportunity was the agency set up by LBJ to wage war on poverty.)

There was genuine grief and a sense of bereavement and loss when John Kennedy was assassinated. There was sadness after the death of Dwight D. Eisenhower and Harry S. Truman, but it was alleviated by the conviction that both men had lived long enough to feel vindicated and honored by their contemporaries and assured of a favorable verdict from posterity. In LBJ's case, there was the sadness of a Greek tragedy—of a great but flawed man who had been driven from the office of the presidency; a man whose name was mentioned in party conclaves with embarrassment, and whose photograph was placed where, it was hoped, television cameras would not focus upon it.

When Kennedy died, the mourners in Congress who knew

him personally wept out of their own grief. They seemed to feel sorry for themselves. In the rotunda this day, they seemed to be sorry for Lyndon Johnson, not for themselves. Yet the world they lived in had been reshaped by the manic drive and extraordinary expertise of this man in bending others to his will and pushing through landmark legislation on an unparalleled scale.

Johnson would have been one of Thomas Carlyle's "heroes," for he was a perfect exemplar of the great men who have shaped destiny. In this book, I have discussed the role of happenstance, the interplay of personalities, and the impact of an extraordinary personality in the making of history as I have witnessed it first hand. Johnson, by all odds, best illustrates that last category.

To compress the life, achievements, and failures of Lyndon Johnson in one chapter would be comparable to engraving the *Book of Common Prayer* on the head of a pin. Perhaps it will be enough to attempt on a small scale to give a portrait of the rangy Texan and a glimpse into his will to power, both as legislative leader and as president.

He was a man of extraordinary vanity and outsize ego. On entering the antechamber of his majority leader's office, one was immediately confronted by a life-size portrait of Lyndon Johnson, posed standing up in front of a fireplace, his right elbow leaning on the mantelpiece. His initials had to be everywhere, on his cufflinks and as the initial letters of the names of his wife and two daughters—though it involved abandoning his wife's first name, Claudia, and resurrecting her childhood nickname, Lady Bird.

At the same time, he was extraordinarily unsure of himself. Despite his myopia and astigmatism, he refused to be photographed with his glasses on. If a photographer entered the room where he was holding forth with newsmen, he'd stop talking, pull off his glasses, pose rigidly—favoring his left profile—and snap, "All right, take your picture." Some photographers like George Tames of the *New York Times* would lower their cameras and walk out of the room.

He could not take criticism. Combing through even the most encomiastic article, Lyndon would look for what he called "the needle" aimed at him. Honest differences with his strongly held opinions were difficult for him to grasp. They were evidence, especially if they came from friendly sources, of "disloyalty." Lyndon so identified his own convictions with the national interest that a serious challenge to them could not be viewed as good faith.

In face-to-face conversation, Lyndon was one of the most persuasive men alive. He knew almost instinctively the motivations, the drives, the beliefs of the man he was trying to convince, and his auditor would emerge from the talk almost glassy-eyed. Lyndon's staff called it "Treatment A."

It was this kind of legerdemain that persuaded some of the smartest newsmen in Washington that Lyndon really didn't seek the presidency in 1960. Lyndon would put his arm around the shoulder of the reporter, broaden his Texas accent, and say: "Why, Ah know that no man from the South can ever be nominated for the presidency in mah lifetime. And if he was, Ah don't think he can be elected. Ah've been in the legislative branch for thirty years. Ah know it and Ah like it. All Ah want to be is the best senator Texas ever sent to Washington, and to be the best damn majority leader in the history of the Yew-nighted States Senate. Ah'm a candidate for the Senate in 1960 and nothin' else."

One shrewd reporter thus dazzled was Washington columnist Rowland Evans who, after one such "Treatment A" meeting with Johnson, bet this writer that Johnson would never announce he was a candidate for the presidency. LBJ did announce on the eve of the Democratic Convention in Los Angeles. Evans paid off the $5 bet.

Yet at the very time Johnson was persuading Evans and a string of other newsmen that he had no intention of seeking the nomination, his agents in Texas, with the considerable firsthand help of Speaker Sam Rayburn—a fellow Texan and LBJ's principal mentor during his political apprenticeship—were persuading the Texas legislature to enact unprecedented legislation to allow Johnson to run for both the Senate and the presidency so that he wouldn't have to give up the first to seek the second.

Duplicity? It depends on how one views it. LBJ knew he would lose his great grip upon the Senate if his colleagues, who included several presidential aspirants, were convinced he would be an aspirant himself.

Johnson's greatest gift was in the acquisition and use of power. Theodore H. White, in *The Making of the President—1964,* quotes one of the Johnson's "oldest cronies" as saying that

"Johnson's instinct for power is as primordial as a salmon's going upstream to spawn."

Many have forgotten what the Senate was like under LBJ. Never before in the history of that body—and perhaps never again—had one man gathered so much power unto himself.

He was majority leader, so he set the order and pace of legislation. He was chairman of the Steering Committee and made all the committee assignments in that capacity, without consulting anyone else. He was chairman of the Democratic Conference (the caucus of all Democratic senators) and would make unilateral judgments on the calling of such meetings to discuss Democratic policy. Once held at regular intervals to discuss party policy, under Lyndon they were held once a year, at the start of each congressional session, to hear his own State of the Union address. He was also chairman of the Democratic Policy Committee which set the party's policy in that body.

Historically, Senate leaders have shunned additional responsibilities, such as chairing committees and subcommittees. Not so Lyndon.

He was chairman of the powerful preparedness subcommittee of the Senate Armed Services Committee. As Richard Russell's spirits and vigor declined, Johnson became the de facto chairman of the full committee and so had the Pentagon under his thumb. He was chairman of the Senate Appropriations Subcommittee on State, Justice, and the USIA, so the funds for the Department of State, the Department of Justice, and the United States Information Agency were in his control. Top officials from all these agencies were to be found sitting in his outer office, hat in hand, seeking favors. And he made himself chairman of the Aeronautical and Space Sciences Committee, so the agency created for the exploration of outer space, NASA, came under his thumb.

And in the White House sat Dwight D. Eisenhower, who was the least activist of presidents, so LBJ filled the leadership vacuum with such initiatives as the creation of the Space Committee when the country reacted almost hysterically to the Soviet sputnik, a satellite that orbited the planet before we were able to even lob one into the sky.

One man, Democratic Sen. William Proxmire of Wisconsin, challenged Johnson's iron grip on the Senate. On February 23, 1959, he blasted LBJ for his "one-man rule." Proxmire had been in the Senate one year and three months, and had, in his own words, "played no role whatsoever" in his capacity as a senator from Wisconsin. He had served in the Wisconsin State Assembly where he and his fellow Democrats caucused one day a week on the legislative business. He said:

> Our leaders would find out what we wanted, and they'd go out and fight for it. We all had an equal voice. I came here and found that we had one caucus a year—to hear Lyndon Johnson's own State of the Union message. Then we'd adjourn until the next January to hear Lyndon's next message. There was no debate in caucus. We were told what the program would be, and that was it. I felt the people of Wisconsin had voted for me and not for the Senator from Texas.

Proxmire lighted no fires of independence, although he became a hero back home in Wisconsin, the state that bred so many antiestablishmentarians, such as the La Follette dynasty. Most senators stayed cowed. They were beholden to Johnson for committee assignments. He set policy. He determined which of their bills would be called up, when, and in what shape. Not a bill passed unless LBJ approved of it. Not a cent was appropriated for defense, foreign policy, and the enforcement of justice unless LBJ approved of it.

Privately, Johnson fumed. In the cloakrooms, he referred to Proxmire as "Senator Pissmire." A Herblock cartoon in the *Washington Post* angered him, for it showed King Lyndon on a throne with a javelin, labeled Proxmire, sticking through his crown. Beneath were the words: "Methinks the peasants are getting out of hand." By the time Proxmire made his third such speech in a month, Lyndon deigned to make a brief reply. Such attacks, he said, were "easy ways" to get attention, adding that "Senator Proxmire had to be wet-nursed."

Johnson could hold grudges for a long time. Edmund Muskie of Maine recalled his first meeting with LBJ when he left the governor's mansion for the Senate:

> Lyndon called me in to give me some fatherly advice. He told me I would have some adjusting to do. All governors do, he said. As senators they would be so busy, they wouldn't have time to familiarize themselves with all the issues they have to vote on. I recall he said, "Sometimes you won't know how to vote until the Ms are reached on the roll call."

Then Lyndon discussed Rule XXII. He knew the Senate liberals

were going to make a move on the first day of the new Congress to
weaken the filibuster rule. He hoped he'd get my vote to resist such a
move. I didn't say anything. He said, "Ed, you haven't much to say." I
replied, "Lyndon, we haven't gotten to the Ms yet." He gave me a
cold look.

Muskie voted with the liberals in an unsuccessful attempt to
make a strong modification in the filibuster rule. Two days later,
Muskie went to a soiree in the home of the late columnist Walter Lippmann. LBJ came in, walked over to Muskie, and said:
"Ed, if I'd realized you were one of those goddamn liberals, I
wouldn't have walked across the street to meet you."

Muskie gave his committee preferences to the Steering Com-
mittee. In order, they were Foreign Relations, Commerce, and
Judiciary. He got none of them, ending up on Banking and the
District of Columbia. He recalled:

> That was my start. The next two years were pretty goddamn de-
> pressing. Lyndon didn't even speak to me until midsummer when he
> learned I was going to the governors' conference in Puerto Rico.
> Then he came to me and asked me to sound out the governors on
> their 1960 presidential choices. It was then, for the first time, I real-
> ized that despite Lyndon's public utterances to the contrary, he was
> interested in the presidency. Then he put his arms around me and
> presented me with some Senate cufflinks.

Contrasting the Senate under Lyndon and under his successor,
Mansfield, Muskie said,

> Lyndon believed in *deciding* himself what comes out of the Senate
> pipeline. Mike regards himself as *presiding* in order to make it possi-
> ble for the Senate to express *its* will, not *his* will. In the long run,
> Mike's way is healthier for the country.
> Lyndon was unique. He was oversize, larger than life. His short-
> comings and virtues were oversize. When he was generous, he was
> overgenerous. When he was mean, he was cold, mean, and nasty. I've
> experienced the full range of his emotions.

As president, LBJ would mete out the same kind of treatment.
Perhaps none was rougher—or more typical—than the treatment he meted out to Democratic Sen. Vance Hartke of Indiana, whom LBJ had cultivated as a protegé from the moment of
his election in 1958. LBJ gave Hartke the first committee of his
choice, the powerful Finance Committee.

Hartke, a former mayor of Evansville, is a short, stocky, bright-eyed man with an earned degree of Doctor of Jurisprudence and a consuming ambition which led him to make a ridiculous try for the presidential nomination in 1972. He ran well in the rear of the pack in the New Hampshire primary, making his confident prediction of victory there one of the silliest of the political season.

His senatorial defeat in 1976 after three terms stemmed in large part from his fatuous insistence that he did not have to submit to a luggage search at airports like other people because he was a U.S. senator. This was at the height of the hijacking season. Despite these fatuities, Hartke was and is a brilliant man; a man of conscience as shown by his early and risky opposition to the Vietnam War; and, curiously, a man well versed in theology, particularly the writings of Paul Tillich.

While LBJ could occasionally be tolerant of dissent by former colleagues, dissent by protegés was "disloyalty" and he could react with rage. While Hartke was standing in the rotunda, paying his respects to the dead president, he recalled the day of his irrevocable break with him over a very trivial matter. Under the law creating the Federal Aviation Administration, one of the two top officials had to be a civilian. The deputy administrator was a retired military man. LBJ wanted to name retired Brig. Gen. William F. "Bozo" McKee, Vice Chief of the Air Force, to be the administrator. He didn't know McKee. Defense Secretary Robert McNamara proposed him as "an able man." LBJ was anxious to get started on the supersonic transport. He was concerned over the French progress on the Concorde. McKee, he believed, would be the best man for the job.

LBJ asked Congress to pass a bill setting aside this provision of the FAA so he could name McKee. The Senate Commerce Committee quickly approved the bill thirteen to two. Hartke was one of the two dissenters. He thought too many military men were coming into civilian jobs; it was his way of registering his protest.

It was 6 P.M. on a day in late April when the phone rang in Hartke's office. His secretary said, "Senator, the president is on the phone."

"What's this I heard," Johnson roared, "that you have written a minority report? Are you going to fight me? I want you to call it back and tear it up."

"Mr. President," Hartke replied, "it's too late to call it back from the printers. Besides, I believe in this and it doesn't matter to you. Only two of us voted against that bill."

"Look here, Vance," LBJ went on. "I don't know 'Bozo' McKee. I wouldn't know him if he came into my bedroom, took down his pants, and showed me his bare ass. Bob McNamara tells me he's the best man for the SST, and I don't want that son of a bitch de Gaulle to beat us."

When Hartke started to explain that Congress had a valid purpose in mind in writing that feature of the FAA law, LBJ cut in, saying, "That goddamn law was passed by people dead and gone."

"Mr. President," Hartke said, "you were the majority leader when that law was passed."

LBJ's fury then burst its bounds. "Goddamn it, Vance, when I found you, you were just a two-bit mayor of a two-bit town."

Hartke's face got purple and tears came into his eyes as he said, "Mr. President, you can't talk to me that way."

"The hell I can't," Johnson replied and hung up.

A little later, a score of Indiana county committee men and women and their spouses came to Washington. On their itinerary was a visit to the White House and a personal greeting by the president. Hartke telephoned White House aide Jack Valenti and told him that he, Hartke, would stay away if it would embarrass the president. Valenti checked with the president and told Hartke to come along.

When the Hoosiers were assembled in the White House along with their two Indiana senators, they waited—and waited—for the president to appear. Finally, Valenti came out and said, "The president is tied up and cannot see you. He sends his regrets." Subsequently, LBJ's press secretary, Bill Moyers, was asked whether this was a deliberate snub. Moyers replied, "The president doesn't take such actions just because of obstreperous senators."

When LBJ went to the hospital for gall bladder surgery, Hartke sent him a letter, handwritten and hand-delivered, saying that despite their differences, he wanted the president to know he was praying for his safe recovery. The letter was never acknowledged.

Looking at the flag-draped coffin, Hartke mused (as he told me later): "On balance, Lyndon Johnson will be remembered as a sincere humanitarian in the Franklin Roosevelt mold, but with this caveat: the Vietnam War will be hanging over that judgment. Some of the living will forgive him—the dead, never."

At this point in his reverie, he found himself listening again to Dean Rusk's funeral oration. "Today's writers," said Rusk, "are almost too concerned with Vietnam. Historians will take a broader view and think of his initiatives for peace. He was a man of peace."

It seemed an iffy prediction. A much safer one would enshrine his domestic accomplishments as president.

Johnson's record of accomplishment in the first session of the Eighty-ninth Congress—which convened after his smashing victory over Barry Goldwater—has been compared to the achievements of Franklin D. Roosevelt in the one hundred days following his first inauguration. LBJ himself was strongly aware of that comparison and had lists compiled of his own achievements in the first one hundred days of the session so the parallel would not be overlooked.

FDR got through a number of historic and precedent-smashing pieces of legislation. The Agricultural Adjustment Act came just in time to stop the spreading plague of rural bankruptcies. The National Recovery Act stopped the industrial panic and may have saved capitalism itself. The U.S. guaranteed loans to home owners saved the dwellings of millions. The Securities Regulation Act helped repair the very nerve center of the American business system, the stock market. And the Civilian Conservation Corps took hundreds of thousands of unemployed youths off the streets, put them to work doing useful tasks, and taught them useful skills. However, it must be kept in mind that these trailblazing bills were enacted under the whiplash of national distress arising from the worst financial and business depression in our history.

The extraordinary legislative achievements of the Eighty-ninth Congress came during a period of unparalleled prosperity and national unity. These included a $1.3 billion bill providing federal assistance to the primary and secondary schools of the country to cope with the grave crisis in education. The first such measure to pass, it took twenty years from conception to delivery. In itself, its passage would have made it a historic Congress. The same judgment could be applied to the $1.09 billion relief and rehabilitation bill for the economically stricken Appalachian

President Lyndon B. Johnson lies in state in the Rotunda of the U.S. Capitol surrounded by 1,600 men and women from the House, the Senate, the Supreme Court and the Executive Branch. Many of them had shared his triumphs and failures.

His successor, Richard M. Nixon, taking time out from dismantling LBJ's Great Society, solemnly lays a wreath by the flag-covered casket. Had Johnson lived another forty-eight hours, he would have seen the end of the war which ended his hopes.

region. The repeal of $4.7 billion in excise taxes hanging over the economy since World War II and the Korean War was another major achievement.

But even these measures paled alongside two historic bills: (1) a voting rights bill which would do more to implement the promises of the century-old Fourteenth and Fifteenth amendments to enfranchise the blacks than any law ever passed, and (2) Medicare, which not only gave the nineteen million older citizens of this nation hospital and nursing home care under Social Security, but set up an inexpensive insurance system enabling the elderly to pay their medical bills.

And there was more, much more. The national origins immigration quotas, so offensive for so long to a nation of immigrants, were repealed. Assistance to students seeking a college education was enacted as well as loans and grants to allow the institutions of higher learning to expand their plant to accommodate the greater number of eligible young men and women. Taking cognizance at long last that most of America was now urbanized and confronted with still unsolved problems growing out of that shift in our population from the land to the cities, a new cabinet office was created, a Department of Housing and Urban Affairs.

To attribute these unparalleled achievements just to Lyndon Johnson's skill, will, and determination would be a simplistic and quite unrealistic reading of the historical forces at play. On the other hand, to rack them up to ineluctable historical forces alone would be unjust to the role played by LBJ.

Lyndon Johnson's triumph at the polls in November 1964 happened to coincide with the jelling of a national consensus on many controversial issues. And because he had the singular luck to be challenged by the weakest opponent since Alf Landon in 1936, Johnson carried into office with him a Democratic majority large enough to guarantee the votes for his program.

But a consensus and a large majority do not in themselves guarantee passage of a great legislative program. There was a third factor which Johnson could supply in a manner that few of his predecessors could boast. This was a combination of great knowledge of the workings of Congress gained from three decades on Capitol Hill; extraordinary skill in the use of this knowledge which his years as Senate leader helped sharpen; and a determination to succeed that was Brobdingnagian in size and almost psychotic in its intensity.

His sense of timing was extraordinarily acute. He saw he had the votes for Medicare—and he demanded its enactment. He sensed that the public was ready for the compromise on the church-state issue that was the necessary prelude for federal assistance to the nation's schools—and he acted.

When John F. Kennedy proposed an $11.5 billion tax cut, even if it meant a deficit, as a necessary stimulant to the economy, there was much shaking of heads in and out of Congress. The measure moved slowly while Kennedy was alive. Johnson got it through by making the necessary budget-trimming gestures to help conservatives in his own party save face. And when the shocking Kennedy tax cut proved to be successful in its thrust and acceptable to the cynics, it was afterwards easy for Johnson to propose the removal of the excise taxes.

As we have seen, he was quick to sense the nation's sudden readiness to accept sweeping removal of the barriers to black voting rights after Selma.

His determination to succeed led him to employ as president the wiles, inducements, and threats he used as a Senate leader; he did not hesitate to ignore the fact that Congress was supposed to be an equal and coordinate branch of government.

No president before him used the telephone to such an extent for direct communications with legislators. To save the rent-subsidy feature of his housing bill, he personally telephoned thirty House members. One of them was Democratic Congressman Thomas P. "Tip" O'Neill (later to become Speaker), who was thinking of voting against the rent subsidy. Johnson shouted into the phone, "You still have that navy yard in Boston, don't you?" Other East Coast navy yards had been shut down already for economy reasons. Tip voted for the rent subsidy.

Johnson's use—his often ruthless use—of the telephone contrasted sharply with that of Dwight Eisenhower. Before LBJ, the only telephone call that Democratic Sen. Stephen Young of Ohio received from a president was made by Eisenhower—and then it was a mistake. It was obvious from the trend of Ike's conversation that he thought he was talking to someone else of the same name, Republican Milton Young of North Dakota.

Stephen Young said, "Mr. President, this is Senator Steve Young of Ohio."

Whereupon Ike roared, "Goddamn it." And hung up.

There was no small talk when Johnson got on the phone. He

didn't say, "This is the president." He didn't identify himself in any way, assuming, correctly, that the man on the other end of the line recognized the voice instantly.

Even winning was not enough for Johnson. As Democratic Sen. Eugene McCarthy of Minnesota put it at the time: "Lyndon not only wants to win, but he wants people to agree with him." Johnson's extraordinary efforts to win Eugene McCarthy over to support of the Central Intelligence Agency illustrated this tendency to overcome disagreement no matter how minor. McCarthy had advocated the creation of a special Senate committee to oversee the operations of the super-secret agency—a proposal strongly resisted by every president since the CIA came into existence. It took major scandals more than two decades later to accomplish this.

Johnson learned McCarthy was in Austin, Texas, to deliver a speech and invited him over to the LBJ ranch to meet Vice Adm. William F. Raborn, Jr., whose nomination to head the CIA he intended to make public that day. The president sent a helicopter to bring McCarthy to the ranch.

When McCarthy arrived, the president took him aside and said, "I know you've been worried about the CIA. I want you to give it some attention. I want the CIA to do a good job." McCarthy was baffled. He didn't serve on either the Armed Services or Appropriations committees and consequently had virtually no direct influence upon the agency. Furthermore, only a very small minority of senators favored congressional supervision of the CIA. In fact, McCarthy hadn't even offered his bill that year.

The president wasn't finished with his attempt to win McCarthy over to the CIA. When the president administered the oath of office to Raborn, McCarthy was one of the invited guests. Subsequently, he was invited to CIA headquarters for breakfast on one occasion and for lunch on another.

It was this desire, not only to win in actual votes, but to win over those who disagreed with him on any issue, that led to his furious anger at dissent and criticism. And few things got under his skin more than disagreement from within his own party.

When, only a few months after his election victory, criticism over his Vietnam policy erupted on the Senate floor among Democrats, the president telephoned Everett Dirksen in Aurora, Illinois, to complain: "When it's the loyal opposition, you can say, 'Oh what the hell' and take it. But when your own party sticks the knife in your guts, what are you to think? I'm being clobbered on my side of the aisle and it's demeaning to look to your side of the aisle for support."

He never hesitated to "chew out" Democratic senators in a face-to-face confrontation—perhaps "nose-to-nose" would be an apter phrase because of his habit of pressing his nose almost up against the other man's in such moments. A complex, even devious man, he often employed subtler ways of making his displeasure felt.

Democratic Sen. Frank Church of Idaho, an early critic of the Vietnam War, was surprised to learn from press reports the day after he had been to the White House, of a conversation he allegedly had had with the president. The subject of Vietnam had come up, and when Church said, "As Walter Lippmann said . . .," the president supposedly interrupted him to say, "If you want any more dams for Idaho why don't you go to Walter Lippman?"

But no such conversation took place, even though it was given out by "White House sources." Church even took to the Senate floor to deny there had been any such conversation. Then the answer occurred to him. "That's what the president would like to have said if he had thought of it. He didn't. And after I left, he probably told Press Secretary Bill Moyers to put it out."

A few days later, when Church had another occasion to go to the White House, the president said, "Have you built any more dams in Idaho?" Church, getting his own back, replied, "Not yet, Mr. President, but the first one to be finished will be named after Walter Lippmann." Nevertheless, Church admitted that "standing up to the president is like standing on a railroad track when an express train is bearing down on you."

The quintessential Johnson as a legislative manipulator can be illustrated by an episode that occurred in the eighth month of his elected presidency, involving a minor bill. The scene was a White House breakfast meeting with his legislative leaders to discuss the progress of his program in Congress. Suddenly, in the middle of a cordial conversation, the president grew angry. His voice rising, he asked rhetorically, "Are you kidding?" This outburst came when Speaker John McCormack mentioned very casually that the highway beautification bill, still in the House and Senate Public Works committees, was "dead."

The attitude of the committee members, McCormack said,

ranged from cool to hostile. Most of the testimony already heard
was adverse to the measure. The general disposition in both
houses was that the president had been given nearly everything
he had asked for and it would do no harm to bury the bill for this
session at least.

Johnson was taken by surprise by this information. He hadn't
been paying close attention to highway beautification lately because of his preoccupation with more pressing domestic and international matters. He had assumed that all was going well.
The measure was a "must," the president said. It was "Lady
Bird's bill." It had priority status in his legislative program, and
he was determined to see it enacted—and enacted without
emasculation—in *this* session.

In his State of the Union address he had promised to introduce legislation to control billboards and junkyards. The very
general content of the initial speech had been made more specific in his budget message. The overall reaction had been good,
he recalled; the newspapers had been filled with favorable comment.

This common approbation had reached a peak on May 24
at the White House Conference on Natural Beauty. Among the
fifteen panels concerned with aesthetic enhancement of the
American scene, four were devoted to some aspects of beautification and scenic development of highways. Two days later, the
president transmitted the draft legislation for highway beautification to Congress. In his message, LBJ said:

> The federal-aid highway system is one of the great achievements of
> this nation. . . . In a nation of continental size, transportation is essen-
> tial to the growth and prosperity of the national economy.
> But that economy, and the roads that serve it, are not ends in them-
> selves. They are meant to serve the real needs of the people. . . . And
> those needs include the opportunity to touch nature and see beauty,
> as well as rising income and swifter travel.

Then, while the president turned his attention to other things,
and the beauty lovers and conservationists who had attended
the White House conference went home thinking all was virtually accomplished, the hard-core lobbying against the proposal
began. The state highway departments, fearful that any money
spent on beauty would decrease the amount spent on construction, began pressuring Congress. The National Association of

County Officials, close to the grass roots where the voters are, pitched in. The billboard and junkyard lobbies mounted an effective letter-writing campaign. Then the strongest lobbies, such as the American Road Builders Association and the Association of General Contractors, blasted the legislation on a "we-are-for-beauty-but" basis. In the public works committees on each side of the Capitol, the attitude toward the proposal soon turned sour.

After LBJ spoke his mind to his legislative leaders, they conveyed his words to the committee members who, in turn, communicated with the lobbies, advising them to alter the tenor of their attacks. The president, the lobbyists were told, had made enactment of a strong bill a matter of personal prestige. It was going to get committee approval, and it was going to pass. Any thought, they added, that the president could be persuaded to be content with all the bills already passed and to let this one go, could be forgotten.

Once the industries and lobbies involved learned that the president was determined to pass the bill, the tactics changed. Wires began pouring in urging speedy enactment of the bill—with appropriate safeguards, of course. Many of these would effectively gut the bill.

It wasn't alone the knowledge that a strong president, with heavy majorities in Congress, was determined to get highway beautification that caused the affected industries and state groups to change their tune. They began getting a bad press too. Rex Whitton, the federal highway administrator, telephoned members of the American Association of State Highway Officials and told them, "You guys are looking for trouble. It's bad public relations to be against beauty."

The Johnson administration really unlimbered its big guns on this one. Even Mrs. Johnson did some bold-faced though lady-like lobbying with telephone calls to key legislators, and with White House teas for their wives. At morning and night conferences, the president's chief congressional liaison aide and soon-to-be postmaster general, Larry O'Brien, was up on the Hill, usually in Majority Leader Mike Mansfield's office near the Senate chamber, conferring with senators on minute details of the legislation. The bill was scheduled for Senate action first.

Often, when new obstacles arose, the president's press secretary, Bill Moyers, was on the telephone. On the eve of Senate floor action, when the bill and the report were assumed to be in final form, the president forced changes. At that late hour, a conference was called in Mansfield's office. Present were Moyers, O'Brien, and the bill's floor manager, Sen. Jennings Randolph of West Virginia. The president, they were told, still wasn't satisfied with the bill. There were five amendments— three of them substantive—for which Randolph had fought in committee but been trounced. Like a good soldier, Randolph was prepared to pass the bill as it emerged from committee.

But no. The president wanted him to offer those five amendments again when the debate started. This was embarrassing to Randolph, but he knew when his arm was being successfully twisted. When the Senate convened, the senators found on their desks copies of the bill, the committee report, and the five amendments which Randolph now insisted would have to be adopted. Veteran Senate aides said they couldn't recall a precedent for this situation.

This caused some members to holler foul. One of them, Republican Norris Cotton of New Hampshire, threw a brief scare into the Democratic leadership by threatening to have the bill recommitted for further committee study of the amendments which were in Xerox form (there hadn't been time to print them).

Even while the bill was under debate, the president summoned Randolph from the floor to the cloakroom for telephone discussion on the situation confronting the various amendments. The president told Randolph that the House Public Works Committee was in closed session on the bill to write it in its final form. He wanted every change adopted on the Senate floor telephoned to the House group so that it could be incorporated in the House version of the bill. Johnson also told Randolph he was determined to have a bill reported from the House committee and passed in the House so close to the Senate version that no time would be wasted on a Senate-House conference.

Returning to his desk from one of these conversations with the president, Randolph, a battle-scarred veteran of many legislative battles, shook his head and told a colleague sotto voce, "I've never seen an operation like this one."

The bill, tailored to LBJ's—and Lady Bird's—taste, passed both houses by wide margins. It provided $320 million for the next two years for highway beautification and required the states to provide effective means of control of outdoor advertising and junkyards on the interstate and primary highway systems. Landscaping was to be part of the cost of highway construction.

Johnson was aware of his incredible drive to succeed and of the ruthlessness with which it was often manifested, but he identified that will to succeed with the public interest. Unless that trait of Johnson's is grasped, the essence of the Johnson personality is lost. He was utterly convinced that the bills he drove through, the appointments he made, the opponents he crushed, the bald-faced lies he would tell to mislead or confuse the opposition were all indulged in *not* to pamper himself, feed his ego, or line his pocket with wealth.

Because of his total identification of himself with the public interest, he couldn't tolerate opposition and criticism. The concept of a free press eluded him. The Johnson logic was a simple one: if he were acting only in the public interest, any criticism of that action became a threat to that public interest. He never changed.

Back in the Capitol rotunda, the services, which had started at 3:30 P.M. when the casket was brought in through the doorway leading to the Senate wing of the Capitol, came to an end at 4:05. President Nixon shook hands with the members of the Johnson family, and then he left with Mrs. Nixon and their two daughters.

The crowd dispersed slowly and then, at 4:30, the citizens who came to pay their respects began filing in. The people, two and three abreast, stretched seven blocks back. The line did not break until 3:30 A.M. and after that, the citizens continued in a straggle until 8 A.M. when it was time to remove the casket. It was a quiet line. In all, more than 40,000 had come to pay their last respects. There was no disorder, no sign of disrespect. It wasn't as big as Ike's, but some 15,000 larger than the line that went through for J. Edgar Hoover.

All in all, LBJ would have been pleased.

CHAPTER 15

Oleomargarine,
Mare's Urine, & a
Teamsters' Endorsement

The operations of that complex organization, the Congress of the United States, that sometimes approach the Byzantine can often be best illuminated by stories that history overlooks as well as those that engage the attention of chroniclers.

Most of us have already forgotten that one of the mightiest legislative battles of the century was waged over the right of housewives to buy colored margarine without paying a heavy tax designed not for revenue, but to discourage its competition with butter.

Just about everyone is unaware of the role played by pregnant mare's urine in stopping a strong trade protectionist drive that could have played havoc with America's trading relations with the rest of the world.

And few realize that the failure thus far to come to grips with the awesome threat of nationwide transportation strikes was due to a last-minute change of signals by a president intent on getting a labor union endorsement he didn't really need to win a reelection race.

These stories are perfect paradigms. In the telling, they contribute to an understanding of why the Congress acts in mysterious ways its wonders and follies to perform. The heart of the matter is seldom clarified in textbooks. Not just foreigners, but

Americans often ask, "Why the hell does Congress act like that?"

The first federal margarine law was enacted in 1886. It took sixty-four years to remove this thoroughly unfair, inequitable, and punitive piece of legislation from the books. It took that long to break the grip of the dairy bloc in Congress, and then it came about only when the cotton and soybean growers of the South overcame their sectional isolation by finding allies in the Midwest and in the growing urban centers of the North. And even then, it wasn't easy.

The 1886 law imposed a manufacturer's tax of two cents on each pound of margarine, and required manufacturers, wholesalers, and retailers to secure licenses upon payment of fees in the amounts of $600, $480, and $48 respectively. A separate license was required for each place at which the licensee carried on his business.

It had to be labeled "oleomargarine" even though only two percent of it was made from edible tallow. As the years went by, about ninety-five percent of the margarine on the market was made from cottonseed and soybean oils alone. But "oleo oil" was a useful pejorative for the dairy bloc, so that name remained officially "oleomargarine."

The constitutionality of the tax was upheld by the U.S. Supreme Court in 1887, which ruled that the act upon its face was "an act for levying taxes" and therefore "its primary object must be assumed to be the raising of revenue." The Court refused to look behind the label of the measure at the legislative design to suppress the margarine industry rather than to raise revenue. And once established as a taxing matter, its constitutionality was assured since the Court had previously held that "the power to tax may be exercised oppressively upon persons."

Under the rules of the House of Representatives, all revenue-raising measures must originate in the Ways and Means Committee. The dairy bloc had succeeded in bending those rules so that margarine legislation would have to come from the Agriculture Committee upon which the dairy bloc had a solid grip. The dairy bloc had the power to cripple a competitor and now had the high court's blessing to get away with it because it was a revenue measure.

In 1902, the dairy bloc delivered what it hoped would be a

death blow to the margarine industry. For the first time, a legal distinction was made between colored and uncolored margarine. The tax on "artificially" colored margarine was increased to ten cents a pound. The Supreme Court upheld this, too. To get around this prohibitive tax, margarine producers manufactured a product "free from artificial coloration" which could then be sold tax-free. They used cottonseed and coconut oil treated in a manner to bring out their natural color—which was yellow.

To meet this situation, the dairy bloc pressed for and got an amendment of the law to make the color restriction more stringent. Thereafter, all margarine would be held to be yellow in color when it was of a tint or shade containing "more than 1.6 degrees of yellow or yellow and red collectively." So now colored margarine, whether artificially or naturally yellow, was brought within the ambit of the law.

By the early spring of 1948, the outlook for repeal of the discriminatory taxes began to look bright. The public was aroused on this issue as never before, goaded by the spectacle of butter at a dollar a pound. The Democrats on the Agriculture Committee, who had played the dairy bloc game for so long, were changing their minds; soybean and cottonseed oil were looming large now in the Southern economy.

But they didn't control the committee. This was the Republican-controlled Eightieth Congress, and Republicans were in control of the committee. They were a troubled lot, since soybean crops were beginning to grow in importance in the Midwest, and some of the more principled members were bothered by the inequity of a tax directed against one domestic product for the benefit of another competitive product.

There was an additional reason for feeling the time was ripe for repeal. Butter had become the least profitable source of revenue from dairy products. In 1936, for example, butter represented twenty-five percent of the total income from dairy products; in 1947, it was only fourteen percent. Though the butter price was high as compared with that of vegetable fats, it was low in terms of the labor and feed that went into its production. There was more money to be made in fluid milk, cheese, and ice cream, and the consumers' dollars were flowing readily into these channels.

With this roseate assessment in mind, the margarine forces

went into action. The National Association of Margarine Manufacturers, the National Cotton Council, the American Soybean
Association, and the Best Foods Corporation, which made a
margarine called Nucoa, laid out $52,000 and hired the high-
powered publicity firm of Selvage and Lee. The publicity firm
went to work. It prepared speeches for congressional friends on
both sides of the aisle, and supplied data for those who wanted
to compose speeches in their own style. Every time a friendly
speech was made, copies by the thousand went out to newspaper editors, radio commentators, retail grocers' associations, labor unions, consumer groups, and women's organizations.

The pressure mounted and began to have effect. Never before had the members of the House Agriculture Committee received such a flood of mail on margarine—and it averaged
eighty percent for repeal of the taxes. Editorial comment
achieved a startling unanimity in the demand for repeal. And
these editorials were to be found in newspapers published in the
heart of the stronghold of the dairy interest. The *Wichita Bea-
con,* in the district represented by Kansas Congressman Clifford
Hope, chairman of the committee, published a full-page editorial demanding that he report out a repeal bill.

Repeal bills began piling up in the legislative hopper. Nearly
half were sponsored by Republicans. It was the first time any
Republican had sponsored a margarine tax repeal. And for the
first time, the dairy lobby was thrown on the defensive. It sent
out a call for help to all the milk sheds in the country and the
united, well-disciplined dairy farmers responded with letters,
telegrams, and even personal visits to their congressmen.

It was now clear that a repeal bill would pass—if it came to
the floor of the House. But the first obstacle had to be overcome: getting the measure out of committee.

Congressman Hope, whose sympathies lay with the dairy interests, was opposed to any committee hearings. To force his
hand, a young, impassioned freshman Republican, E. A. Mitchell
of Evansville, Indiana, organized a luncheon in the Speaker's
dining room. Mitchell, a processed food manufacturer, had tak-
en a dislike to margarine taxes years ago when he handled the
stuff as a grocery truck driver. He objected to the many forms
he and his customers had to fill out and the constant snooping of
Internal Revenue agents who were quick to penalize the slight-
est, most innocent error on the part of the purchasing grocer.

Mitchell attacked the problem with a single-minded fervor, buttonholing members with such persistence that some were ready to flee when they saw him. Often, his face would grow white with rage as the members refused to heed his logic. Frankly, he didn't give a damn whom he antagonized (to use his own words) so long as he got some action.

To this luncheon, Mitchell invited all legislators who had introduced repeal bills or announced their support of such legislation. In addition, Mitchell invited representatives from the League of Women Voters, the Home Economic Association, the National Council of Jewish Women, the National Consumers League, the American Dietetic Association, and the National Women's Trade Union League. They all turned up.

Donning a chef's cap, Mitchell opened the luncheon by demonstrating with aluminum tureen and spoon the nuisance and difficulty of coloring a pound of margarine. He asked his colleagues for support on a nonpartisan basis, and he appealed to the women present to notify their memberships to flood the Agriculture Committee members with demands for open hearings.

The pressure succeeded. The four-day hearings drew standing-room-only audiences, largely of women, who not only stood against the walls of the committee room but spilled out into the corridors.

Witnesses testifying for repeal were harassed with irrelevant questions and lengthy speeches by dairy bloc congressmen. Do you want to injure the dairy industry? they were asked. What do you know of the profits of the margarine industry? Isn't milk the best product for human consumption? And when a biochemist from the University of Southern California described exhaustive tests made upon rats which were fed on margarine and thrived on it, he was dismissed with the statement, "You can't tell me margarine is as good as butter."

The arguments of repeal proponents were cogent and well presented: the taxes imposed a burdensome restriction on margarine; they were not needed to discourage fraud since there's a Food and Drug Administration which checks on such matters—besides, the butter seizures for food-law violations were a hundred times greater than margarine seizures; margarine suffers a heavy tax because it is artificially colored, whereas butter is colored eight months out of the year without penalty. If you tax margarine for the benefit of the dairy industry, why not a tax on

Democratic Senator Paul Douglas of Illinois, left and below with President Johnson, stopped a strong protectionist drive in the Senate by denouncing a proposal to give tariff protection to mare's urine. A brilliant man, author of a shelf of books, he often failed because he was in advance of the times. Measures and programs which he introduced and which apparently sunk without trace would be surfaced by others years later and passed.

*A national Teamsters' strike, stopping
trucks bearing food and other essentials,
could bring the United States to its knees.
In 1972 Senator Bob Packwood of Oregon
had the votes lined up to pass the bill,
urgently sought by President Nixon, to ban
such strikes. At the last minute Nixon
ordered the bill killed—and picked up the
Teamsters' endorsement.*

rayon and other synthetic fibers for the benefit of cotton? Taxes
and license fees amounted only to $10 million a year, hardly jus-
tifying their existence for revenue purposes; low income groups
were penalized and their cost of living raised; and cottonseed
and soybeans are discriminated against.

The argument of the anti-repeal witnesses, especially veteran
lobbyist Charles W. Holman, a short, stocky, balding man with a
fringe of gray hair who represented 400,000 well-organized
dairymen: butter is better; it comes from a cow; repeal will hurt
the dairy farmers; margarine should not be permitted to imitate
butter.

But the arguments that won the day had nothing to do with
the nutrition of rats or the inherent inequities of the law. August
Herman Andresen, a wily dairy-bloc congressman from Minnesota, said the same thing in private conversations to each of his
Republican colleagues on the committee.

> This is an election year. We're going to win in November, sure
> enough, but why take a chance on jeopardizing that victory? The
> dairy centers are Republican strongholds now; why take a chance on
> losing that support? If this bill gets on the floor, it will split party ranks
> wide open; why present the electorate with the spectacle of a disunit-
> ed party? Don't let the GOP down now.

After he let that sink in, Andresen proceeded to tell them that
defeat of the legislation meant much to him personally. Chairman Hope would probably become secretary of agriculture
when the Republicans won in November and he—Andresen—
would move up to the chairmanship. A chairman is in the position of doing favors, such as naming subcommittee chairmen
and helping along legislation particular members were interested in.

His tactics won the day. When the vote came, the score was
sixteen to ten to bury the repeal legislation. And they did it in
such a fashion that it could not be reconsidered unless there was
a unanimous committee vote. One committee Republican told
me, "I still feel sick about my vote, but in the face of a plea for
party unity, I went along." William S. Hill of Colorado told his
Republican colleagues, "I'm going along with you, but I tell you
we can't hold the lid on indefinitely. We can't stop progress.
Eventually, these taxes will be repealed."

In fact, action in the House came sooner than anyone had anticipated—within two months, as it turned out, aided principally by an incredible blunder by the triumphant dairy interest. The day the committee pigeonholed the repeal bills, butter prices jumped seven to eight cents. The nation's housewives flooded the Congress with letters of protest. It was a spontaneous response, not one generated by lobbying forces.

This response convinced Mitchell, the zealous and thoroughly unpopular freshman defender of margarine—he was to serve only one term, for his dairy constituents never forgave him—that he could get repeal legislation to the floor through an act of parliamentary force majeure.

There is a device for getting floor action on a bill bottled up in committee: a discharge petition signed by 216 members, a majority of the House. It is a device that rarely succeeds. The leadership always opposes it, for it tends to undermine committee structure and authority and with that, the loss of effective control over the unwieldy body of 435 members.

For this effort, Mitchell teamed up with L. Mendel Rivers of South Carolina, a dyed-in-the-wool Southern Democrat who heightened his resemblance to John Calhoun by letting his hair grow long. Rivers would get up at 5 A.M. to proselytize the early-to-work members at the House cafeteria breakfast tables. He knew the uses of power and never hesitated to employ them, as a high-ranking member of the Armed Services Committee.

It was easier to get Democratic signatures because of the Southern concentration of cotton and soybean growers. Also, even Minority Leader Sam Rayburn overcame his opposition to discharge petitions because of constituent pressure on this issue, and he took the entire Texas delegation along with him.

Charles Halleck of Indiana, the Republican leader of the House, worked behind the scenes to discourage the rank and file Republicans from signing the petition, even though he had a growing number of soybean farmers in his district. He felt that such a controversial issue must be kept from a divisive vote in the House, just months away from an election the Republicans expected to win.

The Mitchell-Rivers effort worked, even though the last signature was obtained only after the two seized the arms of a reluctant member, Hamilton "Ham" D. Jones of North Carolina, and literally dragged him up to the rostrum where they refused to let him go until he signed. Crowing in triumph, Rivers quoted from William Jennings Bryan: "The humblest citizen in the land, clad in the armor of Right, can prevail against the whole host of error."

The debate when the bill came to the floor was almost unprecedented in its bitterness, name-calling, and threats of retaliation. The show was a good one, and for the two days it ran, it played to a standing-room-only House. The galleries were packed, and those who couldn't get in, queued up in the corridors. Those lucky enough to obtain seats were privileged to witness democracy in action with the element of dignity noticeably absent.

House rules of decorum were honored more in the breach than the observance. Harold Knutson of Minnesota, a dairy bloc member, called his dissenting Republican colleagues "poor misguided saps" and Chester Gross of Pennsylvania called them "suckers" for aiding Democrats in the repeal drive. John Rankin of Mississippi called Gross a "misfit."

Rising to Gross's defense, Knutson shouted that he was going to remove the import limitations on cotton if the oleo drive succeeded, because "it is my good fortune to be the chairman of the committee that can do it." Echoing the late Adolf Hitler, he added, "If you pull us down, by the Eternal, we will pull you down with us." This was too much for Tom Abernathy of Mississippi, who said he was ready to leave not only the House of Representatives but the country as well, if Congress was going to keep on acting this way.

Gross wasn't finished by any means. Clutching a small bottle in his hand, he took the floor again. "Here I have a little bottle full of worms taken out of cottonseed," he said. "If I took them in my hand and squeezed them, juice would run out of my hand. That goes into cottonseed oil." Rivers retorted, "Anyone who knows anything about the subject knows that no boll weevil ever gets into the seed, because the seed is not formed at the time the boll weevil is active."

Mitchell got into the act now, citing milk and butter seizures by the Food and Drug Administration because they "consisted in whole or part of a filthy substance, by reason of the presence of insects, insect parts, insect fragments, rodent hair, cat hair, moth scales, and nondescript dirt." Thruston Morton of Kentucky tried to restore some measure of sanity to the debate: "We have been told margarine is full of worms and therefore unfit for human consumption," he said. "We have been told that butter is a filthy product and a carrier of tuberculosis and other disease germs. If the housewives of America give any credence to the arguments advanced during this debate, most of us will eat apple butter for the rest of our lives."

Hill of Colorado offered an amendment to lift the tax only as long as margarine was packed in triangular shape so the restaurant diner would not think he was eating butter when the label was removed. Francis Case of South Dakota had another idea: the tax would be lifted if the patty was circular. To prevent its being trimmed into another shape, the law would require it to be round "down to the last cut or drop."

The amendments, all of them beaten down, were clear signs of the desperation of the dairy bloc, which knew it was going to be beaten. By the end of the second day of debate, the margarine forces won by a resounding vote of 260 to 106. But there was a stay of execution. The Senate, in a rush to adjourn, didn't take up the bill.

The Democrats won the White House and the Congress in November. The battle was renewed in the House the next year, but the zest for battle in the dairy bloc was gone. Hopes, however feeble, lay in the Senate.

The public was now apathetic about the issue. Butter was twenty cents a pound less in January of 1950 when the Senate took up the bill, so the housewives were no longer indignant. But everyone knew how the battle would come out: margarine would win after sixty-four years.

Consider the statistics at the time of looming victory. On the one hand, you had 558,609 dairy farmers, 3,500 creameries, and 40,000 dairy processing plants. On the other hand, there were 1.5 million cotton farmers and 500,000 soybean growers.

Margarine was the second largest outlet for cottonseed oil. More than 450 million pounds of cottonseed oil were used, the equivalent of one and a half million tons of cottonseed—about fourteen percent of the gross cash income from the cotton crop. Margarine was also the second largest outlet for soybean oil, consuming 235 million pounds. About sixteen percent of all soybean oil produced in this country went into margarine that year, influencing the price of the entire production.

The butter lobby took on an air of desperation. It brought thousands of horny-handed dairy farmers to Washington, uncomfortable, many of them, in their ill-fitting "store-boughten" clothes, to tell their senators their livelihood would be destroyed if the tax was repealed.

Then it resorted to a series of potentially emasculating amendments. One would repeal the margarine taxes but forbid the movement of margarine in interstate commerce, thus forcing the establishment of a margarine factory in every state. When this ploy failed, the cigar-chomping William Langer of North Dakota, a predominantly dairy state, offered a series of civil rights amendments guaranteeing fair employment practices and outlawing the poll tax and lynching. Senators would have to vote on these amendments before they could reach the margarine tax repeal and, for a while, it was touch and go.

The Democratic leadership in the Senate was able to circumvent this threat by holding a party caucus in which there was unanimous agreement that all nongermane amendments—that is, not pertinent to the main matter—would be voted down, whatever their merit. The leaders of the final Senate debate were Hubert Humphrey of Minnesota, on behalf of the dairy bloc, and J. William Fulbright of Arkansas, a great soybean-producing state.

Humphrey was very much on the spot with his fellow liberals, representing predominantly urban areas in the North, who wanted the tax repealed. He rationalized his stand in a typically liberal fashion. He attacked the margarine bill on the ground that it fostered monopoly. Since there are only 29 margarine companies as against 3,500 creameries and 40,000 dairy processing plants, he argued that the issue was one of small business versus big business—of the farmer and consumer in opposition to monopoly.

His argument fell flat when Fulbright interrupted him to point out that while six companies control five percent of margarine production, eight dairies control seventy-one percent of the milk production. Quoting from a Federal Trade Commission report, Fulbright said that two dairy corporations, National Dairy Products Corporation and the Borden Company, hold respectively 27.5 and 21.4 percent of the industry's net capital assets. "There is nothing comparable to this in the field of margarine manufacturing," he said. Humphrey changed the subject.

When the tumult and shouting died, the Senate repealed the sixty-four-year-old tax by a top-heavy vote of fifty-six to sixteen.

Eight years later, in 1958, trade protectionists took a beating comparable to that of the dairy bloc, though for a while it appeared as though they would set back the clock on reciprocal trade legislation. The fever of protectionism has always been endemic in this country. Sometimes it has soared out of control, as in the enactment of the Smoot-Hawley tariff bill which most economists agree today helped precipitate the worst depression in American history.

Enacted in 1930, the Smoot-Hawley Act raised import duties to an all-time high. It reflected the then-prevailing view that high tariffs would assure domestic prosperity. In three years, U.S. imports dropped from an average of $4 billion a year under the Tariff Act of 1922 to $1.4 billion, while exports had slipped from $4.6 billion to $1.6 billion. In a word, Smoot-Hawley was a memorable disaster.

Expansion of exports became a major goal of the New Deal's recovery program. It was embodied in the Trade Agreements Act of 1934 which gave the president authority to lower tariffs to up to fifty percent of the rates established in 1930. This peeling back of Smoot-Hawley worked so well that, despite continuing cries from unreconstructed protectionists, the tariff-cutting authority was extended on seven different occasions.

On December 3, 1957, President Eisenhower informed a bipartisan group of legislative leaders that he planned to seek a five-year extension the next year with even greater duty reduction powers. Speaker Sam Rayburn shook his head dolefully and told Ike, "It will take blood, sweat, and tears to get the program through Congress."

Protectionist sentiment was never stronger than at the time the new session of Congress opened. The spread of textile manufacturing into the South had transformed many hitherto low-tariff areas into protectionist strongholds. The importation of low-cost Venezuelan oil strengthened the protectionist forces within the oil- and coal-producing states, while the recent fall in

the prices of lead, zinc, and copper produced protectionist sentiment in the states of the West where these nonferrous minerals
were mined.

So strong was the protectionist sentiment that early in the session it was believed by many observers that President Eisenhower would be lucky if he could get a straight one-year
extension of the present law. For a while, Senate leaders even
doubted the Finance Committee would report out a bill. This
would have meant an automatic return to Smoot-Hawley.

World events helped relieve the gloom of the opponents of
protectionism. The sudden intensification of the cold war with
the Soviet Union made it appear more necessary than ever to
hold onto our friends, even if it meant that some domestic industries must suffer as a consequence.

But this alone would not have been enough to stem the protectionist tide. The protectionists overplayed their hand. In the
Senate Finance Committee they forced a broadening of the national security provisions of the Trade Agreement Act to permit
special protection for a wide range of domestic industries.

Here's what they did: Under the existing, expiring law, any industry hurt by competing imports could seek relief from the
U.S. Tariff Commission under the so-called "escape clause." In
addition, where imports endangered an industry vital to the national security, the president, upon the recommendation of the
Office of Defense Mobilization, could order some kind of tariff
relief. The protectionists broadened the national security provision so that just about any industry could seek help on the
ground that the *economy* of the country was vital to national security. Any industry that suffers obviously causes the economy
to suffer. Hence, that industry is vital to the national security.

The protectionists thus fell into a trap—a trap neatly laid for
them by Sen. Paul Douglas of Illinois. Douglas had made a study
of all the industries that had sought relief under the escape
clause in the ten years in which this clause had been in operation. These were the industries which could now, under the
proposed change in the law, apply for relief on national security
grounds.

He found there were forty-eight commodities covered. He
took the Senate floor for a brief speech. It was one of the increasingly rare occasions when one speech could turn things

around. It was devastating. It delivered a blow from which the protectionists never recovered. Douglas read the list with pertinent comments:

> Spring clothespins, which can hardly be regarded as essential to national security.
> Wood screws, which would not seem to be an industry of appreciable importance.
> Blue mold cheese, which is delectable, but which would not be a major item. . . .
> Groundfish filets.
> Glacé cherries, which I would not think would be an essential industry to the national security, however delectable they may be. . . .
> Pregnant mare's urine. I am at a loss to understand the importance of this industry, or precisely how much of a protective tariff it needs, or how the domestic supply should be protected, and what if it were not protected. . . .
> Coconuts. I had not realized that we grew a large quantity of coconuts in the United States. . . .
> Garlic. I think the vast majority of Americans do not feel emotionally involved with regard to the domestic fortunes of that industry. The garlic habitués would probably have their desires satisfied by French or Italian garlic.

It was the pregnant mare's urine that particularly piqued Douglas's interest. He returned to it in a speech in the Senate the following day: "Now we really have something for the birds," he said. "I stared at that item for a long time and could hardly believe my eyes. It is difficult for me to understand how this product can be protected. Why does it need protection? This is tariff protection with a vengeance."

This is the story behind the pregnant mare's urine situation: A few years earlier, a man named Roy E. Jones, of Farmer City, Illinois, organized a pregnant mare's association, It was a trade organization of Midwest farmers engaged in collecting pregnant mares' urine for sale at a dollar a gallon to pharmaceutical houses which extracted estrogens from it. Estrogens are female hormones often used in the treatment of illness related to the onset of menopause.

Then foreign competition entered the picture. Some farmers in Canada got together and began marketing the urine at sixty-five cents a gallon. Jones thereupon petitioned the Tariff Commission for relief under the escape clause. The petition was rejected by four of the six commissioners on the ground that relief could not be granted because there weren't any tariffs on pregnant mare's urine to be raised *or* lowered.

By this time other factors entered into the picture. Scientists discovered that estrogens could be extracted even more cheaply from a plant grown in Mexico. That is how the colorful industry of the collecting and gathering of pregnant mare's urine fell upon hard times.

But if the protectionists had not overplayed their hand, this unique industry would have received tariff protection on grounds of national security. Ike got a four-year extension of the law, only one less than he had asked for, but one more than the Senate was initially willing to give him.

The oleo battle epitomized the conflict of commodities and attendant regional loyalties. The tariff struggle was one of a series of never-ending battles between domestic industries and foreign competitors. Compelling arguments involving the national interest could be advanced on either side, though the equities might be out of balance. But the failure of Congress to legislate effective restraints on national transportation strikes, which could bring the country to its knees, can be laid squarely to one factor: a double-cross by President Richard M. Nixon.

In 1970 and again in 1971, Nixon urged Congress to enact legislation enabling the president to deal with national emergencies arising from strikes in the transportation industry. Before the calling of the strikes, he proposed resolving labor-management differences by:

1. Extending the cooling-off period for an additional thirty days after expiration of the usual eighty-day period provided by the Taft-Hartley Act.
2. Allowing only a partial strike or lockout by the disputing parties.
3. Or by directing "final offer selection" whereby labor and management would each submit a final offer and one alternative plan to an arbitration panel that would then choose one of the proposals without change or modification.

In his 1970 message, he pointed to the failures of both the Railway Labor Act and the Taft-Hartley Act: "Past events and recent experiences demonstrate the failure of . . . the Railroad

Labor Act," he told Congress. "Since passage ... 45 years ago, the emergency provisions have been invoked 187 times—an average of four times yearly. Work stoppages at the end of the sixty-day period have occurred at a rate of more than one per year since 1947. Twice the president has had to request special legislation from the Congress to end a railroad dispute, most recently in 1967."

Nixon said the law actually discouraged genuine bargaining because little meaningful bargaining takes place before the Emergency Board set up by the law becomes involved. Nor did the Taft-Hartley Act work in other transportation industries, such as the maritime, longshore, and trucking industries. The president has virtually no options if the strike takes place after the eighty-day cooling-off period has elapsed—"something that has happened in eight of the 29 instances in which this machinery has been invoked since 1947."

There was even more urgency in his 1971 message:

> The urgency of this matter should require no new emphasis by anyone; the critical nature of it should be clear to all. But if emphasis is necessary, we need only remember that barely two months ago the nation was brought to the brink of a crippling railroad shutdown, the strike being averted only by legislation passed after a walkout had actually begun. That legislation, we should also remember, settled little; it merely postponed the strike deadline. A few weeks from now another railroad strike over the same issues which precipitated the last one is a distinct possibility.
>
> I believe we must face up to this problem, and face up to it now, before events overtake us and while reasoned consideration is still possible.
>
> Time and again, as the nation has suffered major disruptions from a transportation shutdown, voices have been raised on all sides declaring emphatically that this must not happen again—that better laws are needed to protect the public interest, and that the time to enact those laws is before, not after, the next crippling emergency.
>
> But with the same regularity, as each emergency in turn has passed, the voices have subsided—until the next time. So nothing has been done, and emergency has followed emergency, at incalculable cost to millions of innocent bystanders and to the nation itself.

Organized labor opposed the legislation. AFL-CIO President George Meany, testifying against the proposal, said, "We regard compulsory arbitration of emergency disputes as an anti-labor measure masquerading as public interest legislation, and we intend to fight it out with all the strength at our command."

Republican Sen. Bob Packwood of Oregon, a state whose ports had been plagued with lengthy longshoremen strikes, was the sponsor of the legislation to curb transportation strikes. "You mean to say, Mr. Meany," Packwood asked incredulously, "that the federal government has no right to intervene and say there is an interest beyond yours and the employers?"

"That's right," Meany replied. "That's my position."

As Packwood said later, he couldn't believe his ears. He pressed on: "Now are you serious, Mr. Meany, that no matter what the consequences to the rest of this nation may be, the right to strike is paramount over any other economic decision?"

Meany said, "That's right. This country can do what they did in New York during the taxi strike."

"What's that?"

"Let 'em walk."

The Teamsters, of course, were opposed to the legislation. It had long been the dream of the late Jimmy Hoffa, the Teamsters' president, to negotiate nationwide agreements, immeasurably increasing his union's power to bring the entire transportation system to a grinding halt. In 1964, Hoffa negotiated the first nationwide agreement between 400,000 truck drivers and warehousemen and their trucking companies. Unlike other industries—automobiles, for example, where a few companies could stand together against the union—there are some 12,000 trucking companies, most of them undercapitalized, which must stand up to a powerful union. (On April 1, 1976, Hoffa's successor, Frank Fitzsimmons, called the first nationwide trucking strike in history. The united front of the truckers broke in twenty-four hours. The settlement produced a 34.4 percent increase in wages, pensions, and benefits over a three-year period. It became known in the industry as "a suicide pact"; more than one hundred companies closed down or were merged.)

Despite massive labor union opposition, the bill was making progress, in no small part due to the almost single-minded efforts of Bob Packwood. Packwood is one of the brightest young men the Republicans have elected to the Senate in decades. At the age of thirty-six he met the four-term veteran, Wayne

Morse, then sixty-eight, in public debate in Portland, Oregon, and clearly outpointed the master debater himself. Morse, who had confidently expected to demolish the young upstart, never recovered from that experience.

A moderate of strongly held opinions, Packwood was not only among the first in his party to express his disgust with the Nixon administration over Watergate, he has taken on the potent right-to-life lobby by campaigning in Oregon and all over the country for "zero population growth" at every opportunity. He had no qualms about taking on organized labor; in fact, he took on the task in that instance with relish.

On July 17, 1972, Packwood was close to victory. The bill was scheduled to be debated that day. A careful vote counter, Packwood in the past week had counted forty-seven "sure" votes, forty-five opposed, and eight "undecided." With a little shove from the Nixon administration, he was confident he would pick up the needed votes.

When he arrived at his suite in the Dirksen Office Building that Monday morning, his phone was ringing. This, in itself, was surprising, since it was only 8:15. Despite a long drive from his home in suburban Maryland, Packwood invariably arrived before his staff and before the importunate phone calls would start. This practice allowed him some time for uninterrupted work, and this morning he had to prepare a major speech for his bill.

The caller was Undersecretary of Labor Laurence Silberman. "Senator," he said, "this is Larry. I've got to see you as soon as possible."

Puzzled, Packwood said, "Come right on over. I can see you now."

At 8:45, Silberman arrived. He looked obviously distressed as he told Packwood, "Bob, the signals have been changed. The administration will support your bill—but it won't push it at this time."

Silberman didn't have to specify the bill. Conferences between the two men had been going on for months on the Packwood bill—the Transportation Crisis Prevention Act of 1972, to give it its official title. It was an administration "must." Packwood had met eight times with President Nixon's chief congressional liaison aide, Clark MacGregor, who had assured him that this measure was one of the four major domestic programs on which the president insisted the Congress must act before adjournment in this election year.

It was in conference with MacGregor that Packwood had devised the strategy for getting a vote on his bill which labor could have bottled up if it went the normal committee route. Packwood was going to offer it as an amendment to one of organized labor's "must" bills—the bill to raise the minimum wage.

Two sets of lobbyists went to work on the Senate on behalf of the Packwood bill. Tony Ogerdahl, a Washington attorney, was retained by the transportation industry to coordinate the industry lobbying. He had a total of fifty lobbyists working under his direction. Clark MacGregor's lobbyists included not only the White House crew, but officials from the Labor and Transportation departments.

On the eve of Silberman's telephone call, Packwood not only had the forty-seven "solid" votes but had been informed by MacGregor that the White House had lined up six Republicans, among the eight "undecided," who would, albeit reluctantly, vote with Packwood.

"Then, bam, it had all evaporated," Packwood told me later. "Larry Silberman said to me, 'We do have some questions on timing and procedural developments.' And I knew we were down the drain. Without administration help, those six 'unannounced' votes were gone."

For the explanation of events, we go back three days, to July 14, to a favorite hangout of the top echelon of the Teamsters— the La Costa Hotel and Country Club about twenty-five miles north of San Diego and about thirty miles south of Richard Nixon's San Clemente home. It has a challenging twenty-seven-hole golf course, twenty-five tennis courts, an Olympic-size swimming pool, and is surrounded by 5,600 carefully manicured acres.

Twenty Teamsters' board members had bellied up to the bar for a serious discussion on whether to endorse Nixon's reelection. There was a little dissent. Vice President Harold Gibbons insisted there was no way he would support Nixon's reelection. His colleagues' pleading went on all night long, but Gibbons refused to change his mind. He was joined by another vice president, Einar Mohn, who complained about Nixon's proposal to curb national transportation strikes. "How can I support a man whose bill will cripple our union?" he asked.

According to Stephen Brill, author of *The Teamsters*, Nixon's White House counsel "and Fitzsimmons's chief White House handholder," Charles Colson, was at La Costa to round up endorsement for Nixon. (Colson, who was afterward to serve time in prison in connection with the Watergate crimes, was given the lucrative Teamsters' account when he left the White House to go into private practice.) Colson looked up and asked, "What bill are you talking about?" He was told. Colson said he'd take care of it. At 8 the next morning, Colson called Mohn and told him the bill had been withdrawn.

With Gibbons the lone holdout, the Teamsters' board voted nineteen to one to endorse Nixon. Packwood didn't know what lay behind Silberman's curious intervention until he saw the story on the Senate news ticker that afternoon.

As Brill reported, immediately after the vote of the Teamsters' board, the twenty board members piled into five black rented limousines and drove to San Clemente to give the president the news personally. Nixon gave every visitor—including the holdout, Gibbons—a barbecue lunch, drinks, an autographed presidential golf ball, and an invitation to play on his three-hole golf course.

"I guess I should take this philosophically," Packwood told me that evening, "but it's hard to see something so close to me raped. I spent a whole year sweating blood, pleading, cajoling, and persuading."

Nixon's own 1971 message to Congress still holds true. "So nothing has been done, and emergency has followed emergency, at incalculable cost to millions of innocent bystanders and to the nation itself."

CHAPTER 16

A Reporter's Role

———————

Werner Heisenberg's principle of uncertainty, in which the very act of measuring an elementary particle keeps it from being accurately measured—and knocks hell out of causality in the subatomic world—might be extended to the world of politics.

The problem has not only occurred to responsible journalists, but, on occasion, disturbed them. To what extent does the reporting of an event shape that event? Total objectivity is impossible. The inherent shapelessness of reality forces the reporter to select and rearrange its parts to make an acceptable story.

One does not report that Jane Roe, wearing a green dress, took the stand as a prosecution witness, placed her hand on the Bible, and swore to tell the truth, the whole truth, and nothing but the truth so help her God, and answered "yes" when asked if the defendant, John Doe, shot the decedent in her presence. The reporter rearranges the sequence and writes something like this: "John Doe, on trial for his life for the murder of Raymond Smith, was identified today as the murderer by the chief prosecution witness, Jane Roe, in testimony delivered in Federal District Court."

On some occasions, the reporter, wittingly or not, can shape or alter history by direct intervention. In my career, this has happened twice: I helped save a United States senator from an impending defeat, and I was instrumental in salvaging the career of a congressman who afterwards became the thirty-eighth president of the United States. Lest this be viewed as heroic posturing, let me hasten to add that I had no idea at the time that my role, which events thrust upon me, would prove to have much more significance than I then realized.

The senator was William Proxmire of Wisconsin, a Democrat. The congressman who was to go on to become president was Gerald Ford of Michigan, a Republican.

It was about noon, Sunday, October 25, 1964, when my phone rang at home while I was dutifully making my way through the thicket of the *New York Times.*

"This is Bill Proxmire, Sam," the voice said. "I'm calling from Madison. Excuse me for bothering you at home."

"Not at all, Senator," I replied. "What's on your mind?"

"I'm in trouble and I need some information and advice," he said.

"Don't be silly," I said. "Yours is one of the safe seats. I'm not even paying any attention to Wisconsin."

"It *was* a safe seat, Sam. I'm not exaggerating or panicking when I say that I'm in real danger of losing the race, and the election is only nine days away. I've already lost the endorsement of fourteen papers in my state, all of which had come out for me and now turned against me."

"I don't believe you're in real trouble," I said, still incredulous. "Why are you calling *me*?"

"What do you know about the *Pageant* poll?" he asked. I told him I had never heard of such a poll, though I was vaguely familiar with a magazine of that name. Wasn't it of tabloid size, sold in chain grocery stores, and given to printing articles on how to improve one's sex life despite marriage? I was making a joke of it.

"That's the one, Sam. In fact, the lead article is 'Kissing After Marriage: Why Women Want More and Why Men Want Less.' But that's not what I'm calling about. It's got a poll of what it calls 220 key members of the Washington press corps—the reporters, broadcasters, and columnists who chronicle the day-to-day activities of the lawmakers. And I'm listed in the poll as the fourth worst senator.

"It was first reported on October 14. Just listen to this eight-column, front-page headline in the *Wisconsin State Journal:* 'Senator Proxmire, Fourth Worst Senator, Poll Shows.' "

I told him to slow down, for by now I was taking notes as fast as I could. He went on, at length:

"My opponent has mailed over a hundred thousand photostatic copies of this article throughout the state. He's been on television displaying this article for TV viewers. It has been reproduced and carried as a display ad in several of the daily papers here.

"I stand in front of a football stadium for the purpose of distributing my literature and shaking hands with people, and there are my opponent's aides handing out copies of the *Pageant* poll by the thousands.

"Now just listen to these endorsements for my opponent. The *Wisconsin State Journal* leads off its editorial page with this: 'Proxmire Ineffective. Wisconsin Needs Wilbur Renk as its Spokesman in Senate.' The *La Crosse Tribune:* 'Renk Has the Right Tag for Proxmire.' The *Milwaukee Journal:* 'For Senator: Renk.'

"Let me read you what the *Journal,* the biggest paper in the state, says: 'The *Milwaukee Journal* has come to the conclusion that it favors the election of Wilbur Renk to the United States Senate on November 3. Senator Proxmire is able, intelligent, articulate and a tireless campaigner. However, his accomplishments in seven years in Washington have been few.' "

"Bill," I told him. "Let me call you back within the hour. I never heard of the poll. In the first place, I don't believe responsible Washington correspondents respond to such polls, even though we're often deluged with them, even from high school papers. Secondly, if *Pageant* was going to poll so-called 'key correspondents' who cover Congress, it should have polled me. I'm not only *Newsweek*'s chief congressional correspondent, but I'm also secretary to the Periodical Correspondents Gallery Association which accredits periodical reporters on the Hill. Let me check around."

I checked with the AP and UPI correspondents assigned to the Senate. They had not been polled. The same was true of *Time* and *U.S. News and World Report.* (Incidentally, weeks later I found two reporters who *had* been polled by *Pageant:* Milton Berliner of the now defunct *Washington Daily News,* for which he was the movie critic, and Sarah McClendon of the *El Paso Times*. Neither had listed Proxmire as one of the worst senators.) I called Proxmire back and told him, "It looks like a classical Roorback." (A Roorback is a last-minute smear resorted to in political campaigns. Even if it's an outrageous and transparent lie, it can cause damage because there isn't time to refute it effectively.) I told him all the checks I had made and said, "Bill, this poll is a fraud and a phony."

"Sam, may I quote you?" he asked.

"Hell, yes," I replied blithely. It wasn't until after I hung up that I realized that I might be laying myself open to a slander suit by the publisher of *Pageant*. I might also be embarrassing *Newsweek* by precipitating myself into the Wisconsin senate race. Then I shrugged my shoulders and went back to the *Times*.

Somehow, I didn't realize what a furor I would be stirring up. Proxmire went on statewide radio and TV hookups quoting me. He ran ads in every paper in the state quoting me. I quote here from one of his broadcasts:

> My staff asked Radio Press International, a service that reports congressional news for radio stations throughout the country. This service made a survey of the Senate Press Gallery in late October and could find no one among the reporters covering the Senate who had replied to the *Pageant* survey.
>
> I asked Sam Shaffer, chief congressional correspondent for *Newsweek* and secretary of the Periodical Press Gallery, the organization that accredits magazines such as *Time, Life, Newsweek* [*Pageant*—if they had a Washington correspondent, which they don't] to the press gallery.
>
> Shaffer, who has covered the Congress for *Newsweek* for seventeen years and has served as secretary of the periodical accrediting committee for a number of years, conducted as comprehensive a survey of the press gallery as was possible in late October. He not only queried periodical correspondents but also newspaper, television, and radio network reporters. He concluded, and I quote: "I was not polled and to my knowledge no one in the Senate Gallery was polled. Such polls are held in utter contempt by responsible members of the Senate press corps. They are utterly without stature. The *Pageant* poll was a phony."

Four days before the election, the Wilbur Renk organization fell silent about the poll and used it no more in the campaign. That same day, I received a phone call from Renk's campaign manager. "Since when does *Newsweek* endorse Senate candidates?" he asked me. There were no friendly overtones in his voice.

"*Newsweek* doesn't endorse candidates," I replied. "Nor do its correspondents. Proxmire called me about the *Pageant* poll and asked me what I knew about it. I checked around and concluded it was a phony. I would have done the same for your man had the situation been reversed."

Proxmire wasn't the only senator or representative smeared in that poll, but nowhere else was it to become such a major and threateningly decisive issue. At the request of the late Democratic Congressman Hale Boggs of Louisiana, who was also rated low, a congressional investigation was launched in the dying days of the Eighty-eighth Congress.

The testimony revealed that *Pageant* had done no polling on its own but had purchased the poll from a free-lance writer in Ohio. Subpoenas were served on the *Pageant* publisher and the alleged pollster by the House Special Committee to Investigate Campaign Expenditures. In his official letter of complaint to the committee, Proxmire wrote:

It's hard for me to conceive of a Wisconsin voter who missed the "Proxmire—Fourth Worst Senator" message. My own personal campaigning has for 12 years concentrated on seeing just as many people personally as I possibly can see at factory gates, shopping centers and sports events. Never in these years have I observed such a stunning and devastating impact on a candidate from any issue. Again and again I would be confronted by former supporters who told me they could not support me because of the cold evidence of the *Pageant* poll. The *Pageant* article became the prime issue, the very heart of my opponent's campaign against me.

We tried our best to counteract the poll by radio, television and newspaper ads, reporting the opinion of well-known Washington newspapermen about the poll. We had some success in counteracting it. But the *Pageant* article undoubtedly had a devastating effect.

Prior to the publication of the *Pageant* article, polls, including a professional poll by Oliver Quayle, showed me running far ahead of my opponent. Polls taken after the October 14 revelation by *Pageant* showed that I had dropped far down and had become, instead of a relatively "safe" prospect for re-election, a marginal candidate.

Because of my big initial advantage I eventually won by some 112,000 votes. But I am convinced that my margin would have been at least 200,000 greater, perhaps much more, if it had not been for

the *Pageant* article. I am also convinced that this article has perma-
nently damaged my reputation in Wisconsin. The damage is serious
and irreparable.

Proxmire was wrong; the damage did not turn out to be irreparable. He won in 1964 with 53.3 percent: in 1970, with 70.8 percent; and in 1976, with a whopping 72.2 percent.

Meanwhile, the committee's subpoenas never got served. The
United States marshals entrusted with the task could not locate
either the publisher or the pollster, both of whom managed to
be away from their offices, homes, and usual haunts. However,
the committee did receive a letter from the pollster stating he
had destroyed the polling sheets to protect the confidentiality of
those polled. With the end of the year and the adjournment of
Congress, the investigation just petered out. It was not renewed.
The point had been made: the poll was worthless.

Proxmire is one of the most fascinating men in Congress. He
has been called eccentric, even flaky. About one thing there can
be no dispute—his driving energy. He has established an all-
time record for making consecutive roll call votes—more than
6,000 and more than double the previous record established by
Margaret Chase Smith. An advocate of the long-stymied geno-
cide treaty, he has made a five-hundred-word speech urging its
ratification every day the Senate has been in session for the past
eleven years. In 1972, he became the first member of the Senate
to have a hair transplant and for more than a week appeared on
the Senate floor wearing a turban-like bandage. (Strom Thurmond of South Carolina subsequently had a hair transplant too.)

An indefatigable runner, in politics as well as on the track,
Proxmire ran three times for governor of Wisconsin, failing each
time. He was then elected to the Senate on his first try in November 1957. Proxmire runs—not jogs, but runs—five miles daily from his home in northwest Washington to his office where
he works at a standup desk until it is time to go to committee or
to the floor. In the winter of 1974–75 he ran the 700-mile perimeter of the state of Wisconsin over a three-month period, averaging thirty miles each day he ran. On some days, especially
when he was paralleling the shore of Lake Superior, he ran in
thirty-degree-below-zero weather.

To acquaint himself with the occupations of his constitutents, he has taken time out to work as a garbage collector, painter, bank teller, and gasoline filling station operator.

He has become the Senate's watchdog on governmental and, in particular, military wasteful spending. He exposed the multibillion-dollar overrun in the C-5A air transport plane and led the fight against the supersonic transport plane which its builders wanted the federal government to finance. Since March 1975, he has achieved particular prominence by his Golden Fleece of the Month award to recipients of governmental grants, particularly in obscure corners of the scientific world. It hasn't endeared him to the world of Academe, but it delights the frugal constituents of Wisconsin.

A few days after the election, I received a call from Proxmire asking me to lunch with him and his pretty wife, Ellen, on their return to Washington. We met in the Senate dining room. She embraced me, kissed me full on the lips, and said, "Sam, you elected a Senator."

I had been sufficiently rewarded.

In the case of Gerald Ford, the element of fortuity was far greater and actually hinged on finding a sheet of paper in a rented cottage on Newfound Lake five miles north of Bristol, New Hampshire, on Tuesday, August 3, 1965.

That morning, on a grocery-shopping expedition to Bristol, I came across a day-old copy of the *New York Times* and discovered that Gerald Ford had come under serious attack by President Johnson for allegedly violating a presidential confidence involving national security matters. I knew that Ford's hold upon his House Republican leadership post was shaky and could now be in jeopardy.

I also knew at first hand that the president was—to put the most charitable construction upon it—in error, and that Ford was innocent of the charge. Then I began wrestling with a problem familiar to journalists: what is the reporter's responsibility in such matters? In this instance: what was the responsibility of a reporter who was on vacation with a wife and three children, and who wanted to put the hurly-burly of Washington as far away as possible for a month?

At this point in my narrative, I have to backtrack to Thanksgiving week in November 1964. On the third of that month,

Senator William Proxmire, shown
here smiling under a new hair
transplant and campaigning back
home in Wisconsin, has been called
eccentric, even flaky. There is no
dispute about his driving energy
and ability. He runs—not jogs, but
runs—five miles daily from home
to office. Averaging thirty miles a
day, he ran the entire perimeter of
his state, some 700 miles.

Johnson had scored a sweep over Barry Goldwater, carrying forty-four of the fifty states. Republicans lost 36 House seats, reducing their number there to 140—the lowest since Franklin D.
Roosevelt's 1936 election, when they held onto only 89 seats.

The survivors were in a mood to replace their leadership in
the House. A small handful of conspirators gathered in the office
of Congressman Robert Griffin of Michigan (afterwards to become a senator) to plot the overthrow of House Republican
leader Charles Halleck of Indiana. The Republicans needed a
new image. Halleck, with the help of these same conspirators,
had unseated his predecessor, Joe Martin of Massachusetts, six
years earlier. The argument at that time: fresh blood was needed in the leadership. Now the argument was advanced against
Halleck himself, who had an excellent record as an "obstruction-
ist" to Democratic initiatives.

Griffin and the others wanted someone who could present
"constructive alternatives" as a way of rebuilding the shattered
party. They also wanted a "new, fresh face." Charley Halleck's
increasing resemblance to comedian W. C. Fields—aided by a
frequent resort to the bottle—presented a bad image for the
party in the age of television. They settled on Jerry Ford, a former all-American football star. He was, the conspirators admitted, an attractive person, but no ball of fire and somewhat
hesitant about charging windmills unless he had advance assurance his lance could wreck the windmill.

After checking with his wife, Betty, and sleeping on it, Ford
announced his candidacy. Halleck, who did not initially believe
the challenge would be made, cut short his Florida vacation and
began calling his Republican colleagues from his Washington office. Halleck was alone in his effort. Griffin's office was manned
by thirty volunteers—a measure of the party's disaffection with
Halleck.

It developed into a bitter struggle. On the eve of the Republican caucus, where the vote on the leadership would be done by
secret ballot, Halleck thought he had eighty-four votes—thirteen more than a majority. Ford's managers told him he had six-
ty-one "solid" and twenty "leaning."

The vote was close: seventy-three to sixty-seven. Ford won
with just a six-vote margin. It was far short of a mandate. In fact,
when in his first official act he sought to replace Minority Whip

Les Arends, a long-time party hack, with a bright young Republican, Peter H. B. Frelinghuysen, Ford suffered a setback.

For months, Ford's hold upon the leadership was tenuous. Halleck was bitter over the defeat and did nothing to ease Ford's role. Nor did Lyndon B. Johnson, who liked Charley Halleck. They had been drinking companions for years. Even after Halleck's defeat, Johnson went out of his way to reward him by elevating Halleck's son to the District of Columbia bench, despite serious questions about young Halleck's qualifications for the judgeship raised by the local bar association. In fact, Halleck failed of renomination to a second term on the bench after the District of Columbia Commission on Judicial Disabilities and Tenure found him "barely qualified."

The virulence of Johnson's attack upon Ford the following August may be explained in part by the president's friendship for Halleck. But aside from that, LBJ just didn't like Ford. He often spoke of him contemptuously. "The trouble with Jerry Ford," he would say, "is that he used to play football without a helmet." His quip that "Jerry Ford is too dumb to walk and chew gum at the same time," continued to plague Ford even after Johnson's death and after Ford became president. Clio, the Muse of History, will probably correct the record someday. In this more permissive age, I can report that this remark has been bowdlerized. What Johnson actually said was, "Jerry Ford is too dumb to fart and walk at the same time."

On Sunday, August 1, White House correspondents traveling with the president were summoned to a press conference held on the front porch of his ranch house on the Pedernales River near Johnson City, Texas. In remarks that made page one all over the nation, Johnson described as "untrue and perhaps malicious" reports that the opposition of influential Democratic senators had dissuaded him from calling up the reserves or taking other measures that would have significantly broadened American participation in the war in Vietnam.

The president said that these reports had been based on a "background" session for reporters by a Republican who had thereby "broken" the president's confidence and "distorted" his true position. He didn't name the Republican, but all the stories filed from Johnson City did, based upon "guidance" from LBJ's aides. That's how Ford's name leaped into the headlines.

The previous Wednesday, Johnson had held a formal press conference at the White House in which he announced an increase of 50,000 men for U.S. forces in Vietnam. At the same time, he rejected the idea of calling up reserves and said he would depend entirely on increased draft calls.

On the eve of that press conference, he had summoned the bipartisan leadership of Congress to the White House to set forth what he planned to announce publicly the next day. At that meeting, Senate Majority Leader Mike Mansfield, a consistent opponent of our involvement in Vietnam, read a three-page paper noting that many of his colleagues were unwilling to risk facing the consequences of a rapidly expanded war and declaring that there was much more opposition to the war in private than could be seen in public. But Mansfield said nothing about the possibility of calling up reserves—a far more serious situation than increasing draft calls.

At noon, Thursday, the day after the White House press conference, Jerry Ford had a small group of newsmen to lunch in the Capitol. I was one of those present. It was the first of a series of such luncheons planned by Ford so that newsmen could get to know him better. Everything was on the record except for a question dealing with the congressional leadership meeting at the White House. On a background basis, Ford mentioned the Mansfield letter, but little else. He said nothing about calling up reserves.

The morning after Ford's luncheon, several news stories appeared stating that President Johnson had been dissuaded from calling up the reserves because of Mansfield's statement. These stories did not state their source, but Johnson leaped to the conclusion that Ford was responsible.

At the press conference on the banks of the Pedernales (pronounced Perdenales for some reason) River, Johnson was asked by Richard Strout of the *Christian Science Monitor:*

"Mr. President, there is a story in some papers that you were dissuaded from taking a stronger line in Vietnam because of something Mike Mansfield said."

Johnson had anticipated the question and was ready with his reply. "That was the result of a man who broke my confidence and not only broke it, but distorted it.

"I read Senator Mansfield's statement very carefully following a backgrounder held by one of the prominent members of another party, and I found nothing to justify that statement. And I would brand it untrue and perhaps malicious. Senator Mansfield never mentioned reserves, and it was not in any of his discussions, and the discussions did not have anything to do with the reserves, as his paper will show.

"Most of the people you deal with, and we dealt with several dozen, perhaps a couple of hundred, including the governors, all of them respect the confidence. But once in a while an inexperienced man, or a new one, or a bitter partisan, has to play a little politics. I think they keep it to a minimum, generally speaking, but one or two of them will do it. And boys will be boys."

Ford replied in a stiff formal statement which read in part:

"Communist leaders all over the world would be happy to see a bitter, name-calling contest develop between President Johnson and congressional leaders at this crucial time. Mr. Johnson's remarks made during his Sunday press conference in Texas, if he was referring to me, are the possible result of a misunderstanding which I trust the White House will correct.

"I refuse to be baited into a verbal Donneybrook with the Commander in Chief that would play into the hands of Hanoi, Peking and Moscow."

The White House did not "correct" the "misunderstanding" as urged diplomatically by Ford.

My initial reaction when I read the story in New Hampshire was to do nothing. Certainly, I thought, some of the other newsmen at the luncheon—there were about a dozen—would correct the record. Back at the somewhat grandiloquently named Golden Winds Cottage, I found I couldn't get rid of the nagging thought that a terrible injustice had been done to a decent man who had been my host at a luncheon. I discussed the matter with my wife and then said, "If there's any stationery in the cottage, I'll write Jerry a letter and try to straighten this mess out."

I had brought a typewriter but neglected to bring paper. After some search in the cottage, I found one yellowed sheet of paper. I wrote the following letter:

Dear Jerry:
    I have learned belatedly, here in the distant reaches of New Hampshire, of the President's wholly unfair criticism—presumably of you—

of an alleged violation of confidence concerning the alleged contents and influence of Sen. Mansfield's statement, read at the White House briefing on Vietnam.

I was one of your guests at the background luncheon. It was I who asked you about the Mansfield statement. I said I had learned that Sen. Mansfield had read a two-page statement critical of Vietnam at the White House meeting and asked you for details. Your only comment, as I recall it, was that the statement seemed to you to be longer than two pages.

You said nothing—I repeat nothing—to the effect that Sen. Mansfield argued against calling up the reserves or that this had any influence on the President's decision.

I was struck at the luncheon by your great sense of national responsibility when you told us that though you had been advocating a different course in Vietnam from the President's, you were going to support our Commander-in-Chief in the decisions he had made.

The President has been ill-informed—perhaps by inaccurate or tendentious reporting by some newsmen. Please feel free to make this letter public or to send a copy to the President.

Ford followed up both suggestions in the last sentence. Together with Senate Republican leader Everett M. Dirksen, he called a press conference in which he distributed copies of my letter. He sent my letter to the president with a note saying, "I must respectfully request a conference with you to determine on what basis you were erroneously informed as to my views."

Bill D. Moyers, White House press secretary, said later that day that the president had no plans for a special meeting with Ford. He said he had not seen the communication from Mr. Ford, although excerpts from the press tickers had been read to him. Pressed for comment on my letter, Moyers said, "There is nothing I can contribute to that correspondence between Congressman Ford and his friend. Nor can I add or subtract anything from the accurate response to Mr. Strout's statement and query in Texas."

Note the subtle dig in those words "his friend." Ford was not then, as he later became, a friend of mine. He was just a news source, and considering the diminished number of troops he was able to command after he was chosen leader, not an important news source at that.

Recounting the episode some weeks later, Larry King, a freelance Washington writer, wrote, "Sam Shaffer is either the bravest man in Washington or he has his income taxes in order."

After all, at best, I called the president misinformed; at worst, a liar.

I had no idea of the consequences of my letter until my return to Washington when Ford took me aside to express his gratitude for my timely intervention. "For three days, Sam," he said, "I wandered about in a daze. I couldn't put my mind on anything. My leadership position was wobbly enough. Now I felt it had been destroyed. The President of the United States had said in almost so many words that I was undermining the national security. I had made up my mind to resign as minority leader. The morning I made that decision your letter arrived. I shall never forget it."

The White House never mentioned the allegations against Ford thereafter. He remained as leader and went on to become vice president and president.

After the 1976 elections and his defeat by Jimmy Carter, my wife and I set out for New York City to celebrate my retirement as a journalist after forty years. One evening, while dining with friends in a sixth-floor walkup apartment on Christopher Street in Greenwich Village, I called my hotel to learn whether there were any messages for me.

"You have a message, sir," said the hotel operator, "but I think somebody is putting me on. The message is for you to call the president at the White House."

I put through the call, and he came on the line, his voice booming, "Congratulations, old-timer." "On what, Mr. President?" I responded. "On your retirement," he said. I hadn't the faintest idea how he learned about it, but when he did, he was determined to talk with me by phone. I began taking notes to report the conversation later to my hosts and wife.

"We've had a great relationship, Sam," he went on. "You're a great man and a great reporter. I can't thank you enough for all you've done for me. I just want you to know that. I want you to know I hadn't forgotten."

I wanted to make him feel good too, so, moving the discussion around to the election, I said, "Mr. President, if there's any consolation, there are so damn many more Democrats than Republicans in the country."

But the president didn't grasp at that straw. Instead, and quite realistically, he said, "No, Sam, the people wanted a

change. We have a clear conscience. We worked like hell and
did the best we can."

"Well," I said, "there is consolation in this: like Eisenhower,
you will be leaving office with the affection and good will of the
American people. I don't think there is anybody in the United
States who dislikes Jerry Ford."

Almost wistfully, he responded, "Yes, history will treat us
kindly."

There was more along this line. Replying to my question
about *his* plans for retirement, Ford said, "We'll be active—aca-
demically, philanthropically, politically, and maybe in the business world. I want to see some young people and answer their
questions and take a good look around America."

"Can we get together and have a good chat?" I asked.

"Oh, yes," Ford said. "After we get all this crap out of the
way."

I like to think that whoever left that yellowing sheet of paper
behind in the Golden Winds Cottage unwittingly had a hand in
changing the course of history.

Did I do the right thing by history? My answer can best be
given in the opening words of Jimmy Carter's inaugural address:
"For myself and for our nation, I want to thank my predecessor
for all he has done to heal our land."

CHAPTER 17

The Abdication
of Richard Nixon

~~~~~~

This book has been devoted primarily to the Congress and only incidentally to the presidency. The abdication of Richard M. Nixon on August 9, 1974, belongs in this narrative because it was a resurgent Congress, whose powers he had deliberately set out to emasculate after his landslide victory on November 7, 1972, that brought him down.

In addition, the resignation in disgrace of a president who only twenty-one months earlier had carried every state but one is worth recounting in itself—especially if one has some fresh details of a "lofty scene" that will certainly "be acted o'er/ In states unborn and in accents yet unknown" (to quote Shakespeare's *Julius Caesar*).

When we think of Watergate, we think of perjury and obstruction of justice stemming from the burglarizing, on orders from on high, of the headquarters of the Democratic National Committee and of a psychiatrist's office; of illegal wiretapping; of conspiracies to "launder" campaign funds; of compiling lists of "enemies" to be harassed by the awesome power of the federal government; of the steady stream of lies by the president to the American people; and of the effort to corrupt the FBI and the CIA. These offenses were serious enough to institute impeachment proceedings in the House and to drive Nixon from office before he could be convicted in the Senate and stripped of his presidency.

But in this writer's opinion, Nixon's efforts to render impotent the powers of the Congress were far graver, though subtler, in import, for they struck directly at the constitutional framework of the government. The Founding Fathers gave Congress the power of the purse. In addition, they stated unequivocally that if a bill vetoed by the president is still approved by a two-thirds vote of both houses, "it shall become law." Nixon found a way to nullify both the power of the purse and the effectiveness of a veto disapproval.

Nor was this all. Congress cannot legislate effectively in a vacuum. It needs information before it can write or reject a law. To obtain that information, it must have virtually the unrestricted power to investigate the need, if any, for a law. Even when no particular legislation is in sight, the right to investigate has been consistently upheld by the courts.

To enhance this prerogative, Congress employs the power of subpoena. It has the power to jail recalcitrant witnesses—even on the premises of the Capitol if it so chooses, though it rarely does, preferring to turn the miscreants over to federal prosecutors and the courts. Even cabinet officers must respond to committee invitations to testify. But there is a gray area, covered by "executive privilege." White House aides are protected from the congressional power to compel testimony. A president cannot function if he is unable to protect the confidentiality of his closest advisers.

What Nixon tried to do was cripple the congressional power of the purse and restrict the power to investigate. In the first instance, he deliberately ignored the congressional will despite the overriding of his vetoes; in the second, he sought to extend the mantle of executive privilege to his cabinet departments.

And he might have gotten away with it, for his methods were subtle and the issues not the kind to stir Congress into impeachment proceedings. Who could fault a president for refusing to spend the money Congress appropriates—unless he possessed the level of sophistication to grasp the constitutional problem involved? The same would apply to the "executive privilege" shield he tried to erect between much of his administration and the Congress.

He didn't get away with this potentially serious assault upon the Constitution because of Watergate.

Despite his forty-nine-state sweep, Nixon did not carry Congress with him. The Democrats retained control of Congress, increasing their majority in the Senate and suffering only minimal losses in the House.

Senate Democratic leader Mike Mansfield left no doubts about *his* interpretation of the November elections when he summoned the Democratic senators into caucus on the morning of January 3, 1973, just before the Ninety-third Congress convened. "We meet today with a new majority," he told them. "We meet with new responsibilities and a new mandate. The recent election tells us something of what the people of the nation expect of the Senate. If there is one mandate to us above all others, it is to exercise our separate and distinct constitutional role in the operation of the federal government. The people have not chosen to be governed by one branch of government alone."

Mansfield's first priority was the creation of a committee, to be headed by the Senate's foremost constitutional authority, Sam Ervin, Jr., of North Carolina, manned by senators who could avoid partisan attack because they clearly had no ambitions for higher office, and armed with all the money and subpoena powers necessary to undertake a thorough investigation of Watergate and the related scandals connected with the 1972 presidential election campaign.

Republicans had no choice but to go along or appear to be part of the cover-up of a rapidly developing scandal. The Senate approved the creation of the committee by seventy-seven to zero. It was to become the instrument for the destruction of the "mandate" Nixon thought he had won in November; the crippling of his presidential powers; and the setting into motion of an ineluctable train of events leading to the institution of impeachment proceedings and flight from office. In the beginning, this was not Mansfield's purpose. After it was all over, I said to him one day over a cup of coffee in his office, "Mike, you realize that you toppled a president." He replied with a dour smile, "Well, that wasn't my purpose. I just wanted to find out what happened at Watergate."

Though all the elements for the historic clash between the

president and the Congress were present from the start, their magnitude was not immediately apparent. In fact, there were solemn pledges of cooperation from both sides: Two weeks before the session began, Ted Kennedy told a Los Angeles audience at a $500-a-plate testimonial dinner, "There is more good will in Congress now toward Mr. Nixon than perhaps at any time in his career in public life. I, for one, will extend the olive branch to the administration in the coming Congress." And, in his State of the Union message, Nixon said: " . . . I pledge to do my part to achieve a constructive working relationship with the Congress. My sincere hope is that the executive and legislative branches can work together in this great undertaking in a positive spirit of mutual respect and cooperation."

The confusion over who got the "mandate," and just what that mandate was, inevitably produced the incendiary friction. Nixon interpreted that mandate as an endorsement of his New Federalism philosophy, first enunciated on August 9, 1969, by which "funds and responsibility will flow from Washington to the States and to the people." The Democrats, not inaccurately, interpreted this Nixonian effort to reorder the nation's domestic priorities as an attempt to undo Lyndon Johnson's Great Society, John Kennedy's New Frontier, Harry S. Truman's Fair Deal, and Franklin D. Roosevelt's New Deal.

The Democratic Congress would have no part of the New Federalism. As Speaker Carl Albert put it when he saw the extent to which the president planned to curtail federal programs in the fiscal 1974 budget, "Congress will not permit the president to lay waste the great programs which we have developed during the decades past." So Nixon resorted to an extraordinary and extralegal method of reordering domestic priorities: he would impound the money voted by Congress. And if it overrode his veto, he would still refuse to spend the money.

Thus Congress would become a nullity. As various sectors of the nation's economy would wake up to the fact that money voted would be spent only at the president's will, they would turn to the White House, not Capitol Hill, for relief. Power would flow steadily westward down Pennsylvania Avenue from the halls of Congress to the presidential mansion.

Of course, there's nothing new about impounding funds. What was new was Nixon's abuse of the power. Other presidents, going all the way back to Thomas Jefferson, have impounded

funds. Jefferson impounded $50,000 which Congress had appro-
priated for fifteen gunboats on the Mississippi. "A favorable and
peaceful turn of affairs," he reported to Congress, "rendered
immediate construction unnecessary." He took a little more
time and built better gunboats with the money. Reviewing the
history of impoundments, Democratic Sen. Birch Bayh of Indiana told the Senate:

> The impoundment actions of the current administration are basi-
> cally outside these historical precedents, for they seek to reorder do-
> mestic priorities in a manner antithetical to the priorities set by the
> Congress in its legislation. And these impoundments cover a substan-
> tial portion of federal spending: approximately seventeen to twenty
> percent of controllable funds have been impounded since 1969.
> We can hardly consider Congress as a coequal branch of govern-
> ment if the legislation it passes may be ignored by the executive
> branch through the procedure of impoundment.

That's not the way Nixon viewed the election. Speaking to reporters at Camp David three weeks after the election, he said:

> ... The tendency is for an administration to run out of steam after
> the first four years, and then to coast and usually coast downhill. ...
> What I am trying to do is to change that historical pattern. The only
> way that historical pattern can be changed is to change not only some
> of the players, but also some of the plays. ...
> The American people are never satisfied with things as they are.
> The American people want change. I think they want change that
> works, not radical change, not destructive change but change that
> builds rather than destroys. It is the kind of change that I have tried to
> stand for and I will continue to work for over the next four years.

By midyear, Nixon had impounded $16.7 billion voted by
Congress, sometimes over his veto. He used the impoundment
weapon to terminate two percent Rural Electrification Administration loans; the Farmers Home Administration's water and
sewer grant program; and the Environmental Protection Agency's water pollution control funds, just to cite a few instances.
The $6 billion in water pollution control funds had been ap-
proved unanimously by Congress.

When the Department of Agriculture, under presidential orders, announced the termination of the water and sewer grants,
Congressman W. R. Poage of Texas, chairman of the House Agriculture Committee, asked the department to state its legal justi-

fication for impounding money voted by Congress. The department replied that the action taken was lawful because the appropriation bill was "permissive in nature." No one had ever employed such a dodge before. The usual language in bills is "the President is hereby authorized to spend. . . ." The word "authorized" has never been viewed in the entire span of American history as "permissive." So the Congress reenacted the bill to make the expenditure mandatory: "The President is hereby directed. . . . " Nixon vetoed the bill on the ground that the mandatory spending proviso created "grave constitutional questions" about the separation of powers. The House sustained the veto. Here we had the unprecedented spectacle of a president effectively nullifying the laws he didn't like by impounding the funds and then effectively employing the weapon of the veto to frustrate further the will of Congress.

White House congressional liaison aides were quite candid in discussing Nixon's use of the veto weapon with legislators. One of them told me, "Call it government by veto, if you will. The fact remains that though the Democrats have the majorities in Congress, all we need is one-third-plus-one to have our way."

In its frustration, Congress tried two methods to restore its legislative powers. It went to the courts to strike down Nixon's actions as illegal, and it wrote legislation to limit sharply his powers to withhold funds Congress authorized to be spent.

The first court test of the president's power to withhold funds appropriated by Congress resulted in a victory for Congress when the Eighth U.S. Circuit Court of Appeals ruled on April 2 that the administration illegally withheld construction money apportioned to the state of Missouri under the 1956 Federal Aid Highway Act, which established the Highway Trust Fund. In a two to one ruling, the court held that funds appropriated by Congress "are not to be withheld from obligation for purposes totally unrelated to the highway programs." The Nixon defense was that the expenditure would be inflationary.

By early September, about thirty impoundment cases had been decided, primarily at the federal district court level. The Nixon administration was on the losing side in all but five.

Simultaneously, a bill was slowly wending its way through Congress to put a halt to such impoundments. It was slow going because Nixon's "government by veto" was working, and enactment of the proposed restraint had to wait until his power was eroded by the Watergate developments. The steady decline in the margin by which the House sustained his vetoes was an indication of the decline in Nixon's fortunes directly traceable to Watergate. He had fifty-one votes to spare on April 10, when the House sustained his veto of the rural water and sewer grants. This had shrunk to just five on August 1, on the veto of the Emergency Medical Services bill.

Meanwhile, let us look at parallel developments on the Watergate front. The Watergate cover-up began to unravel March 23, the day Judge John J. Sirica had set for passing sentences in the criminal trial of the seven Watergate defendants—all of them small fry in the scandal whose dimensions were only just becoming apparent. Sirica read a letter in court which one of the defendants, James McCord, had written to him earlier in the week charging that perjury had been committed, that other persons besides those convicted had been involved in the break-in, and that political pressures had been applied to make the defendants plead guilty.

Once McCord started to talk, the story of the cover-up began to unfold steadily, first in the form of leaks to the press, and then as hard news as the Ervin committee got under way.

Even before the Ervin committee hearings began formally on May 17, the unraveling was proceeding. Jeb Stuart Magruder, a former White House aide and Nixon's deputy campaign director, was the first to resign. On April 25, he quit his $36,000-a-year job at the Commerce Department.

Three days later, White House counsel John W. Dean III was linked in press reports with the Watergate cover-up. In a statement which was not cleared by the White House, he asserted he would not be made a "scapegoat" in the affair.

On April 30, Nixon announced the resignations of four of his closest aides: Bob Haldeman, John Ehrlichman, John Dean, and U.S. Attorney General Richard Kleindienst.

On May 22, Nixon issued a 4,000-word statement on the Watergate case in which he conceded for the first time that there had been "wide-ranging efforts" in the White House to cover up aspects of the case—but denied that they took place with his approval or knowledge.

On June 25, John Dean took the stand before the Ervin committee and became the first person to implicate the president directly in the White House conspiracy to cover up the Watergate scandal. He began his testimony with a 245-page statement that took him six hours to read. Accompanying the statement were some fifty documents that he turned over as supporting evidence. One set included lists of "political enemies"—persons singled out for retribution because of opposition to administration policies. Techniques such as Internal Revenue Service audits and the denial of federal grants were proposed as weapons.

During his testimony, Dean listed a number of specific conversations he had had with the president which indicated presidential knowledge of the cover-up. The dates became vitally important after a subsequent revelation by the Ervin committee that all presidential office conversations were taped.

If one were to pick a date when the turn in Nixon's fortunes, in his tests of strength with Congress, could be considered decisive, it would be June 28—three days after Dean began his damning testimony. That was the day when Congress, for the first time in American history, used its ultimate weapon, the power of the purse, to stop a war—and succeeded beyond its wildest hopes.

Two days earlier, Congress had approved an amendment to the Second Supplemental Appropriation Bill, barring the use of all funds in this and all other bills previously enacted from being used to support combat activities in or over Cambodia and Laos. It would, in short, stop the bombing of Cambodia which had been going on for years, nineteen months of these in total secrecy from the American people and their representatives in Congress. Nixon vetoed the bill in twenty-four hours, maintaining that the bombing prohibition would "cripple or destroy" any chance of reaching a negotiated settlement of the Cambodian conflict. He also let it be known he would veto any other bill to which an immediate bombing halt was attached. The House sustained the veto, and Mike Mansfield declared the Senate would keep right on adding the prohibition to other bills "again and again and again until the will of the people prevails."

A new factor entered the equation. On June 30, the United States government would be unable to pay its obligations if the temporary debt ceiling increase was not extended. Also, the government itself would be without funds to operate if a so-called "continuing resolution" was not passed by Congress. (At that time, the fiscal year ended on June 30. Congress had not yet completed action on the regular money bills to run the government. Following past practice, it would pass a continuing resolution for a given number of weeks, allowing the government to keep spending at last year's rate, until it could vote the money bills.) So, on the day Nixon vetoed the supplemental bill, the Senate added the bombing prohibition to a bill extending the debt ceiling. Meanwhile, the House added the same prohibition to the continuing resolution.

To employ a cliché, Congress and Nixon were now eyeball-to-eyeball. Congress was in a mood to force the government to come to a dead halt. Millions of civil service workers would not receive their paychecks. Payments on government contracts could not be made. Social Security checks couldn't be cashed. Soldiers, sailors, and airmen would go payless. It was Nixon who blinked.

He offered a compromise: a bombing halt by September 1. No, said Congress. A forty-five-day compromise was worked out. As a result of the congressional use of the purse strings, the bombing of Cambodia at long last came to a halt on August 15. Assistant Senate Majority Leader Robert C. Byrd stated flatly that the bombing halt would never have been voted by Congress had Nixon not been weakened by Watergate.

There was a greater legislative humiliation to come.

On November 7, both houses of Congress finally voted to override a Nixon veto—thirteen votes to spare in the Senate and four in the House. The override did not come on a minor bill, but on one of the most important in the history of the country. The action came on the War Powers Bill, a measure to restrict presidential warmaking powers. The bill, now law, which the president had denounced in his veto message as both "dangerous and unconstitutional," sets a sixty-day limit on the president's powers to commit the armed forces of the U.S. At any time, Congress can stop this with a concurrent resolution, an action that does not require presidential approval. The law also requires the president to consult with Congress before acting and makes him report in writing within forty-eight hours after he does act.

"The time was ripe," commented Democratic Congressman Clement J. Zablocki of Wisconsin, manager of the War Powers Bill in the House. Beyond the merits of the bill itself, Zablocki cited the Watergate scandal, the firing of special prosecutor Archibald Cox which so outraged the nation, and the controversy surrounding the Watergate tapes. In the Senate, Nixon loyalist John Tower of Texas, who led the futile effort to sustain the veto, said, "I realize this is a time when everyone can with impunity kick the president, because he is at a low ebb in popularity, and many people are calling for impeachment or resignation."

Congress wasn't through with the business of reasserting its powers. It enacted legislation to restrict presidential impounding powers. Any refusal to spend had to be agreed to by a vote of both houses; any withholding or delay could be overcome by a resolution passed by either house disapproving the president's action. (In order to hold the Republican votes in line against a veto, the Democrats agreed to reform badly needed congressional budget procedures. Budget committees would be created in each house to set target totals for appropriations, spending, taxes, the budget surplus or deficit, and the federal debt.)

The other idea that Nixon had to curb congressional power was couched in the form of executive reorganization in order to achieve "a trimmer federal government." Six government departments, embracing Interior, Commerce, Labor, Health, Education and Welfare, Housing and Urban Development, and Transportation would be reorganized into four departments: Community Development, Natural Resources, Economic Affairs, and Human Resources. On the surface, the proposal was plausible. But there was a catch which few recognized at the time: The cabinet officers heading these all-embracing four new departments would also be White House counselors. This meant that at any time the president could prevent congressional grilling of these cabinet officers by flinging the mantle of executive privilege around them.

Congress would have no part of such a reorganization, principally because it would radically upset congressional committee jurisdictions. As Nixon's strength waned, he made no effort to push the proposals which would have faced resistance in the best of times.

Summarizing the session for his colleagues, Mansfield said at the end of the year 1973:

> It was not an uncommon view in this city at the time [when Congress convened] that Congress had all but ceased to have relevance in this government. At the start of the year, the beginnings of contempt

for the constitutional role of Congress were clearly to be seen in the ruthless resort to impoundment practices and in the abuses of executive privilege.

That is what the Ninety-third Congress confronted when, in early January, it assembled for the first time. Frankly, I have never known members of the Senate to be more concerned about the security of constitutional structure of the government than they were at that time. There was fear of what was transpiring but, I am happy to say, there was also a determination to halt the erosion.

Though the erosion of congressional power was halted and reversed, the diminution of presidential power continued unabated for Richard Nixon. On October 20 there was the memorable "Saturday Night Massacre." Nixon ordered his attorney general, Elliott Richardson, to fire Archibald Cox, the special prosecutor. When Richardson refused, he was fired. For the same reason, he fired Deputy Attorney General William D. Ruckleshaus. Solicitor General Robert H. Bork, next in line, became acting attorney general and fired Cox.

Indignation swept the country. The deans of seventeen law schools signed a petition asking Congress to create a committee to "consider the necessity" of impeaching Nixon. And Speaker Carl Albert agreed to have the House Judiciary Committee begin an inquiry into the grounds for impeaching the president.

Republicans, looking ahead to the elections a year away, became frantic. Most of them could not bring themselves to believe that Nixon was part of the Watergate crimes and cover-up. All of them believed his only salvation lay in, as they put it, "letting it all hang out." What was needed, they insisted, was "Operation Candor."

At their request, Nixon began meeting with groups of Republican senators whom he invited to ask him anything and "to pull no punches" either in questions about Watergate or in their advice to him. And they pulled no punches. They asked him why he didn't pay more income taxes and whether Tricia Nixon was getting a special tax deal. He was asked whether International Telephone and Telegraph got a favorable antitrust decision out of the administration because it had promised a $400,000 underwriting of the 1972 Republican National Convention in San Diego. He was asked whether he had increased the milk subsidy in return for a heavy campaign contribution.

He was advised to resign. He was urged to submit voluntarily

The last moments of the thirty-seventh Presidency are poignantly portrayed here as Nixon finishes his farewell to the White House staff. He fights to hold back tears; Pat Nixon can no longer restrain them. The off-the-cuff remarks will long be remembered as troubled, meandering, and maudlin. A little later that day, while flying to temporary exile in San Clemente, California, his Presidency expired.

The most solemn message ever conveyed to a President was brought to Nixon by these three Republican leaders. Opposite from left to right: Senators Hugh Scott of Pennsylvania and Barry Goldwater of Arizona and Congressman John Rhodes, also of Arizona. They told him there was no way of heading off an impeachment vote in the House and that a trial and conviction in the Senate was a certainty. Nixon had no choice but to resign his Presidency.

Below, while a military honor guard stands stiffly at attention and the soon-to-be thirty-eighth President Gerald Ford, far right, looks thoughtfully into an unknown future, Nixon stands in the door of the White House helicopter and gives his familiar victory gesture. It was a memorable, if inappropriate, stance, but it demonstrated that President Nixon's resiliency had not been destroyed by his tragedy. He flew to San Clemente and home.

to impeachment proceedings. He was told he couldn't restore a badly shattered credibility without some such dramatic action as appearing before a joint session of Congress and answering questions from the floor, or going before the Watergate committee either on the Hill or in the White House and answering questions on live television.

The proceedings had an air of unreality about them. One of those who felt this was freshman Republican Sen. Pete Domenici, a hardworking young moderate from New Mexico. To add to the unreality, his chair collapsed under him during a tense moment, the back falling off and the legs breaking. He brought home a piece of a broken leg to show his wife. It was more than a souvenir; it was evidence that such a meeting had really taken place.

To grasp the extraordinary events of the week of "Operation Candor" it would help to set the scene at one of them. Shepherded by Senate Republican leader Hugh Scott, a group of fourteen senators in alphabetical order was ushered into the "California" Room.

Scott, a suave and debonair native Virginian who became a Philadelphia lawyer, served sixteen years in the House and eighteen in the Senate before retiring in 1976. He was a passionate collector of Chinese art and the author of several books, including *The Golden Age of Chinese Art.* He was a vigorous seventy-six when he retired and went back to practicing law—this time in Washington. An early supporter of Dwight Eisenhower, he was in the "progressive" or moderate wing of the Republican party. He supported Nixon until late in the unraveling of the Watergate scandal when he suspected—correctly—he was being "used" by the Nixon crowd. "I'll be goddamned if I'll be played for a patsy," he said as the awful truth about Nixon dawned belatedly on him.

Harry S. Truman often had his cronies in the "California" Room for poker games, recklessly trying to fill inside straights, running out of money, and borrowing small sums from Democratic Sen. Clinton Anderson of New Mexico, a regular member of these games. Anderson never figured out how he could properly remind a president that he hadn't paid him back. Fortunately, Truman himself remembered—on occasion. Dwight D. Eisenhower, who took some pride in his culinary attainments, cooked beef stew there for intimates. Little Caroline Kennedy used it as a schoolroom. In the Johnson years, Lucy and her fiancé, Pat Nugent, dated there and danced to rock 'n roll records.

After the Nixons moved in, they began using it as an occasional and informal dining room. When Julie Nixon and David Eisenhower wanted to eat dinner alone or just listen to the stereo, they would preempt the room. Officially, the room, a relatively small circular room on the top floor of the White House, is called the Solarium. A huge picture window looks to the south. The view is one of the finest in Washington. One can see the Washington Monument and the Jefferson Memorial and the hills of Virginia across the Potomac. Pat Nixon on occasion stepped onto the porch behind the railings to sunbathe.

For some reason still baffling to the White House staff, the Solarium suddenly acquired an unofficial name during the week of Operation Candor. Some staffer referred to it as the "California Room" and the name stuck. Perhaps it was the decor that suggested the name. Two yellow sofas, covered with an orange and red floral print, were placed along the wall. There was a small yellow table in the center of the room surrounded by yellow wicker chairs. The rest of the walls was lined with similar chairs; the four normally around the center table were lined up against the walls with the others for the extraordinary, historic, unprecedented—to many of those participating, almost unbelievable—series of meetings starting at 5 P.M. and running from two to three hours.

At one meeting, the senators entered the room promptly at 5:00. The center table was loaded with canapés and hors d'oeuvres. Waiters carried in trays of drinks. For fifteen minutes the senators chewed on tidbits, swallowed their drinks, and chatted. Then the president entered the room, shook hands all around, and asked his guests to sit down. He had a broad smile on his face which looked freshly shaved and relaxed. He wore a light blue cashmere jacket with dark trousers, which drew mumbles of praise from some of the senators. He sat down on a chair so that he was facing the broad window. He started out with a review of the situation in the Middle East, Kissinger's trip to China, and the energy crisis. Marlow Cook of Kentucky muttered, "Mr. President, we didn't come here to hear about these things."

Nixon heard Cook. The following evening, with another group of senators, he started right in on Watergate. While the president was talking, Cook discovered that he himself was playing with a two-bladed knife that he always carried on him. It suddenly occurred to him that he was sitting right next to the president with an open knife in his hands, absentmindedly opening and closing the sharp-edged blades. Praying that the Secret Service would not suddenly descend on him, he closed the knife and hurriedly tucked it into his pocket.

The president turned first to Howard Baker of Tennessee and asked him to speak. Baker, who was very tense and nervous throughout the meeting, told the president bluntly: "We're in a hell of a lot of trouble. You're in trouble and we're in trouble. We've got to find some means of getting it all out—of letting it all hang out.

"I think you should come before the Watergate committee, either at the Capitol or in the White House, and you should answer questions on camera regardless of how many days it takes. It would be one way by which your credibility could be established."

The president said he was considering a number of options. Baker shot back, "A press conference won't do it, Mr. President."

The president, maintaining an outwardly calm demeanor, turned to Cook and asked, "Marlow, what do you think?"

"Mr. President," Cook replied, "I've always been of the opinion that you should have called Sam Ervin after John Dean testified and said, 'Sam I'll be there at ten in the morning.' If you had, you wouldn't be facing this situation.

"The way you have handled this is comparable to a father saying to his kids that you can't open the presents until Christmas night. You know how impatient they would get. The American people have waited too long for the facts. We're beyond the point of a response to everything new that's brought out. The executive branch has worked by reacting to events.

"I totally disagree with your lawyers who tell you that you can't release the tapes and other memoranda in your possession until the courts give you that permission. The owner of the tapes can release them at any time he wants to. I can't for the life of me figure out why your lawyers can't find a way to get them out, especially if they contain the evidence, as you say, to prove John Dean a liar." (The next morning, Cook's position was upheld in a ruling by Judge Sirica.)

The president turned to Edward Brooke of Massachusetts. "Ed, you're next."

It was a tense moment. Brooke had already stated on a nationally televised program that the president should resign because "he has lost the confidence of the people." Brooke, the Senate's only black member and, by a long stretch, its handsomest, was defeated in 1978 after twelve years in that body. Considered unbeatable for years, he foundered because of a messy divorce proceeding which turned up personal financial practices so questionable that even the Senate Ethics Committee had to look into them. The "clearance" given Senator Brooke was patently equivocal.

Brooke said, "Mr. President, your administration will be known for great heights and great depths. It's now in a great depth. You need to restore your credibility. The only way is to tell the truth. You've got to come across to the American people with all the facts. They've got to believe you. It may take a miracle. You have worked miracles, such as your initiatives in China and the detente with the Soviet Union. Maybe you can work one here." And then, after a slight pause, he added, "And that's what it will take."

Brooke suggested that the president consider appearing before a joint session of Congress and answer questions raised on the floor. The president said this was among the options which had been presented to him, but he indicated he didn't like the idea.

"Mr. President," Brooke went on, "I came to my suggestion on resigning very reluctantly because of the destruction of public opinion that has taken place, and I've seen nothing to change my position since. You can't restore the public confidence in a meeting with fifteen senators.

"I know of no impeachable offense you have committed, and I hope none will ever come to light. But that's not the issue. The issue is public confidence. I think these investigations will continue. They'll never stop. There will be years of trials."

Nixon interjected, "I know that." He then turned to James Buckley of New York who told him, "The problem, Mr. Presi-

dent, is so serious, I'm not sure you understand just how serious
it is. You should open up everything in the White House down
to every shoebox."

Buckley, whose closely cropped hair was as old-fashioned as
his rigidly conservative philosophy, was the first Republican to
call publicly for Nixon's resignation. Long before Nixon's culpa-
bility was clearly established, Buckley felt the president's useful-
ness was at an end because of "the erosion of his moral
authority." Buckley was defeated after one term.

The president tried to lighten the moment by turning back to
Brooke for a quip. "Ed, I can't always do what you want, such as
saving the Boston navy yard." Brooke didn't smile. He had an
anguished expression on his face as he said in a soft voice, "You
know what I said on the TV program. I said I thought you had
three options. One is impeachment, but I was against that because it is a very long and tortuous process and could take
months and possibly years and it would divide the country. The
second was that you would stay in office and limp along for the
next three years. And the third course is resignation."

Those who have had occasion to study Nixon under stress can
always tell when his tension builds up. Unlike others who raise
their voices, Nixon, when he is feeling most tense and is holding
it in check, lowers his voice and keeps it at that level for a long
time. Nixon's voice was significantly lower when he said, albeit
with a strained smile, "I know what you said, Ed. I bear no malice against you. I understand your reasoning. That would be the
easy way out. I won't resign."

Norris Cotton of New Hampshire, a member of the Senate for
twenty-eight years, who retired in 1976, advanced the impeachment idea as the best way of "clearing the air" because he didn't
think there were the votes for impeachment. The president
came down very strongly against the proposal. He was harsher
in his condemnation of the impeachment approach than of any
other proposal advanced.

The president in his reply to Buckley—and in comments
made during the quite frequently unstructured dialogue
that developed—made his now familiar rebuttals to the numerous charges: His intervention in the ITT case was a result of his
belief that bigness alone is no excuse for antitrust action and that
in some cases, such as competing against Japanese cartels, big-

ness is required. The raise in the milk subsidy was in response to congressional dairy bloc pressures. He said he was going to get all the facts out, from Tricia's alleged income tax manipulations to the break-in of Daniel Ellsberg's psychiatrist's office. He said that once the March 21 tape was made public, it would prove that Dean was telling him then for the first time about the Watergate scandal's involvement with the White House.

Nixon admitted the accuracy of the wire service story in which his chief aide, General Al Haig, quoted him as saying, "Oh, my God" several times as the president listened to that tape. "I hope," Nixon said, "people won't think I was taking the Lord's name in vain."

Whereupon Cook said, "Mr. President, I don't think the American people will think any the less of you for that. Frankly, I think you ought to cuss a little more." Henry Bellmon of Oklahoma, silent up to then, added, "A lot of people in Oklahoma would like it if you just stood up and said, 'I'm gonna straighten this goddamn thing out.'" (The revelations of the kind of language Nixon actually used nearly all the time in the Oval Office were still in the future.)

There was only one other light moment to break the tension in the meeting, and that was when Domenici's chair broke and the president quipped, "Those chairs are hand-me-downs from other administrations."

Bob Dole of Kansas, who had been Nixon's stoutest champion on the Senate floor until the Watergate situation got too hot even for him, complained about the "lack of continuity" in the Watergate matter. Something unanticipated was always turning up to embarrass the president's defenders. "When the people in Marshall County, Kansas, start speaking out, Mr. President," he said, "you better look out."

Nixon said, "Bob, you don't have to worry about that. You were chairman of the National Committee during the campaign, and everybody knows you had no connection with Watergate."

"That's what I keep trying to tell the people of Kansas," said Dole, who was running hard for a second Senate term.

Tall, handsome, and highly articulate, Bob Dole was reelected after pulling a Roorback on his Democratic opponent, a Topeka gynecologist and U.S. congressman named William R. Roy. At

the last moment of a statewide televised debate supposedly limited to agricultural issues, Dole suddenly accused Roy of per-
forming abortions. It was too late for the flabbergasted Roy to
reply effectively that, as a physician, he had performed perfectly legal and proper therapeutic abortions to save the lives of his
patients. President Ford picked Dole as his running mate at the
Kansas City convention in 1976. Dole's reputation as a hatchet
man did not help the ticket appreciably and may have hurt
Ford's election chances. Three years later, Dole, with character-
istic vigor, plunged into the Republican presidential nomination
race.

Bill Brock of Tennessee added his voice, "Those who support
you are bottled up. There's no effort by the White House to get
out the facts. The people want the facts out so they can get on
your side. Hell, I make speeches defending the administration,
then pick up the morning paper, read something new, and I feel
like a fool."

After two hours and fifteen minutes, the president turned to
Baker for concluding comments. Baker was almost beside himself with frustration, and his manner and words showed it. One
senator told me later, "I have never seen Howard so emotional,
so upset."

"Mr. President," Baker said, "I'm frustrated. I'm going out of
this meeting without knowing where we're going. I want to
urge you to remember that this comes from friends of yours who
love their country. I hope that your friends will share in your decision."

The president said, "That's what this meeting is all about. And
when I do [reach a decision] I'll meet with the leadership."

"Mr. President," Baker said, "I mean *when* you meet with
them, not *after* you meet with them."

Nixon, slightly taken aback, said, "That's what I said."

The next meeting with Republican senators came twenty-four
hours later. It lasted three hours and ten minutes. Going directly
into the Watergate matter, Nixon said firmly he was not going to
resign. "I won't walk away from any problem."

Mark Hatfield of Oregon, who had pondered the remarks he
would make to the president for several days, said, "The country
has been deeply wounded. Basically, it is a loss of trust and confidence in your administration. Frankly, the communications thus

far from your administration have been the mixture of belliger-
ence and defensiveness and not of strength. Therefore, these
have been interpreted as guilt.

"The American people respond when people indicate a need
for help. To reverse the present situation and restore the credibility of the administration, there should be some statement of
regret and sorrow that the country is in the condition it is today.

"At least, you could admit your mistake in strategy and ask for
help in restoring the trust. In order for them to respond, they
need the facts. I don't feel you need my help or the help of the
Republicans in the Senate."

Hatfield, a deeply religious man who had been, successively, a
political science professor, governor of Oregon for eight years,
and a member of the Senate since 1966 where he was a leader
of the moderate wing of the party, had written these words out
the night before and memorized them. In 1968, he had hoped
he would be picked as Nixon's running mate. Afterwards he
counted himself as fortunate for being passed over. Hatfield
now urged Nixon to invite the Ervin committee to the East
Room of the White House and answer the questions—on television. If there were still unanswered questions, the president
should call in a panel of distinguished newsmen. "This," Hatfield said, "offers you the opportunity to get the facts across that
you say will clear you and move you toward some kind of recon-
ciliation with the people."

Nixon indicated he would respond at a certain point, but that
there were certain legal problems involving people whose cases
were still to be settled in court.

"Do we want the truth, Mr. President," Hatfield asked, "or
convictions? If this is the only way to get the truth, I'd opt for
that. Convictions are less important."

Most of the participants in Operation Candor, as the effort
was tabbed, were strong allies of the president. But there wasn't
one who didn't agree that the situation was extremely bad for
the president and had to be changed. Not only did it continue to
be extremely bad, but it got worse. By the first of August, the
impeachment of Nixon by the House of Representatives was
considered a certainty. The debate was to begin August 19.
There were still some last-ditch Republican defenders who insisted the case lacked direct, specific, hard evidence. They

maintained that there had to be what they called "the smoking gun." In the late afternoon of Monday, August 5, the "smoking gun" came into play and Nixon was done for.

The White House announced the president was releasing the transcripts of three recorded conversations on June 23, 1972, six days after the Watergate break-in, with H. R. Haldeman, then his chief of staff. The tapes had been turned over to Judge Sirica in compliance with the unanimous decision of the U.S. Supreme Court. In an accompanying statement, Nixon acknowledged that he had withheld the contents of the tapes from his staff and his attorneys despite the fact that they contradicted his previous declarations of noninvolvement and lack of knowledge of the Watergate cover-up. The transcripts showed clearly Nixon's participation in the cover-up, approving the invocation of CIA involvement as a means of obstructing the FBI investigation of the Watergate break-in. Nixon took full responsibility and expressed deep regret for "this . . . serious act of omission." He made plain that neither his staff nor his counsel, James D. St. Clair, had known of the contents of the June 23 conversations.

In both houses, the anger, outrage, and disgust that swept through offices, corridors, and cloakrooms soon came to be known as "Firestorm Two"—the first being the reaction to the firing of Archibald Cox.

"Hell cannot contain the fury of a congressman who feels he has been had," said Republican Congressman John Anderson of Illinois. In his office, Barry Goldwater stormed, "This man must go." GOP Congressman Charles W. Sandman, Jr., of New Jersey, who had leapt overnight from obscurity to national prominence by his television performance as President Nixon's most tenacious and acerbic defender on the House Judiciary Committee, dashed off a letter to be hand-delivered to the president, stating: "These conversations contain specific, clear and convincing evidence constituting the criminal charge of obstruction of justice, leaving me no recourse but to support impeachment on Article I of the Articles of Impeachment." He concluded with a request that the president now consider resigning as "the only course of action" that he can take "in the best interest of the nation."

The demands for Nixon's resignation poured into the press galleries in both houses as fast as the photocopy machines could turn them out. Members trooped up to the radio and television studios at each end of the Capitol to voice their demands on the air. But Nixon apparently had no intention of resigning, and this only added to the anger of the legislators, especially the Republicans who were facing an election only a little more than two months away.

The next day, the Senate Republican Policy Committee held its regular luncheon which all Senate Republicans attended. At a $3 tab, each had a choice of chopped steak, fish, or roast beef. The asparagus tips were undercooked; in fact, none of the food was tasty that day.

Vice President Ford attended the luncheon. John Tower asked Ford for a summary of that morning's cabinet meeting. Ford said the president had made a statement that he would not resign. Most of the ninety-minute cabinet session was devoted to a discussion of a proposed "summit meeting" on the economy.

Maryland Sen. J. Glenn Beall was astonished. "Is that all the president had to say about impeachment?" he asked.

Barry Goldwater stood up. He was angry and his rising voice showed it. He said, "I'm not yelling at you, Mr. Vice President, but I'm just getting something off my chest. The president should resign. It's not in the best interest of everybody to have to face an impeachment trial."

Ford rose and said he thought he should excuse himself at this point. There was warm applause for him as he left.

"My great concern," said John Tower, up to now an ardent Nixon defender, "is that the president does not comprehend the hazard he faces in coming to trial in the Senate here. There is an erosion here—an erosion on the part of those who had supported the president all along."

It became apparent that nearly all present wanted Nixon to resign but that he wouldn't unless someone told him what he faced. Several asked, "Who's going to bell the cat? Who's going to tell the president?"

Then followed a series of meetings, in the office of Republican Hugh Scott, of the Senate leadership hierarchy plus two "elder statesmen" representing the liberal and conservative wings of the party, respectively Jacob K. Javits of New York and Barry Goldwater. Scott opened the meeting. "We're here to discuss whether, in the interest of country, the party, and the president himself, we ought to take some steps to warn the president of the seriousness of the situation so far as the Senate is concerned. We should also report to him about our communications from home. The whole country is in a state of jitters if not a nervous breakdown about the whole thing."

There was wide disagreement on selecting just who would "bell the cat." The first suggestion was that the six members of the elected Republican hierarchy do the job. Robert Griffin of Michigan said he would have to be excused because he had called for Nixon's resignation before the "smoking gun" turned up. His presence would be an irritant to Nixon.

Someone suggested that all forty-two Republican senators should go. At this, Norris Cotton of New Hampshire, a man with a short fuse, exploded. "It'll be hard enough to sneak in the Senate leaders through the back door without alerting the press," he said. "If you send all forty-two Republican senators down, you might as well hire a band and march down Pennsylvania Avenue."

Tower suggested that just one senator go. "Let Barry find out if the president will see him. He could slip in the back door and have a frank talk with the president." Hugh Scott didn't like the suggestion. If only one senator was to be designated, then it should be the highest elected leader, to wit, himself. But then Tower pointed out that the president might not like having Scott tell him he should resign. After all, the president had once pointed out with some degree of annoyance that Scott had voted seventeen times against administration programs.

At this point, Goldwater said, "Look, if it is the decision of this group that I be selected to talk to the president, I'm perfectly willing to do so."

A call was put through to William Timmons, the chief White House congressional liaison aide. He was told about the discussion and the urgent need to send an emissary or emissaries to the White House to tell the president he must resign or face certain impeachment in the House and probable conviction in the Senate.

"Oh, not today," Timmons cautioned. "The president is in no frame of mind to listen to anything like that."

"Well, let's adjourn now until the call of the leadership," said Scott, ending the inconclusive meeting. "Let's let it simmer."

Midmorning on Wednesday, Hugh Scott received a telephone

call from General Haig, telling him to hold himself in readiness for an invitation to the White House. Haig said, "The president is leaning strongly to the conclusion that his only available option is resignation. The president doesn't want the country tied up in turmoil for six months more. If the invitation does come through, just remember that the president needs a triggering mechanism. He wants to hear from the leaders just how bleak the situation really is."

It was Nixon who solved the problem of the delegation makeup. At 1:30 P.M. Timmons came to Scott's office to deliver the message that the president wanted to see Scott, Goldwater, and John Rhodes of Arizona, the House Republican leader.

"Give him an honest evaluation, Senator," Timmons said. "It will trigger his decision. He needs to feel he has exhausted all remedies."

The meeting was set for 5 P.M. At 4:45, the three legislators assembled in Haig's office. He had asked them to meet there fifteen minutes early to discuss the situation. Timmons and White House counsel Dean Burch were also present.

Haig said he, Timmons, and Burch had given the president the "damage assessment." It was the general feeling of the staff that resignation was the best course, Haig told the legislators, and that was what they had conveyed to the president. "The president is up and down on this thing," Haig said. "Please give him a straight story. If his situation is hopeless, say so. I just hope you won't confront him with your own demands."

The handsome, brilliant Haig, a general who resigned a promising career that could have led to chairman of the Joint Chiefs of Staff to become Bob Haldeman's successor as chief of the White House staff, was credited with keeping a sinking ship of state from foundering. President Ford later named him Commander in Chief of the NATO forces.

Promptly at 5:00, the three legislators entered the Oval Office. The president was on his feet, shaking hands with each of the three and asking John Rhodes, "How is your son doing on the bar exams?" Rhodes, surprised by the question, answered that his son was doing well, he hoped.

The president sat down, put his feet up on his desk, and asked the three to sit down. Then he started reminiscing about how kind President Eisenhower had been to him. Then he reminded the three that there were no living ex-presidents, adding, "If I were to become an ex-president, I will have no ex-presidents to pal around with." He said this with a small, grim smile. Then he said, "I am going to make my own decision. Whatever decision that I make I shall make in the national interest. Please raise no collateral issues. I'll raise none myself, such as the benefits accruing to me. That's not part of the issue here." The president did not define "collateral issues" further, but all three understood him to be referring to the question of immunity from prosecution. Then Nixon said, "Well, what do you want to say?"

Scott and Rhodes turned to Goldwater to give his assessment of the situation in the Senate. "Mr. President," Goldwater said, "if it comes to a trial in the Senate, I don't think you can count on more than fifteen votes."

The president turned to Rhodes and asked, "Not more than ten in the House, John?"

Rhodes replied, "Maybe more, Mr. President, but not much more."

The president said, almost as an aside, "And I really campaigned for a lot of them. But that's all right. That's politics. Now, Hugh, what's your assessment of the Senate?"

Scott replied, "I'd say twelve to fifteen, Mr. President."

Goldwater cut in to add, "I can vouch for only four or five who would stay with you right to the end."

Scott said, "Oh, there may be more than that."

The president said, "Well, Hugh, what do you really think about the situation?" Scott replied, "Gloomy." Nixon, again with that small, sour smile said, "I'd say damned gloomy."

The president, still with his feet on his desk and still radiating a calmness and self-control that surprised his visitors, reminisced some more about Ike's kindness to him and Lyndon Johnson's kindness too. Then he said, "I guess that's it. I thank you for giving me your views. Remember, when you go out there, you'll talk to the press. I guess there's no way to avoid that. I think you should tell them that whatever I do will be grounded in the national interest."

As the three got up to leave, Scott said, "These are sad times, Mr. President."

Nixon replied, a little sadly, "Don't bother about that, Hugh. Do your duty and God bless you."

Later that same day, at 7:30, Scott, Rhodes, Sen. James O. Eastland of Mississippi, and Speaker Carl Albert met with the president at his invitation in his office in the Executive Office Building across the street from the White House to be given a preview of his television speech to the nation at 9:00. Nixon asked them whether they would like a drink. None accepted. The situation struck them as too tense for a social drink. It was anything but a social occasion, even though the president tried to put them at their ease. He said, "I'll capsulize the speech for you. It will come as no surprise to you. All of you by now know what I'm doing." Then he said, "Who's ranking here? Oh, it's you, Carl. You take this seat in front of me. You, Jim, take the sofa. The rest of you sit down, please."

In summarizing his speech, Nixon said that the president and Congress have to devote full time to the problems of the nation. It was obvious that if an impeachment trial was held, it would take at least four months. His lawyer, St. Clair, estimated it would take six months. At any rate, he couldn't give leadership to the country, nor could Congress, over this length of time.

"This wouldn't be fair to the nation," he said. "If I followed my own inclination, I would follow the constitutional process to the end. That's what my family wants. But I have to consider the national interest and the national interest will be best served if I resign.

"Jerry Ford will make a good president. He will heal the wounds of Watergate and give the country a chance to go forward again."

There were no interruptions while he talked. When he finished, Eastland took his cigar out of his mouth and said, "You've been a damned good president."

Carl Albert said, "I hope you don't think that I have added to your problems by anything I have said or done."

Nixon smiled and said, "You've been great, Carl. That goes for all of you. I have no complaints, not even against those who opposed me. You all know Jerry Ford, how good he is. He will be a good president and you can work with him."

Albert said, "Oh yes, Mr. President, we sure can."

It was his farewell to them, and he walked out in full control of himself. How turbulent his emotions were became evident just thirty-five minutes before he went on television. He had just concluded an emotional farewell in the White House Cabinet Room with forty-six of his closest friends in the Congress.

"I just hope you don't feel that I let you down." he said to them. His eyes filled with tears. He rose wordlessly and disappeared from the hushed room through a side door.

The new president, Gerald Ford, asked several congressional leaders, in advance of the swearing-in ceremony, to meet with him immediately afterward in the Red Room. After the ceremony, Ford went into the Red Room and was shortly joined by Scott, Albert, Mansfield, Rhodes, and John McFall of California, the House Democratic Whip. Their wives, meanwhile, joined Betty Ford at the entrance to the State Dining Room for the reception line.

Ford asked Scott to sit down on the sofa with him on his right. Albert was asked to sit on his left. The others distributed themselves on the two sofas in the room. Ford then turned to his aide, former Congressman John Marsh of Virginia, and said, "I wonder if we can have a picture taken of this occasion?" Marsh responded, "I'll see to that right away, Mr. President."

Leaving the White House later, Scott said, "He didn't realize he was president. Instead of saying 'call in a photographer' he asked whether he could have one."

After the picture was taken, the new president said, "The hallmark of the new administration will be openness and accessibility. Now, shall we join the ladies?"

The wounds of the Nixon era were beginning to heal.

EPILOGUE

During the height of the Vietnam War, Sen. J. William Fulbright, a pessimist by inclination and conviction, told the Senate: "There is nothing inevitable about the survival of the United States." When we recall the rise and fall of great empires and the humbling of powerful nations, it is difficult to cavil with that prognosis.

The Republic thus far has lasted only half as long as it took to complete the spires of the cathedral of Chartes. The exquisite south tower was erected in the twelfth century; the magnificent flamboyant Gothic north tower was built in the sixteenth century. Nevertheless, two centuries of survival of a democracy dedicated to life, liberty, and the pursuit of happiness are worth bragging about. The system of checks and balances may not produce the most efficient government, but it is conducive to freedom under law.

We have seen how it can contain bouts of national hysteria as in the McCarthy era. We have seen how it was able, however tardily, to complete the enfranchisement of blacks before civil disorder got totally out of control. And we have shown the world how we can get rid of a corrupt president and achieve a smooth, healing transfer of power to his successor.

To tell all that happened in Congress in the thirty years I spent covering it as a reporter would be far beyond the purpose of this book.

Many Americans don't know much about how their government operates. The textbooks give the anatomy but somehow miss the spark of life.

A few years ago, a political science professor, on leave from his university to become a staff director of the Senate Republican Policy Committee, decided the time had come to go back to teaching.

As the returning professor was saying farewell to his friend Max Kampelman, then the legislative counsel to Sen. Hubert H. Humphrey of Minnesota and now a successful Washington attorney, he commented, "Max, I'm going back to teach a course in government. Shall I tell them the truth about the legislative process? Shall I tell them what *really* goes on?"

I don't know what the disillusioned professor told his students but I have tried in this book to report what really went on in the halls of Congress during my three decades as a correspondent on Capitol Hill.

PICTURE CREDITS

The author wishes to thank the *Washington Post* for providing many of the photographs used in this book.

Further acknowledgment and thanks are made to the following for permission to use their photographs:

U. S. Army (General R. Zwicker) p. 37, Wide World Photos (Klaus Fuchs) p. 42, The National Archives (Churchill, Roosevelt, Stalin) p. 69, The *Boston Globe* (Morrissey family & Sen. E. Kennedy) p. 127, Wide World Photos (President & Mrs. Richard Nixon) p. 282

INDEX